A-Z OF CARS
OF THE
1920s

**THIS WORK IS PUBLISHED WITH THE ASSISTANCE OF
THE MICHAEL SEDGWICK MEMORIAL TRUST**

Founded in memory of the great motoring researcher and author
Michael Sedgwick (1926-1983), the Trust is a registered charity
formed to encourage new research and the recording of
motoring history. Suggestions for future projects and donations
should be sent to the Hon. Secretary of the Michael Sedgwick Memorial Trust,
c/o John Montagu Building, Beaulieu, Hampshire SO4 7ZN, England.

A-Z OF CARS
OF THE
1920s

Nick Baldwin

With an introduction by William Boddy

Published 1994 by
Bay View Books Ltd
The Red House, 25-26 Bridgeland Street
Bideford, Devon EX39 2PZ

Typesetting and computer make-up by Chris Fayers

ISBN 1 870979 53 2

Printed in Great Britain by
Butler & Tanner Ltd, Frome, Somerset

Acknowledgements

Numerous marque experts, companies, enthusiasts and helpful friends
have assisted in the project, just some of whom are listed below:
The Automobile and many of its knowledgeable readers, Dr J Alderson,
the late J H Baldwin, R Barraclough, J G Bissett, W Boddy, B Bonnett, J Boulton,
C Bugler, R Carter, J Collins, the late Peter Cole, J Coombs, D Culshaw, CWS,
A B Demaus, A I Dick, J Donaldson, B Dowell, M Draper, H Edwards,
D Evans, J Evans, M C Evans, R Forss, C Fontane, B Foster, G N Georgano,
J Goldsworthy, D Good, K Good, S Hallett, D Hales, Sir D Hall, T Harding,
P & B Hart, B Heath, B & C Herridge, P Higgs, P Horne, Humber Register,
M Jenner, M Longmore, E M Lowndes, K Marvin, L Mather, T K Meredith,
Lord Montagu, J Moore, National Motor Museum, R O'Callaghan,
D H Pearse, C Petts, Phillips Auctioneers, B Price, G Ravenscroft, A M Rodgers,
Rover Sports Register, the late M Sedgwick, Sedgwick Memorial Trust,
J Sharples, N Simpson, G Skillen, B Smith SMM&T, J Spicer,
Rev. L C Stead, J Stringer, A Sully, D Thirlby, R Tyrrell,
Ulster Folk & Transport Museum, VSCC, M E Ware, E Warmington,
W R Warne, M Webb, M J Worthington-Williams, R A Young

CONTENTS

Key

Information is presented at the beginning of
each model entry in the following order:

**MODEL DESIGNATION. Years of manufacture
(production figures). Price. Engine configuration,
number of cylinders, valve gear, cubic capacity.**

Abbreviations

S	–	in-line engine
V	–	vee engine
HO	–	horizontally opposed engine
SV	–	side valves
OHV	–	overhead valves
IOE	–	inlet over exhaust valves
OHC	–	overhead camshaft
DOHC	–	double overhead camshafts
TS	–	two stroke

Introduction
Motoring in the 1920s

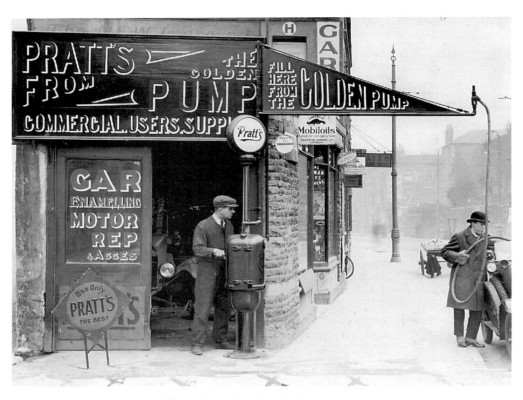

Filling up from a hand cranked Pratt's pump.

This painstaking book, in which Nick Baldwin recalls the great and complex variety of the cars that blossomed in the long-ago 1920s, may not, perhaps, recall quite how motoring itself was then. Present-day drivers can hardly be expected to visualise just how free from traffic congestion and anxiety those days were, or what fun motoring must have been to those coming new to it after the First World War. Service personnel with gratuities to spend, not to mention those made rich on civilian profits from the fearful hostilities, were getting out and about on the then truly "open" road. Even those who now own and enjoy veteran and vintage cars can hardly fully comprehend what carefree days those were, unless they experienced them personally. No motorways, few bypasses, easy parking, certainly no traffic wardens or wheel clamping! It was, had they known, a golden age for the New Motorists, as they cranked up their cars and went off in search of fresh scenes and good touring country.

It was possible to experience the sense of adventure which motoring engendered without aiming for impressive journey times. In fact, speeds were generally low, at all events in the first half of the decade which this enthralling book covers. Especially in Scotland, Wales and the West Country, lanes were narrow and high hedged, their bends blind. Crossroads were likewise a hazard, unguarded apart from the more important town crossings, traffic lights unheard of – until the first experimental ones blinked their warning in Wolverhampton in 1928. Added to which, until the advent of four wheel brakes around 1924-25, the stopping power of many cars was minimal and drivers were often still obsessed with the anxieties of skids, and the "dreaded side-slip". In wet weather the external contracting back wheel anchors found on several American automobiles lost much of their power, and although the Austin Seven had brakes on all its wheels from its advent in 1922, these did not give the stopping power of good two wheel brakes, even after they had been coupled front to rear. Indeed, it was some time before anyone trusted four wheel brakes. I recollect an uncle who proclaimed that he would never ride in a car so equipped, as to do so was to invite a trip into the ditch. Yet not many years later his Austins had such brakes, which stopped skidding as well as lowering pull-up distances. However, that distrust of brakes on the wheels which steered the car tended to persist. Some designers kept these for emergencies, not connected with the rear wheel or transmission brakes, and those like HE who did move with the times in some cases went to considerable mechanical complexity to ensure that braking on the inner front wheel did not interfere with cornering.

On the whole, therefore, travel times were unimpressive in the earlier part of the 1920s, unless you were a young undergraduate intent on establishing some local "record" between your college and a London night-spot. Conscientious drivers gave hand signals until semaphore arms, illuminated with pea-bulbs, made arm-flapping unnecessary, Georges Roesch boxing his arrow indicators in on the 14/45 Talbot of 1926.

I recall how a morning might be occupied driving 16 miles out and back on holidays in South Wales in a 1920s Overland, or before that in a Chevrolet, its chauffeur tooting on a bulb horn before every corner, ready to haul on the hand brake should an obstruction be encountered. Yet on arrival in Cardiff, where the ladies insisted on the inevitable coffee stop, it was possible, in those peaceful times, to park for as long as necessary in the main street, outside Howell's, unmolested.

Road users were more hardy then, closer to the weather. If the aforesaid expedition happened on a rainy day the luckless chauffeur would have quite a difficult time unbuttoning the side curtains and moving the rear compartment windscreen forward to let us out. In London, open-top 'buses were the norm, their upper decks demanding unfurled umbrellas on wet days. Even when it was fine, 35 to 40mph was about the comfortable pace for an open car; at speeds higher than this the wind buffeted the occupants and hats and caps were apt to blow off. Another curb on speed, at all events in the first half of the decade we are considering, was the menace of the chars-à-banc. These enormous vehicles, most of them still on solid tyres, had become very popular for tours and summer seaside outings. I think that even Nick, who knows about commercial vehicles, must join me in expressing wonder that anyone could control such juggernauts, with 30 or more passengers on board in separate compartments each with its own door, the front occupants crowding the driver, who had the body overhang to add to his problems. Not surprisingly, these motor coaches travelling at 20mph for miles on end were impossible to overtake, unless you were in an accelerative sports car and encountered a piece of straight road. Even this was unwise if the merry coach party had been imbibing and had empty bottles to throw overboard...

Many were the letters to the motor papers complaining, and to the chara menace could be added slow lorries with minimal acceleration, and the chance of meeting round a corner a traction-engine or steam wagon taking on water from some convenient river or stream. These are some of the reasons why average speeds were not unduly high. There was, however, a theory that average speed represented roughly half your car's maximum, i.e. that a 70mph sports car should be able to average 35mph and an 80mph road-burner 40, whereas the average light car, flat out at about 50mph, would not be able to put much more than 25 miles into an hour's coaxing.

Another restraint on speeding was the universal 20mph speed-limit, introduced in 1903 and not abandoned until the end of 1930 – but no Radar convictions until 1959! Drivers lived in hope of not being caught on a stopwatch-checked piece of road with its hidden policemen, but those who had wisely joined the AA would be warned of what lay ahead when the Scout omitted his usual salute, which otherwise made a 1920s motorist feel akin to minor Royalty.... Then there were punctures, or even burst tyres. These were exacerbated by speed. I remember as children how, crowded into another Overland tourer for a bathing trip to Porthcawl, we would persuade the jolly father who was driving to see if he could wind up the ribbon speedometer to 60mph; inevitably, as he tried, would come the crack of another burst Dunlop or whatever, on the flint surface of what were then main roads.

Until petrol pumps began to be installed at garages you had to prepare for a long journey by collecting a sufficient number of two-gallon cans (now collectors' items). These could be awkward to carry on the car, unless the luggage carrier could be utilised or you had thoughtfully fitted a lazy-tongs side guard to one of the running boards. And how useful were those running boards, since defunct, as seats on the then popular picnics. Ideas of what constituted a long journey varied, of course. Some drivers wrote of their prowess, and that of their cars, in this idiom. But my aforesaid relation, when owning an Austin 12 which had replaced his 1920 Austin 20 Mayfair landaulette (which the chauffeur disliked washing, so made any excuse not to use) regarded a trip from Cardiff to Oxford as too far for the ladies to endure in one day, so an hotel had to be booked halfway...

As the desire to motor grew after the Armistice the circulation of the motor magazines must have benefitted, even though I think many ordered them as part of the New Motoring scene and probably passed them on to their chauffeurs unread. Those were the days of *The Autocar*

The open road...

(every Friday, 4d), *The Motor* (every Thursday, also 4d), and *The Light Car & Cyclecar* with its splendid photographic front cover (Fridays, 3d) which, if visitors had given me a "tip", I would rush off to buy, instead of returning with the expected sweets. In those days editors used to provide their readers with many letters pages and did not curb the length of such correspondence. In those fascinating pages many battles were fought, with, for instance, Louis Coatalen, Sunbeam's Chief Engineer, telling W O Bentley that his cars were based on pre-war racing car design and S F Edge defending any aspect of the AC that had been criticised. In retrospect, it seems odd that in an age when so many people were new to cars and anxious to know how to decarbonise the cylinders, grind-in the valves, even mend the frequent punctured tyres, such advice was very largely ignored. Instead, pages were devoted to descriptions of new cars, road test reports, and especially to racing and other competition events, some in far-away places scarcely known to most readers.

It may have been this, or the love of sport, which caused such activities to be well supported. Brooklands Track, built in 1907, reopened in 1920 and its Bank Holiday Race Meetings would bring crowds of up to 30,000 to watch a series of handicaps in which pre-war Grand Prix cars, stripped sports cars, the latest factory racers and home-devised specials would battle it out. Those living in the Midlands would tend to go to the Shelsley Walsh speed hill-climbs, dating back to 1905, and if you resided further north it might be the sand

races on the beaches of Southport and Skegness that were the sporting attraction. By 1922 K Lee Guinness had lapped Brooklands in the 350hp V12 Sunbeam at over 122mph, and before the 1920s were over the lap record had been raised to 134.24mph by Kaye Don in a far smaller V12 Sunbeam. At Shelsley Walsh the course record was set by C A Bird (of the custard powder family) at 52.5 seconds in yet another Sunbeam, broken six times before the 1920s faded, and then left at 45.6 seconds by Raymond Mays in the 3-litre supercharged Vauxhall-Villiers. The sand races were sufficiently alluring for George Formby to have acted as starter at one of them... And by 1927 200mph had been officially exceeded for the first time, by Major (Later Sir) H O D Segrave, at Daytona, driving a 45-litre twin-engined Sunbeam.

In the 1920s many manufacturers offered sports or speed models, even the light car makers, although some were sporting mainly in respect of the body styling, with little or no engine tuning. But the brave performances of the Bentleys and the wealthy "Bentley Boys" who drove them at Le Mans made the Cricklewood marque a schoolboys' favourite. At Christmas time we could go to stores like Harrods, Whiteleys, and Gamages, where famous Land Speed Record giants might be on display, with Sir Malcolm Campbell, Segrave and Parry Thomas explaining them. While ordinary drivers were content to amble along at 35mph, a Bentley was good for 75-80mph in "Red Label" form, the immortal 30/98 Vauxhall was said to achieve 100mph stripped for racing, and

...and a city snarl-up.

the irresistible 36/220hp Mercedes-Benz did that speed on the road – as I was shown as a 14 year old, in school cap, on the Barnet by-pass.

One thing which made the 1920s so fascinating was that most of the cars could be recognised by their distinctive radiators, as you will see, and some even by their sounds. Keen folk would sometimes take a census of those that went by, Model T Ford and Austin or Morris usually top, and taxi ranks offered many different makes. I used to persuade my mother to hang about until a make I had not ridden in previously came to the head of the rank, to avoid hiring another Unic. Motor cycles with single-cylinder engines represented the "Suck, compress, fire, exhaust" cycle to perfection, unlike today's multi-pot models. It was so much more fun in those long-ago times. The Olympia London Motor Show was supplemented by those marvellous Extra Show Numbers of the weekly motor magazines, and catalogues could be collected in the "Trojan bags" given away at that company's stand.

Out on the highways and byways it was all pretty leisurely. I could show you a photograph of East Grinstead in the 1920s with no white lines, no no-stopping yellow lines, horse-drawn traps and carts mingling with the few cars and a farmer driving his sheep along the middle of the road. But congestion was not far off. Another picture shows a rather busy Newton Abbot, with T-Fords much in evidence and the local Dennis single-decker hemmed in, awaiting its passengers – but only because it was market day. However, Kingston was bypassed by 1927 and soon traffic

was speeding dangerously along it. On Sunday evenings so much traffic was returning into London that the rise into Streatham, to quote one example, held the interesting sight of novice drivers running gently back into those behind, others finding much difficulty in re-starting, as a policeman controlling a five-way crossing, and trams, halted to change from overhead to centre-line pick-up, disrupted things. Late at night, a pilot from Croydon would pass the lot, contemptuously, in an old Mercedes Ninety...

The police remained reasonably lenient for most of the following decade, more interested in the compulsory third-party insurance documents than in bald tyres or opaque windscreens – as I know, from tempting them with a £5 ABC and a well-worn Rhode. Kids grew up used to being crammed into the rear seat of Chummy Austin 7s or even over the back wheel of a Family Morgan. Closed motors were not largely seen in the opening 1920s, but the aristocracy used Daimlers, as did Royalty, the newly-rich flaunting their wealth in Rolls-Royces, as the world's best car. An apocryphal story, perhaps, but certainly it took the more adventurous to appreciate the overhead-camshaft, so called "aero-cars", such as the Leyland Eight, Lanchester Forty, 40/50hp Napier, etc. Change was in the wind, and as the 1920s merged with the 1930s, another fearful war imminent, motoring conditions altered and were never quite the same, nor as much fun, again.

Bill Boddy
Founder Editor, *Motor Sport*

The British Car in the 1920s

A view over the 1919 motor show at Olympia.

In the following pages are outlined the achievements of the hundreds of motor manufacturers who struggled to sell cars in the expanding British market from 1919 to 1930. The era was dominated by the growing influence of the mass producers, but in the year or to following the end of the Great War dozens of hopefuls developed prototypes, of which just a few went on to commercial success. This was the era of the marginal cyclecar, which was quickly beaten by "real cars in miniature", like the Austin Seven, but a few of this spartan brigade, like GN, survived to evolve into the type of light sporting car that MG was to market so successfully from late in the 1920s.

Britain proved to be such a large and lucrative market that several overseas concerns established factories here, encouraged in part by the high level of duty imposed on imported cars. These makers are covered in the A-Z section, whilst those from Canada enjoying import tax exemption are listed in the final section of the book, along with makers from elsewhere in the world who sold cars in Britain.

American firms exerted enormous influence in the decade, yet their products, though generally highly competitive and cheap, could not hope to succeed in a land where from 1921 taxation was levied on horsepower rating. The approved RAC horsepower calculations took no account of stroke but simply of bore size, so some strange anomalies arose. However, as a general rule, cheap American cars were very expensive to tax (the Model T Ford for example being rated at 20hp and thus £20 per year). In 1926 the horsepower band up to and including 8hp amounted to only 7% of the total market but two years later this figure had almost doubled to 11% and it was to continue to grow in the difficult years ahead.

The 1920s saw the arrival or widespread adoption of practically everything we take for granted today, including four wheel brakes, detachable wheels, unitary construction, chrome plating, safety glass, low pressure tyres, saloon coachwork (which accounted for nearly 80% of 1929 sales), front wheel drive, supercharging, full pressure lubrication, independent suspension, small sixes (and indeed smaller, shorter stroke and more powerful fours, often with OHV), all steel bodies, sprayed artificial cellulose which saved many days when compared with hand-painted multi-coats, electric lighting and starting, hydraulic brakes and much more besides. The decade saw the gradual transition from motor firms using outside coachbuilders employing lots of wood in the construction to the in-house pressing of metal panels and welded bodies. From then on built-in obsolescence became a fact of life which helped to increase production runs and reduce prices.

Production line techniques have not arrived in this factory (above) but are being demonstrated (below) at the Wembley exhibition by Ford Model T workers.

It became very difficult for the smaller manu-facturers to match the economies of scale enjoyed by firms such as Austin, Standard, Singer and Morris, and all went to the wall or were taken over unless they had something unique to offer. The 1920s marked the zenith of proprietary car engine makers like Coventry Climax, Coventry Simplex, Dorman, British Anzani, Meadows, Tylor and many others, often of American origin. Various other components were also produced by specialists, notably the makers of springs, steering gear, propeller shafts, radiators, wheels and tyres, glass and electrical equipment.

Once designs had stabilised in the early 1920s it was found that 70% of cars had four-cylinder engines and 21.3% six cylinders. By the end of 1928 six cylinders had overtaken four (at any rate in buyers guides, if not on the road) with respec-tive percentages of 49.6 and 34.6. By then 48.1% had OHV compared with 40% in 1924. Interestingly, in the same year 20% still had non-detachable cylinder heads and virtually all had

magnetos, whereas coil and magneto ignition were equally balanced four years later (and virtu-ally every head was detachable). At the start of the decade the vast majority of gear levers were on the right but by 1929 66.8% were centrally located. By the mid 1920s 95% of cars had electric starters but 47% only had two wheel brakes (com-pared with 100% at the end of the decade). Petrol tanks had moved to the rear from a gravity feed position at the front, and the use of torque tubes was in decline throughout the vintage period, while at the same time spiral bevel axles became almost universal. Steel spoked wheels were losing out to disc and wire types, and semi-elliptic sus-pension was gaining ground over other systems. In 1924 29% of the cars available had cone clutches, 27% plate and 42% disc. For 1929 these figures had become 5.4%, 21.4% and 71.1%, though interestingly the percentage of four speed gearboxes changed little in five years – 54% in 1924 against 58.6% as the decade drew to a close.

The number of private cars on the roads of

Britain in 1919 stood at 109,705. It jumped to 186,801 in 1920 and in 1924 reached 482,356. By 1930 this figure had more than doubled to 1,075,081. As the import statistics given country by country in the "foreign" section at the end of the book show, relatively few cars were direct imports, though lots contained American parts, know-how or capital. Britain's own motor industry produced 71,396 cars in 1923 (the first year in which cars were separated from other types of vehicle). In 1924 the figure was 116,600, in 1925 132,000 and in 1926 153,000. In succeeding years the figures were collated for the twelve months to September, with 164,553 made in 1927, 165,352 in 1928, 182,347 in 1929 and 169,669 in 1930. As only 34,000 of every category of vehicle had been produced in 1913 we can see how much the industry had grown following wartime expansion. This expansion was in terms of both factory space and employment, and was fuelled by more widespread wealth, exposure to motor transport in the 1914-18 war and growing personal freedom. In other words many men and a growing number of women now wanted their own cars.

The figures for car imports to the UK by year, starting in 1922 and rounded to the nearest thousand, were 13,000, 14,000, 11,000, 32,000 (when duties were briefly abandoned August 1st 1924 to July 1st 1925), 11,000, 18,000, 14,000, 11,000 and finally in 1930, 7,000. Of these an average of about 1500 per year were re-exported, in some cases after being bodied by British coachbuilders.

Thus in Britain an enormous choice was available, from hundreds of different manufacturers and thousands of different models, but only a few dozen firms at home and abroad actually made any significant impact in terms of numbers of cars sold.

Hand assembly played quite a big part in even the cheapest mass-produced cars and materials still included a surprisingly high proportion of non-ferrous metals. For years the American industry had been advocating steel pressings and castings but the high initial cost of presses and dies meant that, for the smaller production runs of many British cars, steel fabrication and non-ferrous castings played an important part. Despite the value of brass, copper and aluminium to scrapmen, not least in the drive for war materials in 1939-45, an amazing number of vintage cars has survived. Examples of nearly half the makes, if not half the models, listed in this book exist in Britain, and are admirably catered for by numerous one-make and regional car clubs and by the all-important Vintage Sports Car Club based at 131 Russell Road, Newbury, Berkshire RE14 5JX.

As a matter of interest, Britain's car exports more or less balanced its imports by the mid-1920s and then gradually moved into a healthy surplus by the 1930s. Existing figures for annual exports commencing at a 1924 low of 15,659 motor vehicles and reached a peak of 41,961 in 1929. Australia was by far the largest market, taking between 4,000 and 15,500 vehicles annually. So if you cannot find the car you want "in the metal", the chances are that it exists in Australia which, as well as appreciating British cars, had an amazing thirst for all manner of other European and American types.

Finally a word about sources of information used for this book. Naturally the motoring magazines of the era have been invaluable, as has the book *Automobiles of the World* published in 1921. Specifications have been obtained from the above sources as well as from contemporary sales brochures and trade guides published by Stone & Cox, Fletcher & Son and Motor Technical Records.

Since the 1960s numerous specialist motoring magazines have published accounts of some of the 1920s motor manufacturers. Particularly useful have been Bill Boddy's "Fragments on Forgotten Makes" in *Motor Sport*, and histories by Michael Worthington-Williams in *Old Motor*, *The Automobile* and elsewhere. The late Michael Sedgwick contributed many useful articles to *Veteran and Vintage* and other publications and I am fortunate to have access to his research notes, as well as those of *Old Motor* magazine (where I was formerly joint editor). The index of motoring publications at the National Motor Museum, worked on steadfastly by Michael Sedgwick and successive librarians, has also been most useful.

Production figures have caused quite a problem, except in the cases where clubs, museums or individuals have original construction records. Some of the contemporary trade sources quoted chassis numbers, but these are often inaccurate and are helpful chiefly in giving a general impression of size and importance. A more reliable method, particularly with the smaller "assemblers" of cars, has been to study the engine supply records. Fortunately those of Dorman exist at the William Salt Library, Stafford, whilst thirty years ago I was lucky enough to have access to the Meadows engine records at their maker's factory and made copious notes. Some of these latter records still exist and are being evaluated by the National Motor Museum.

Plainly more information will continue to come to light and I would very much like to receive via the publisher written observations, corrections, photographs and anything else that might help to improve future editions.

Nick Baldwin
March 1994

The A-Z

ABBEY

Earl Street, London SW1

The Abbey Auto Engineering Co. Ltd assembled friction-driven £315 two-seaters powered by Coventry Simplex 10.8hp engines in 1922. Few were built. It has been suggested that in a second incarnation this car became the Lewis.

1922 Abbey Ten.

ABC

Hersham and Walton on Thames, Surrey

Originating as an engine maker, and using the designs of Granville Bradshaw (see also Belsize), ABC had 22 acres of factory by the end of the Great War. Engines, Skootamota cycles and cars were produced, but only the engines lasted into the next decade and the firm was ultimately absorbed by Vickers in 1951.

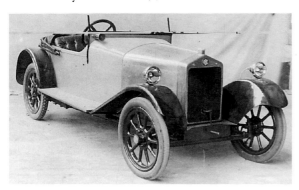

ABC 12hp, 1921.

The two-cylinder cars were light and stylish, contemporary reports speaking of above average performance and handling. Unfortunately early engines gave trouble and tarnished the marque's reputation. Most other components came from

Harper Bean which, like Vulcan, Swift, etc., had sales handled through the ill-fated British Motor Trading Corp. In 1919-20 Bean owned nearly half of ABC's shares and transferred production to Hersham, where 5000 cars p.a. were envisaged.

12HP. 1920-27 (prod: 1500 approx). 1922 sports £255, 1923 four-seater £265. HO2 OHV air-cooled 1203cc (1320cc Super-Sports), single plate clutch, four speed gearbox with vertical gate, spiral bevel axle, quarter-elliptic suspension. Spritely performance thanks to an unladen weight of between three-quarters and half a ton depending on body style. Engine rough and noisy, but improved with larger crank and roller bearings plus bigger bore in 1925. The petrol tank was above the engine, with the filler cap on the realistic "dummy honeycomb" radiator, which could cause havoc if someone mistook the ABC for a water-cooled car! Some raced at Brooklands and were capable of 40mph in third gear and over 60mph in top. E C Gordon England's ABC racer, before he changed to Austin 7s, proved notably reliable in the JCC 200 mile races. Self starter and front wheel brakes were later options. In 1921 the ABC was claimed to be the cheapest "real" light car.

ABF

(All British Ford) Kenilworth, Warwickshire

Despite its title this was not a Model T conversion but a small series of cars built by garage owner and inventor Bertie Ford in the 1918-20 period. He had been an aviation pioneer in Canada and after breaking his legs in an accident turned his attention to carburettors, hospital machinery and cars. Series production was intended but a combination

ABF V4 Sports

of the early postwar slump, competition from better-funded manufacturers and illness ended the project.

Versions with a water-cooled flat twin engine and a V4 sports model (shown above) survive. The former may well be a prototype of the Buckingham cyclecar, whilst the latter had an ingenious two-stroke engine with stepped pistons and atmospheric valves. Most parts were cast and machined in-house.

ABINGDON

Tyseley, Birmingham

The famous maker of the Abingdon King Dick spanner also produced motor fittings and motorcycles (1903-33). Its brief foray into the car business was not a success.

Abingdon 11.9hp. This the portotype two-seater.

11.9HP. 1922-23 (prod: 12). Four-seater from £340. Dorman S4 SV 1490cc, single plate clutch, Wrigley three speed gearbox, torque tube, Wrigley spiral bevel axle, quarter-elliptic suspension. A prototype two-seater was tried for many months before the specification for a high quality four-seater with Brolt electric lighting and starting was laid down. Unfortunately this coincided with financial difficulties for Wrigley, which supplied many of the components, including steering gear, and which in 1924 became the home of Morris-Commercial. Abingdon did not bother to find new sources of supply because sales did not justify carrying on.

AC

Ferry Works, Thames Ditton, Surrey

Makers of tradesmen's three-wheel vehicles from 1907, followed by Sociables for passengers, Autocarriers (1913) Ltd offered more conventional four-wheelers shortly before the Great War. The company name was changed to AC Cars Ltd in 1922, when the workforce totalled about 900 men. Vauxhall had a substantial shareholding until 1925, and AC's founders were also on the board of

the British Anzani engine firm. S F Edge, the racing driver and Napier backer, who was also involved with Cubitt, guided AC's destiny from 1921. He was assisted by J S Napier and A J McCormack, respectively former managing directors of Arrol-Johnston and Wolseley.

The familiar six-cylinder engine, which lasted to 1963, was first seen in 1919, and other familiar vintage features included the three speed gearbox in unit with the back axle for optimum weight distribution, and quarter-elliptic suspension.

In 1927 S F Edge bought the company for £135,000, and it became AC (Acédès) Ltd, accented like Mercédès, but in 1929 Edge and his partner Gillet lost a fortune when the company's financial plight became critical. Edge went home to breed pigs, and the Hurlock family, dealers in surplus machinery and vehicles, acquired the Thames Ditton factory in 1930.

AC 10hp, 1921.

10HP. 1919-20 (prod: 62). Fivet S4 SV 1315cc, three speed gearbox in unit with worm back axle, quarter-elliptic suspension. Revival of a pre-war model, with an increase in engine capacity from 1096cc. Supply difficulties soon killed it, though its engine's bore and stroke of 65 × 100mm were also used on AC's own sixes. As with later models the handbrake worked a disc on the tail of the worm wheel though there were conventional rear wheel foot brakes.

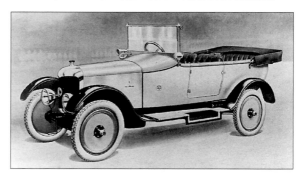

1922 12hp AC Royal four-seater

10HP, 12HP, 12/24. 1920-28 (prod: see below). Chassis 1921 £475, 1928 £255. S4 SV 1496cc, disc clutch, three speed gearbox in unit with worm axle, quarter-elliptic suspension. This model, along with the sixes, had chassis numbers from 5001 in 1920 to 13744 at the end of 1926 (but some numbers may not have been issued). Four wheel brakes became available in the mid-1920s but were still an extra in 1927.

Two thousand engines were ordered from British Anzani but Cubitt was able to build later ones more cheaply. A sustained cruising speed of 45mph was a feature advertised in 1924.

1926 AC Six

SIX. 1921-30 (prod: see 12hp). Chassis 1923 £490, 1929 £310. S6 OHC 1478cc (1992cc from 1922), disc clutch, three speed gearbox in unit with worm axle, quarter-elliptic suspension. Front wheel brakes standardised 1927. This model came in a variety of attractive styles including the Aceca drophead coupé. Initially developing 35bhp, it gained more power and was known as 16/40 (shown), 16/56 and 16/66 (with triple carburettors in 1926).

In 1925 a £630 sports model could do 85mph and in the following year an AC became the first British car to win the Monte Carlo Rally (driven by the Hon. Victor Bruce and photographer W J Brunell).

1929 AC Acédès Magna.

ACEDES MAGNA. 1929-30 (prod: n/a). Coupé £400, sedan £415. S6 OHC 1992cc, plate clutch, three speed gearbox in unit with worm axle. Semi-ellip- **tic front, cantilever rear suspension.** This was a variation on the 16/56 and, thanks to its new front suspension, the first with dumbirons. It had coil instead of magneto ignition and hydraulic four wheel brakes. Performance suffered from overweight bodies but against this had to be counted greater luxury and refinement.

From 1928 a fifth crankshaft bearing improved silence and longevity.

ACCELLERA
see Foster

ADAMSON

Enfield Highway, Middlesex

A wide assortment of belt driven cyclecars was made by haulage contractor R Barton Adamson & Co. in the 1912-24 period, using two- and four-cylinder Alpha engines made in Coventry by Johnson, Hurley and Martin, though the final "Twin Cars" of 1923-24 had British Anzani OHV twins. These had what were effectively two sidecars side by side, with the driver in the offside one, and were made from motor cycle components to reduce costs.

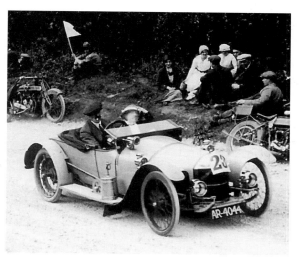

An Adamson on Harting Hill.

11 and Twin Car. 1920-22, 1923-24 (prod: n/a). Complete 1920 £375, 1924 £210. Alpha S4 SV 1330cc water-cooled, from 1923 British Anzani 1075cc OHV twin with air or water cooling, dry plate clutch, belt drive until three speed Burman box on late cars, chain drive, quarter-elliptic suspension. It was a retrograde step going from fours to two-cylinder red and polished aluminium cyclecars, and it was a gamble that did not pay off for Adamson.

AERO CAR

Upper Clapton, London N

A marginal cyclecar made in 1919-20 with 5/7hp air-cooled Blackburne flat-twin engines and a Sturmey-Archer motorcycle gearbox. An American-built 6hp car of the same name in 1921 was driven by a propeller.

The streamlined two-seater Aero Car.

AEROFORD

see Ford

AIREDALE

Esholt, Yorkshire

Nanson, Barker and Co. had built a few JAP, Chater Lea and Dorman powered Tiny cyclecars before the Great War in the corner of a hide and skin yard belonging to Mr Barker Senior.

The more substantial Airedale was made from 1919 to 1924, the first prototype, and possibly next three cars, utilising American Sterling engines.

Other than engines, most parts including gearboxes, differentials and axles were machined in-house, and eight fitters plus an apprentice were employed. Heat treatment was done by a whale oil furnace and all assembly took place on the first floor of a mill, completed chassis being lowered to the ground by block and tackle.

1921 11.9hp Airedale with Dixon all weather single door body.

12HP, 12/24, 11.9HP, 14HP. 1919-24 (production nearly 100). Chassis £425 1919, £360 1924. S4 OHV 1795cc (2120cc 14hp), single plate clutch (multi-plate on 14hp) four speed gearbox latterly in unit (with right hand change), torque tube, spiral bevel axle, semi-elliptic suspension. Approximately 53 cars had Dorman engines, and 33 are known to have had Meadows engines in 1922-23. An unusual offering in 1922 was a limousine at £625. Even an open two-seater cost a high £425 in the standard colour of grey. Such prices, even allied to luxury features like "antique leather upholstery", spelled disaster for this small but enterprising regional car firm and it went into liquidation in September 1924. It was reformed in March 1927, but to no avail.

AJS

Wolverhampton, Staffordshire

This motor cycle maker built seven Meadows powered light cars in 1923 but with the demise of so many smaller car firms in the face of Austin and Morris competition AJS suspended the project. The company introduced a series of high-performance coach chassis powered by Coventry Climax engines early in 1929 and a 9hp car later that year. The £11,600 profits of 1929 marked the last year in which AJS was in the black. Clyno designer A G Booth joined the firm, but this failed to appease the 1200 shareholders.

1931 AJS Nine fabric saloon.

NINE. 1929-33 (prod: approx 3300). 1930 two-seater £210, fabric saloon £320. S4 SV 1018cc, single dry plate clutch, in-unit three, later four, speed gearbox with centre change, spiral bevel axle, semi-elliptic suspension. Some or all engines appear to have been made by Coventry Climax, and overall quality and fitments were above average. AJS was reorganised in 1931, its motor cycle production transferring to London, the cars to Willys-Overland-Crossley at Heaton Chapel, and the Stevens family staying in Wolverhampton to make Stevens motor cycles and three-wheelers.

Many AJS Nines had the fashionable fabric body-work, which tended to look tatty with age and led to many cars being scrapped prematurely. The author owned one that had toured Ireland setting up AJS agencies in its heyday.

ALBATROS

Bedford Street and Croft Road, Coventry, Warwickshire

Available only in 1923-24, the Albatros (said to be the inspiration of one Albert Ross) was an assembled 8-10hp car using Coventry Climax engines.

Chassis numbers started at 201 in 1923 and recommenced at 253 in 1924, though it has been suggested that only about a dozen were actually built (of which no less than two survive – a 1924 8hp being shown).

8 and 10 HP. 1923-24 (prod: see above). Chassis £190, complete £225-£275. Coventry Climax S4 SV 1247cc or 1368cc, cone clutch, three speed in-unit gearbox with centre change, torque tube, spiral bevel axle, quarter-elliptic suspension. A utility version at £200 for a two-seater, falling to £175, was the only one to make do without a differential. Even

the better-equipped cars were quite cheap, but who wants an Albatros round their neck?

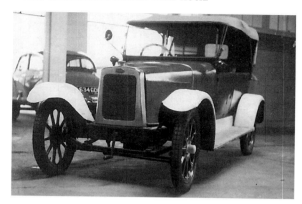

1924 Albatros 8hp.

ALBERT

Vauxhall, London, to 1920, then Chiswick, London

Founded in late 1917, Adam, Grimaldi & Co. made aircraft parts and took over coachbuilders Brown, Hughes and Strachan. Adam had worked for Argyll

Albert 11.9hp chassis, 1921.

and his Albert car (named after its Albert Embankment address) was designed by A O Lord (see Lloyd–Lord and Vulcan) using an engine made by Gwynne. (Three thousand engines had originally been ordered but only 350 cars were made by 1920.) Gwynne bought the makers of the Albert in March 1920 and transferred production to Chiswick. With a Rolls-Royce shaped radiator and well made aluminium coachwork these were expensive cars, virtually all parts being made in-house.

From late 1922 a 14hp Gwynne-Albert was offered, while the Gwynne 8 model was also built as an Albert with appropriate radiator, though reputedly only five were sold.

12HP. 1919-23 (prod: approx 1800). Chassis 1920 £460, factory-built coupé £606. Gwynne S4 OHV 1.5 litres, cone clutch, four speed gearbox with centre change, bevel axle, quarter-elliptic suspension. Beautifully made but expensive cars, with relatively high performance for a 12 thanks to pushrod overhead valves, four gears and ample use of aluminium in the construction. Inherent design weaknesses led the Receiver appointed in July 1923 to axe the model that had gained "a bad name which was never really lived down".

Albert 14GA.

14GA (Gwynne Albert), 14/40. 1922-29 (prod: approx 200). Complete car £575, falling to £220-£495 at end. S4 OHV 1944cc, plate clutch, four speed gearbox, torque tube, bevel axle, semi-elliptic suspension (cantilever at rear on early models). Bigger engined version of 12hp with four wheel brakes from mid-1920s, capable of 40-50mph and 0-30mph acceleration in 12 seconds. Production seems to have been minimal between 1924 and 1926 and then revived briefly as the 14/40 with engine redesigned by C M C Turner.

Like all but the earliest 12s the 14 was built in its entirety by Gwynne, which eventually gave up cars in favour of pumps. French Salmson cars were sold from the same area and possibly the same premises as Gwynnes and Alberts.

ALVIS

Holyhead Road, Coventry, Warwickshire

Founded in 1919 by T G John (1880-1946), who had marine and aero engineering experience. He bought an advanced four-cylinder engine design with lightweight Alvis pistons from Ware and de Freville (pre-war importers of DFP cars) and used it in his first cars. The maker of the subsequent Marseal and Marendaz was involved early on, and T G John was joined by Capt. G T Smith-Clarke from Daimler who, with W M Dunn, created the immortal 12/50 model. Smith-Clarke was responsible for virtually all subsequent models to the end of Alvis car production in 1967. Six thousand Alvis cars were on the road by 1928 (9140 were built to the end of 1931). The firm (T G John Ltd until 1921 and then Alvis Car and Engineering Co. Ltd) was also responsible for production of the Buckingham car to 1923 and the Stafford motor scooter. Most parts for Alvis cars including engines were made in-house, though bodywork was left to specialists like Cross and Ellis. Components were of better quality, and steel of higher tensile strength, than those employed by many contemporaries and overall weight was kept to the minimum, thus helping the Alvis to gain an excellent reputation and endow it with above average performance. The pioneering front wheel drive cars, however, had teething troubles that could have destroyed a lesser firm. Roughly 500 men were employed and output reached 1000 cars in a year for the first time in 1927.

Alvis was an important exporter from late 1922, with, for example, over 300 chassis and complete cars sent to Australia in our period.

The hare mascot became as well-known a trademark as the red triangle badge.

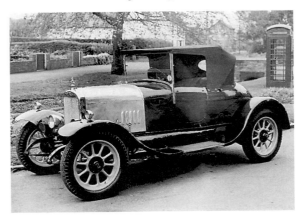

Alvis 10/30, 1920.

10/30, 11/40. 1920-22, 1921-22 (prod: 770, 54). Chassis £450, £470. S4 SV (a few OHV) 1460cc, 1598cc, cone clutch, four speed gearbox with right

hand change, bevel then spiral bevel axle, semi-elliptic suspension. "The car for the connoisseur" started off as a two-seater 10/30 weighing as little as 14cwt and capable of 60mph. Its OHV derivative was known as the Super Sports and could lap Brooklands at 80mph. The 10/30 had a steering column adjustable for rake and was normally finished in blue and grey with matching leather upholstery, while the 11/40 was a 70mph version of it with larger, more flexible engine. It could have various body styles up to a £750 all weather tourer.

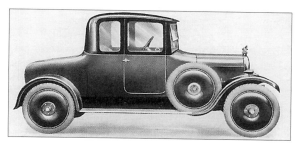

12/40 Alvis with Limousine Coupé body by Grose.

12/40. 1922-25 (prod: 1887). Chassis 1923 £470, 1925 £375. S4 SV 1597cc, cone clutch, separate four speed gearbox with right hand change, spiral bevel axle, semi-elliptic suspension. The 12/40 was an improved 11/40 that sold in larger numbers. It had a direct top gearbox and a honeycomb radiator with solid nickel casing. There was a fully floating back axle and extensive use of heat-treated materials. Front wheel brakes became available on later versions.

Alvis 12/50 ducksback, 1924.

12/50. 1923-1932 (prod: 3705). Complete 1924 £550-£575, 1929 £485-£535. S4 OHV (see below for capacity), cone clutch and separate four speed gearbox on SA-SC and 1925 sports, then single plate clutch and in-unit box, spiral bevel axle, semi-elliptic suspension. The OHV 10/30 (one of which won the 1923 Brooklands 200) developed into this extremely important model, which was made in several series commencing with SA. As a guide, the 1923-24 SA and longer SB were 1496cc, SC 1924-25 1598cc, TE 1926 1645cc, TF 1926 1496cc,

SD 1927-29 1496cc, TG 1927-29 1645cc, TH 1927-29 1496cc, and TJ (coil ignition and shell radiator) 1930-32 1645cc. In 1931-32 there was also a 12/60. The longer-stroke 1645cc cars were devised for luxurious touring. The sportier ones started with a "ducks-back" body style and then came the well known "beetleback" – some of which were good for 80mph. Four wheel brakes were initially optional.

Alvis 14/75

14.75. 1927-30 (prod: 738). Chassis 1928 £550, fabric saloon £795. S6 OHV 1870cc, single plate clutch, four speed gearbox with right hand change, spiral bevel axle, semi-elliptic suspension. First tested in 1926-27 by T G John himself in the Alps, the 14.75 was intended as a non-sporting and ultra-smooth version of the 12/50. Most of these TA/TB series had saloon bodywork with low gearing and had worse overall performance than the 12/50.

However, Smith-Clarke's crankshaft vibration damper helped to make the small six a very refined unit, and the car grew into the well liked Silver Eagle. 14.75 actually meant 14¾ RAC hp, the bhp output being about 60.

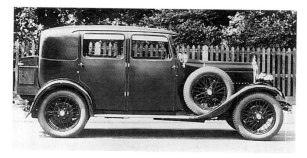

HRH Prince George's 1929 Lancefield fabric bodied Alvis Silver Eagle.

16.95 SILVER EAGLE. 1929-33 (prod: 1929-30 783). Chassis 1930 from £500. S6 OHV 2148cc, single plate clutch, four speed gearbox with right hand change, spiral bevel axle, semi-elliptic suspension.

This was a bored-out 14.75 with the option of its dual carburettors (three in 1930) and the new refinements of dual coil and magneto ignition and centralised chassis lubrication. The hare managed to fend off the eagle mascot until late 1930. 70mph (75mph with twin carbs) and up to 24mpg were possible, and everything from two-seat sports to six-light saloons listed. In the TB/TC series outside our period the engine grew to 2½ litres and 19.82hp.

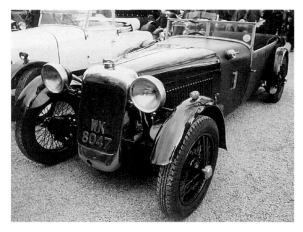

The front wheel drive Alvis 1928-30.

FD/FE series. 1928-30 (prod: 155 including earlier prototypes and racing cars). Chassis 1930 £575, sports saloon £750. S4 OHC 1482cc, single plate clutch, four speed gearbox with right hand change, front wheel drive, quarter-elliptic suspension. Since 1925 Alvis had experimented with front wheel drive cars, initially with a back-to-front 12/50 engine. A straight-eight FWD racer was catalogued in 1926 at £1000, and in 1928 FWD cars finished 6th and 9th at Le Mans. The production road car, with independent suspension, had an overhead camshaft four-cylinder unit and optional Roots supercharger. A straight-eight engine, also of 1½ litres, was available as well. Centre-lock Rudge-Whitworth wire wheels were standardised for the first time on an Alvis. The public was nervous about so much technical novelty and sales were disappointing.

AMAZON

Billiter Street, London EC3

This cyclecar in standard colours of blue and black was made in 1922 and weighed 6¾cwt. For £235 customers got a two-seater with hood. The Amazon had a rear mounted, two-cylinder, air-cooled Coventry Victor horizontal 7hp twin. There was a three speed and reverse gearbox, and final drive to the wire wheels at the rear was by chain. There were quarter-elliptic springs all round and a dummy radiator up front.

ANGLO-SPHINX
see Forster

ANGUS-SANDERSON

Birtley, County Durham 1919-21; Hendon, Middlesex 1921-27

Originally coachbuilders established in 1780, descendants became motor dealers in the North of England with associates making the NUT motor cycle in Newcastle upon Tyne. This factory was used by Sir William Angus, Sanderson and Co. Ltd to make aircraft and then to assemble the first few Angus-Sanderson cars in 1918-19. Later in the year production moved to an armaments factory on a 53-acre site at nearby Birtley which had employed 6000 Belgians on war work. It was reorganised to produce bodywork and assemble proprietory components including Tylor engines, Mechin front axles and frames, and Wrigley gearboxes and drive axles. Wood for the bodywork was grown in the company's own forests.

The vast potential output was never realised and the firm was soon in financial difficulties.

It was reformed, with backing from dealers, S F Edge's British Spyker Co. and Tylors, as Angus-Sanderson (1921) Ltd and soon moved to the Grahame-White aircraft and cyclecar factory at Hendon. An 8hp model followed in 1922, designed by Ricardo with a sidevalve 990cc engine, but very few appear to have been built.

14HP. 1919-27 (prod: up to 3000 1919-21, few afterwards). Tourer 1920 £575, 1926 £365. Tylor S4 SV 2305cc, Wrigley three speed gearbox, cone and later plate clutch (some or all in oil), bevel axle. Semi-elliptic front, cantilever rear suspension. A solid, dependable and good looking car with a radiator shape designed by Cecil Kimber of later MG fame, and initially with wavy disc wheels.

Particularly attractive was the tourer, with its flowing lines, flush hinges and no external handles. Another unusual feature was separate scuttle fillers for main and reserve fuel tanks. The later cars had four wheel brakes and improved engines capable of 27mpg.

ARAB

Letchworth, Hertfordshire

Reid Railton worked on the Leyland 8 designed by J G Parry Thomas and developed a smaller engine using similar valve gear. It was installed in various racing cars before Railton formed Arab Motors in 1925 to create a sleek sports car. They were made in part of a steel foundry and then in the former

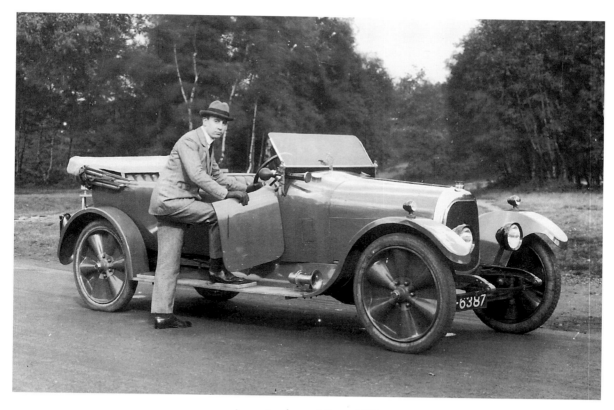

Angus Sanderson 14hp, c.1920.

Phoenix car factory. Fellow directors were two members of the Spurrier family of Leyland Motors, but the project went sour after their friend Parry Thomas was killed in his land speed record attempt in "Babs" in 1927.

Railton then moved to Thomson and Taylor near the Booklands racing circuit in Surrey and was involved with the Brooklands Riley and the Railton car.

Arab Sports.

SPORTS. 1925-30 (prod: about 10). £525 complete or £550 as 90mph low-chassis model. S4 OHC 2 litre 65bhp, single plate clutch, Moss four speed gearbox, ENV spiral bevel axle, semi-elliptic suspension. One of the most interesting British high-performance cars of the decade. Two low-chassis examples seem to have been sold, one of which had fixed-head coupé bodywork.

Possibly only about half a dozen were built at Letchworth and others are thought to have been assembled from spares by Thomson and Taylor near Brooklands. Unusual features included an immensely rigid two-bearing crankshaft cut from a solid billet, leaf valve springs each end of which controlled a separate valve, and an overhead camshaft whose drive chain could be tensioned by a lever behind the radiator.

ARGYLL

Hoozier Street, Bridgeton, Glasgow

Before the Great War Argyll was one of Britain's five biggest car makers, with magnificent factory premises at Alexandria near Loch Lomond. It was building something over 500 cars a year in premises capable of more like 1500, and simply could not sell them all at a profit due to high overheads. In 1914 it was liquidated and the remnants, under the control of J A Brimlow, manager of the repair works, moved into his premises, which were actually the bicycle factory in which the firm had originated in Victorian times.

Argyll cars had been noted for high quality workmanship and material, allied to average performance and price. The company had been one of the pioneers of four wheel brakes in 1911, and was an enthusiastic advocate of single sleeve-valve engines from 1909.

The London service depot of Argyll, which lasted until 1939, also made the RLC car in 1920-21. Postwar Argyll engines were allegedly made by tractor firm Wallace of Glasgow and works truck specialists Greenwood and Batley of Leeds. Sales continued until the early 1930s and a mysterious 18/50 sleeve-valve model was listed about that time.

1921 Argyll 15/30 had sleeve valves.

15/30. 1920-24 (prod: 11). Chassis 1922 £750, 1924 £600. S4 single sleeve-valve 2615cc, cone then single plate clutch, four speed constant mesh gearbox with right hand change, spiral bevel axle. Semi-elliptic front, cantilever rear suspension. This was a revival of a pre-war model without its four wheel brakes, worm axle or wire wheels, but with electric starting and lighting. The engine was said to have 18 moving parts compared with 75 in a poppet-valve type. A price of £900 for an open tourer explains why so few of the model were sold.

Argyll Twelve.

TWELVE, 12/40. 1922-30, 1926-30 (prod: 200-250). Chassis 1923 £400, 1930 £295. S4 single sleeve-valve 1496cc and 1630cc, dry plate clutch, in-unit four speed gearbox with right hand change, spiral bevel axle, semi-elliptic suspension. The smaller engine developed 30bhp and the larger 40bhp. Four

wheel brakes were available in 1926 but the cars were too expensive to sell to more than a few traditional customers, most of whom were sadly wiped out by the aftermath of the Wall Street crash.

ARIEL

Coventry Ordnance, Warwickshire

This well known pioneer bicycle and motor cycle builder also made cars from 1898 to 1915. Its motor vehicle side belonged to Lorraine Dietrich for a few years to 1910 and, after the demise of this involvement, production moved from Birmingham to Coventry, though HQ remained at Bournbrook, Birmingham. Cars were revived in 1922 in the shape of a little two-cylinder lightweight designed by Jack Sangster, son of Ariel's manager. He had previously designed a similar car that became the basis of the air-cooled Rover.

1924 Ariel Nine two-cylinder four-seater.

NINE. 1922-25 (prod: possibly 700). Complete 1923 £235, 1925 from £198. HO2 SV 996cc, dry plate clutch, three speed and reverse gearbox in unit with spiral bevel back axle, quarter-elliptic suspension. The Nine was a lively little car weighing 11cwt, finished as standard in grey, and capable of 53mpg and 53mph. Despite some sources claiming the engine to be a rough and noisy air-cooled unit it in fact had water-cooling!

1924 four-cylinder Ariel Ten.

TEN. 1924-26 (prod: possibly 250), chassis £180. S4 SV 1097cc, cone clutch, rear axle gearbox as Nine, quarter-elliptic suspension. This model normally came in grey too, though a primrose painted sports model capable of 60mph was available in 1925, with 25bhp at 3500rpm. All models had two wheel brakes.

ARMSTRONG-SIDDELEY

Parkside, Coventry, Warwickshire

In 1919 the makers of Armstrong-Whitworth cars acquired Siddeley-Deasy for £420,000 to create Armstrong-Siddeley. The entrepreneur J D Siddeley (later Lord Kenilworth) made a fortune from aircraft, aero engines and cars and regained total control of the business in 1926 for £1.5 million. His first cars had been an amalgam of Deasy and American ideas following his son's visit to Peerless, Stearns, Cadillac, Marmon, Pierce-Arrow, Packard and Hudson. Marmon in particular is said to have influenced the Thirty, and one was imported for evaluation. The "cars of aircraft quality" as they were eventually called (initially "made by the men who make the Siddeley aero engine") soon came to include smaller cars, and all enjoyed

an image somewhat akin to that of Daimler. Indeed the company's adoption and manufacture of the Wilson Self Changing Gear in 1928 brought it into close contact with its Coventry neighbour, Daimler, who bought large numbers, as did Riley, Talbot and others.

To avoid sullying the Armstrong Siddeley name and reputation a cheap utility car was sold under the name Stoneleigh. Most Armstrong-Siddeleys had coachwork built in-house by the Burlington Carriage Co., which had been a subsidiary since 1913.

All cars featured the sphinx mascot – "as silent as the sphinx" – and by 1928 the factory claimed to have built more six-cylinder cars than any in Europe.

THIRTY. 1919-31 (prod: 2700). Chassis 1920 £830, 1929 £750. S6 OHV 4960cc 60bhp, multi-plate clutch, separate three speed gearbox with central change, torque tube, spiral bevel axle. Semi-elliptic front, cantilever rear suspension. An enormous carriage trade offering, though the first tourers cost as little as £960. The Duke of York bought formal styles in 1920 and '21 (and used one for his 1927 New Zealand tour). In 1928 the Thirty was the first model to be tried with the Wilson gearbox, and this

1926 Armstrong-Siddeley Four-Fourteen.

Armstrong-Siddeley Thirty with Penman body, c.1924.

was adopted in the following year. Typical fuel consumption was 17mpg.

A revised monobloc (bibloc earlier) engine with two detachable heads was used from 1925 on the Mk II, which also gained four wheel brakes.

1921 Armstrong-Siddeley Eighteen.

EIGHTEEN and 18/50. 1921-26 (prod: approx 2500). Chassis 1923 £500, 1926 £340. S6 OHV 2.4 litres (2872cc from 1925), dry plate clutch, three speed gearbox with torque tube, spiral bevel axle. Semi-elliptic front, cantilever rear suspension. Effectively a scaled-down Thirty for two thirds of the price – indeed a saloon cost only £525 in 1926, when a Long Eighteen for limousine coachwork was offered. With the larger engine a saloon was capable of 60mph and 19mpg. Four wheel brakes were available from 1925.

FOUR-FOURTEEN and 14/30. 1923-29 (prod: 13,365). Chassis 1925 £260, tourer £360. S4 1852cc OHV, single dry plate clutch, in-unit three speed gearbox, spiral bevel axle. Early cars with quarter-elliptic springs all round, then semi-elliptic. The company's first four-cylinder car and shown to be in a lower class by its flat radiator reminiscent of the Stoneleigh. It had 6-volt electrics instead of the 12-

volt systems fitted to the Eighteen and Thirty.

Four wheel brakes arrived on the Mk II in mid-1925, when a road tester spoke of 24mpg and over 50mph.

As with other chassis the body styles were named after places – Sandown sports, Cotswold tourer, Broadway saloon, etc. Triplex glass was standardised in 1929.

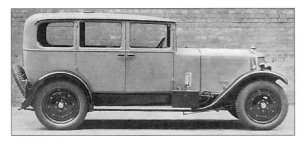

The short model 20hp Armstrong-Siddeley.

SHORT and LONG 20. 1926-36 (prod: 4014 to 1930 plus 983 Long). Chassis 1928 £340 short, £450 long. S6 OHV 2872cc, single dry plate clutch, in-unit three speed gearbox with torque tube, four speed pre-selector gears optional from 1929, spiral bevel axle, semi-elliptic suspension. An important family and professional model that became the firm's top seller. Centralised lubrication came in 1928 and an underslung chassis half way through that year. Dome wings for 1929, and available in Long (10' 8") and Standard (10') wheelbase.

The Armstrong-Siddeley Fifteen.

FIFTEEN. 1927-35 (prod: 3703 to 1930). Tourer 1929 £335, saloon £395. S6 SV 1.9 litres, single plate clutch, three speed gearbox with torque tube, spiral bevel axle, semi-elliptic suspension. An apparently retrograde step with a small sidevalve six, though this is what the market wanted.

Again the radiator was flat rather than the pronounced vee of the luxury models. This model and the rest of the range were fitted with a centralised, footpump-operated chassis lubrication system. The Fifteen was quiet, smooth and flexible, with a top speed of 55mph. Magneto ignition was retained in the vintage period, with automatic advance and retard, though manual control was also fitted.

An Armstrong-Siddeley Twelve. This is a 1930 sunshire saloon.

TWELVE. 1929-37 (prod: 1500 to 1930). Fabric saloon 1929 £295, tourer £250. S6 SV 1236cc, 1434cc late in 1930, when pre-selector gear became available. In-unit three speed gearbox with torque tube, spiral bevel axle, semi-elliptic suspension. "Suitable for the daughters of clergymen" was how Michael Sedgwick once described this smooth and low-powered model. It helped to start the trend to pint-pot sixes. Standard colours were mole and maroon with grey and green interior.

ARROL-ASTER

Heathhall, Dumfries, Scotland

See also Arrol-Johnston and Aster. This combined marque, formed in April 1927 with directors from both companies, lasted for only two years before a Receiver was appointed. It then continued with limited production and sales until 1931. Manufacture of Asters was moved to Scotland, with the London premises retained for spares and repairs until Singer acquired the site. The Galloway was continued, as were the 15/40 and 20hp Arrol-Johnstons (now with Aster-inspired coachwork). The Aster 21/60 and 24/70 carried on, along with a new 17/50 six and a 23/70 straight eight, both with sleeve valves. There was soon some rationalisation in the Arrol-Aster range. In 1928 the firm reconstructed Sir Malcolm Campbell's land speed record Bluebird.

The six-cylinder Arrol-Aster 17/50

The straight-eight Arrol-Aster 23/70

17/50, 23/70. 1927-30, 1928-30 (prod: approx 80). Chassis £498, £698. S6 2370cc, S8 2760cc, sleeve valves, single dry plate clutch, in-unit four speed gearbox with right hand change, torque tube, spiral bevel axle. Semi-elliptic front, cantilever rear suspension. Attractive and rare successors to the Wembley range. A Cozette supercharger was available for £50 on some 17/50s, when 72mph and 17mpg became possible. The Hon. Mrs Victor Bruce completed the 1929 Monte Carlo rally in one. The 23/70, with a large "8" badge on its radiator and an optional free wheel, continued right up to the end when Kryn and Lahy (later K L Cranes of Letchworth) acquired the spares in 1931. The engine was said to be vulnerable if revved above 3400rpm as the wobble-shaft moving the sleeves became over-stressed. The poor steering lock also came in for criticism.

Arrol-Aster 15/40, 1928.

15/40. 1927-29 (prod: n/a). Tourer 1927 £385, saloon £450. S4 OHV 2413cc, single dry plate clutch, in-unit four speed gearbox, torque tube, spiral bevel axle, semi-elliptic suspension. Final version of the 15.9 Arrol-Johnston, which had originally appeared in the teens but now had such modern features as four wheel brakes and OHV. Well equipped, with leather upholstery and rubber-cushioned mountings for the bodywork (which had the shallow windows and other styling features showing the Aster influence).

There were few sales outlets outside the London area, although the firm had its own premises in Birmingham, Manchester and Southport.

ARROL-JOHNSTON

Heathhall, Dumfries, Scotland

One of the three "Big A's" of Scotland (with Argyll and Albion, though the latter wisely stuck to commercial vehicles after the teens), this firm was led from 1909 by the legendary T C Pullinger, who had worked in France and for Humber and Sunbeam. After war work, chiefly involving Beardmore aero engines, the company employed 2400 men at its factories. It had close financial ties with the mighty Beardmore empire and disposed of one of its factories to Beardmore for taxi production. Another made the Galloway car, whilst the ultra-modern ferrocrete structure at Heathhall, with all the latest electric tooling and air lines, made the appropriately named Victory model. This was designed by Beardmore's G W A Brown, formerly of Humber and Clement Talbot, with help from L J Shorter, ex-Humber and Sunbeam. It was not a success and was hastily replaced. From a peak of fifty cars per week, sales of these silent, ultra-conservative cars dwindled and, despite a merger with Aster in 1927, the combined marque died three years later. In the 1920s Arrol-Johnston's managing director J S Napier joined S F Edge at Cubitt. Later Heathhall became the home of North British Rubber, where Alexander Johnston had been MD since earlier in the 1920s.

Arrol-Johnston 15.9hp.

An Arrol-Johnston 15.9hp with "all-weather" body.

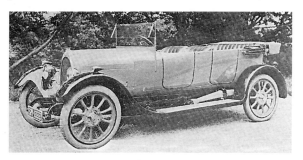

Arrol-Johnston Victory.

VICTORY. 1919-20 (prod: probably under 50). Open tourer £700. S4 OHC 2.6 and 2.8 litres quoted, single plate clutch, four speed gearbox, spiral bevel axle. Semi-elliptic front, cantilever rear suspension. One of the first all-new postwar cars, the Victory was insufficiently developed and attracted bad publicity when one carrying the Prince of Wales broke down in Yeovil. An overhead camshaft was unusual at the time, especially allied to the very long stroke (140 or 150mm), said to have been inspired by the 1908 TT Humber. The engine developed 40bhp at 2000rpm. The Phoenix was said to be a crib of the Victory.

15.9, FIFTEEN (also called 15/40). 1919-24, 1925-27 (prod: 2100 to 1923, then few). Chassis 1920 £620, saloon 1925 £475. **S4 SV (OHV from 1925) 2614cc 15.9hp, single plate clutch, four speed gearbox with right hand change, spiral bevel axle, semi-elliptic suspension.** Revival of a pre-war model as an urgent replacement for the Victory. This and other models, once sold, were catered for at company rallies in the London area in 1921-22, when testers reported on cars whilst owners sipped tea and listened to orchestras! Lots of cars in the middle of the production run had painted radiator shells to reduce costs (a plated 1920 variety is also shown).

Front wheel brakes were adopted in 1925 and the model, now developing 40bhp, had a final lease of life as an Arrol-Aster.

A 20hp Empire model Arrol-Johnston.

12, 14, 20. 1925, 1924, 1924-27 (prod: n/a). Complete £360-£650. S4 SV 1670cc, 2129cc, 3290cc, single dry plate clutch, separate four speed gearbox with right hand change, spiral bevel axle, semi-elliptic suspension. An assortment of short-lived models, involving several mysteries like fifty with Hotchkiss pushrod OHV engines before the above sequence in 1921, and a 1640cc two-stroke chassis at the 1922 London Motor Show. A 1924 20 is shown, at a time when the Galloway shared its engine and many mechanical features with the smaller 12hp model. Sales were slumping and no chassis numbers were quoted after 4001 at the start of 1923.

ASCOT

Pixmore Avenue, Letchworth, Hertfordshire

The backers of this firm (there had been an unconnected Anglo-French car of the same name in 1914-15) included H G Burford (ex-Mercedes, Humber, New Orleans, Burford lorries, etc.). Capital of £400,000 was sought to build a pressed and welded steel car under Hungarian Fejes licence. The lack of castings was intended to keep the price low, and 1500 10hp tourers at £125 were planned for the first year. The factory had formerly built the Phoenix car but only prototype Fejes types emerged due to lack of finance. To salvage the situation a conventionally assembled Ascot Six was hurriedly concocted.

An Ascot Six chassis.

SIX. 1928-30 (prod: n/a). Chassis 1929 £325, complete Gold Cup saloon £435. S6 SV 2423cc, single dry plate clutch, in-unit three speed gearbox with central change, spiral bevel axle, semi-elliptic suspension. Described in an Ascot advertisement as "a simple 2½-litre light six which is built on straightforward lines", the car's 50bhp engine and gearbox are thought to have been from the American firms of Continental and Warner respectively.

Only the earliest cars had the style of radiator shown, afterwards getting a ribbon style, some with side coverings encroaching on the mesh reminiscent of theatre curtains! Standard colours were much brighter than contemporaries' offerings – red or yellow and black, and there was chromed brightwork. Some parts of the car allegedly came from the abortive 18hp Phoenix.

ASHBY

Towcester, Northamptonshire; Barlow Moor Road, Chorlton-cum-Hardy, Lancashire

Victor Ashby and Son (also Victor) ran the Pioneer Motor Works, a garage at Towcester with manufacturing capabilities. Young Victor, returning from engineering service on a motor launch in the Great War, designed a light car which via mutual friends of a Harley Street doctor came to the attention of aeroplane makers Short Bros. Short Bros employed six Ashby men, including a chief draughtsmen previously with GWK, and made Short-Ashby cars for two years before losing interest in the project due to disappointing sales. The Ashby then continued in Chorlton-cum-Hardy during 1923-24.

The air-cooled flat twin Ashby.

ASHBY. 1919-21 (prod: under 50). Coventry Victor HO2 air-cooled 5/6hp or 8hp. Friction drive via discs on end of propshaft working at engine speed and on sleeved axle with reduction gearbox to wheels. Independent front suspension. A prototype is shown on test, with wooden chassis, cylinders protruding through the sides of a narrow bonnet, and a Rolls-Royce shaped radiator.

The car must have had something to distinguish it from the myriad other cyclecars and thus be adopted by Short Brothers.

SHORT-ASHBY, ASHBY. 1921-22, 1923-4 (prod: 130 to July 1922). Two-seater 1923 from £198. Ruby S4 SV 970cc 8hp, four ratio friction drive or Moss three speed gearbox. Transverse leaf front, quar-

The two-seater Short-Ashby.

ter-elliptic rear suspension. Hundreds of orders for the friction car at £275 and the other at £198 were taken at the White City Motor Show overspill in 1921, but most evaporated when payment was due.

After Short Bros abandoned the project a new Ashby Motors Ltd offered the car briefly, but without conspicuous success. The geared car was said to have had unsuitably spaced ratios.

ASHTON & ASHTON-EVANS

Liverpool Street and Floodgate Street, Birmingham

In 1919 an engineering company that made colonial locomotives, tools, castings and aeroplane parts launched this car, designed by E Bailey from Sunbeam. Although a four-wheeler, the rear wheels were only eight inches apart to obviate the need for a differential. The rear "axle" was sprung by a plate on which rested a roller at the end of a quarter-elliptic spring. It was located for driving and braking by a torque tube. There was a constant mesh dog clutch gearbox. Two- and four-cylinder versions seem to have been built, but it was with a more conventional Ashton and then from 1923, Ashton-Evans, that the firm made its name. From 1927 J Ashton-Evans concentrated on his Wonder Mist vehicle polish and on general engineering.

10.5, 11, 11/16. 1920-27 (prod: possibly 250). Chassis 1920 £338, 1925 £235. Coventry Simplex S4 SV 1500cc, cone clutch, three speed gearbox, bevel axle, transverse springs front and rear. Designed by Whitworth Exhibitioner T Bedford, this car, which went under various model designations culminating in 11/16, started at £535 and ended up at £285 complete. The constant mesh gearbox was said to give one of the easiest of vintage changes. The engine developed 21bhp and was guaranteed to give better than 40mpg. The back axle ran on Hoffmann ball

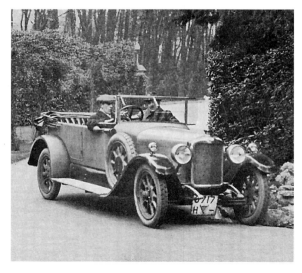

An Ashton-Evans 1½-litre four-seater.

and roller bearings, helping to justify the slogan "the car that glides". The standard early bodywork finished in grey was a three-abreast coupé with two-seater dickey.

ASTER

Wembley, Middlesex

A well-known manufacturer of engines in France established a branch at Wembley in 1898 and later added cars of French origin. In 1913 a limited company was formed in which Lord Invernairn, a major shareholder in the Beardmore and Arrol-Johnston companies, appears to have had an interest.

In 1922, when Aster occupied eight acres in Wembley, a series of expensive, high-grade and particularly stylish cars were introduced which had no counterpart in France.

After merging with Arrol-Johnston in 1927 the combined firm went into liquidation within three years. See Arrol-Aster.

The Aster 18/50

18/50. 1922-24 (prod: about 50). Chassis 1924 £605, body added up to £510. S6 OHV 2618cc, disc clutch, four speed gearbox with right hand change, spiral bevel axle. Semi-elliptic front, cantilever rear suspension. On RAC test an 18/50 covered 2000 miles at 44.17mph, using two gallons of oil. Fuel consumption worked out at 21.07mpg. Four wheel brakes were an early option.

High price made this a very exclusive car. The boss S D Begbie, in impeccable suit and topper, personally inspected each day's operations.

An elegant touring body on the 3-litre Aster 21/60.

The Duke of York's Aster 20/55.

20/55. 1924-25 (prod: 52 in 1925). Chassis from £575. S6 OHV 2890cc, disc clutch, four speed gearbox, torque tube, spiral bevel axle. Semi-elliptic front, cantilever rear suspension. Described as "not for the tyro, but for those that know most about motor cars and for the connoisseur". One such was the Duke of York (temporarily forsaking his Armstrong-Siddeley 30) whose car is shown here. Sports and touring models were listed and all had four wheel brakes. Confusingly, with its starlike name the Aster also resembled the Star car.

The six-cylinder single sleeve-valve Aster 24/70 Weymann fabric saloon.

21/60, 24/70. 1926-27 (prod: 68 in 1926). Chassis £595, £785. S6 OHV 3042cc, S6 sleeve-valve 3460cc, twin dry plate clutch, in-unit four speed gearbox, torque tube, spiral bevel axle. Semi-elliptic front, cantilever rear suspension. The 21/60 was an improved version of the 20/55 with a 2mm larger bore, and the 24/70 had Burt-McCollum licence sleeve valves. Both had an attractive new tapered radiator, and with suitable bodywork 85mph was attainable (certainly not with the 39cwt 24/70 landaulette at a colossal £1,300!). Antique or furniture leather was used for the upholstery.

ASTON-MARTIN

Abingdon Road, Kensington, London W8; from 1926 Victoria Road, Feltham, Middlesex

Under its original makers, Bamford and Martin, this low-production sporting car had a hyphen between Aston, the hill where it had enjoyed competition success, and Lionel Martin's surname. About 60 cars were made between 1915 and 1925, latterly with financial support from Lady Charnwood and Count Zborowski (of Chitty fame).

The firm was reorganised in 1926, moving to Feltham, where for the rest of the decade it did without a hyphen (which however began to creep back in 1930). The new backers were A C Bertelli (see Enfield Allday), W Renwick and Lord Charnwood, followed in our period by others including P C Kidner of Vauxhall and S Straker of Straker-Squire. The company's competition success exerted a strange fascination on rich sportsmen as both backers and drivers.

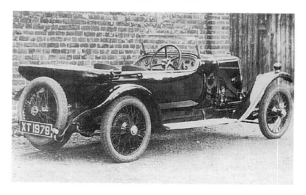

Aston-Martin Standard Sports.

STANDARD SPORTS. 1921-25 (prod: about 50). Chassis 1923 £625, sports £700. S4 SV 1487cc, Hele Shaw multi-disc clutch, four speed gearbox, spiral

bevel axle, semi-elliptic suspension. There was really no such thing as a Standard specification and both single and twin OHC versions were also tried. However, the sidevalve cars earned an excellent reputation and were good for 38-45bhp, about 70mph and 35mpg. The steering column was adjustable and the cylinder head was cast integrally with the monobloc. Pistons came from the makers of the Zephyr car. Front wheel brakes were standardised in 1923.

An Aston-Martin first series 1½-litre saloon in 1928.

A 1930 Aston-Martin coupé.

FIRST SERIES. 1927-32 (prod: 129 by January 1932). Chassis 1927 "S" (short) £495, "T" (touring) £575. S4 OHC 1495cc 56bhp, single dry plate clutch, separate four speed gearbox, torque tube, David Brown worm axle, semi-elliptic suspension. These 1½-litre cars were made under the aegis of A C Bertelli (see Reaba-R&B) at Feltham and came as Tourer, Sports, International and Le Mans (a team ran at this event in 1928 with dry-sump engines). Bodies were built by Bertelli's brother Enrico, and the price for the Standard saloon of 1928 shown here was £675. The cars were sold under the slogan "The premier sporting car" and had twin SU carburettors, an overhead camshaft operating inclined valves, dry sump lubrication on some, and Hartford friction shock absorbers. A more sporting "Ulster" engine cost £50 extra in 1930.

ASTRAL

Thames and Bridge Works, Barking, Essex

Most unusually for a new light car manufacturer in 1923 virtually everything was made in-house. In September 1924 the firm, which traded as the Hertford Engineering Co. with a showroom in New Bond Street, was marked as "gone away", so very few can have been built.

An Astral 12/40.

12/40. 1923-24 (prod: n/a). Chassis £320, two-seater £350, four-seater £365. S4 OHC 1720cc, cone clutch, in-unit three speed gearbox, spiral bevel axle, semi-elliptic suspension. A nicely conceived sporting car with ball-bearing crank and Lucas coil ignition and Dynastart. Presumably it was uneconomic to make at such a realistic price, but one buyer was a banker's son who raced his Astral at Brooklands.

ATOMETTE

Cleveland Street, Wolverhampton

Made by Allan Thomas, AMIAE, in 1922, this was a diminutive three-wheeler with a 3½hp Villiers two-stroke air-cooled engine driving the single rear wheel by belt via a chain driven Burman three speed gearbox. Finished in grey, blue or green it cost 90 guineas and weighed 2½cwt.

The 90-guinea Atomette of 1922.

AUSTIN

Longbridge Works, Northfield, Birmingham

Herbert Austin had established Wolseley's car factory before creating his own in 1906. 1200 cars were turned out in 1912 and there was vast expansion in the Great War. The subsequent one-model policy, based on using 20hp components for cars, tractors and lorries, was not a success. It nearly destroyed the company (which was offered to Ford without success), but the hastily conceived 12hp and 7hp saved the day, and in 1925 8000 workers in 62 acres of factories produced 25,000 vehicles. The output for 1927 was 38,000, of which 20,000 were the amazing 7hp, which by then had wiped out virtually all other light cars.

The London factory of Sizaire-Berwick had been acquired in the early 1920s in an unsuccessful venture to make luxury cars, but these, and all Austin commercial vehicles except tractors and car-derived vans and taxis, were soon discontinued.

Austin made much of its own coachwork and had a workforce of 11,000 by 1929. It had 37% of the British car market as well as impressive exports (36% of British car exports in 1926) and overseas licence production. "You invest in an Austin" was an apt slogan justified by the high quality of components and fittings. All were regarded as more upmarket than most mass-produced types such as the rival Morris, and the Seven had a particularly classless appeal.

Austin 20 laudaulette, 1919.

TWENTY, 20/4. 1919-30 (prod: 15,287). Chassis 1923 £550, saloon 1925 £595, chassis 1930 £405. S4 SV 3610cc 45bhp at 2000rpm, single plate clutch, in-unit four speed gearbox with central change, helical bevel axle, semi-elliptic suspension. Herbert Austin owned a Hudson, and the Twenty embodied many of the best American features including the monobloc six, detachable cylinder head, plate clutch and in-unit gearbox, but with these came the latest European ideas like aluminium pistons. An 80mph sports model was available from 1921. Front wheel brakes were standardised from 1925, when a 1¾-ton saloon on road test in the Cotswolds cruised at 50mph and achieved 17mpg. By the time production ended in 1929 the cars' conservative qualities were becoming old fashioned, and the 20/6 had got into its stride.

Austin 12/4.

TWELVE, 12/4. 1922-39 (prod: 69,444 to end 1930). Chassis 1923 £380, 1929 £188. S4 SV 1660cc 20bhp at 2000rpm, single plate clutch, in-unit four speed gearbox with central change, helical bevel axle, semi-elliptic suspension. Announced (briefly as the Ten) and launched in late 1921 with a five-bearing crank like the Twenty, the Twelve proved to be a virtually indestructible car and had an extended lease of life as a London taxi in the 1930s, a further 15,000 12/4s of all types being sold after 1930. A 1924 test showed light and positive steering and gearchange, 25-27mpg, 40-45mph touring, and effective four wheel brakes. The model became known as the Heavy Twelve Four to avoid confusion with the Light Twelve Six in the 1930s.

1928 Austin 7 two-seater with Avon coachwork.

An early Austin 7 Chummy

1929 Austin 7 Gordon England saloon.

SEVEN. 1923-39 (prod: 123,161 to end 1930). Two-seater 1923 £165, four-seater 1925 £149, saloon 1929 £140. S4 SV 747cc (initially 696cc) 10.5bhp at 2400rpm, single plate clutch, in-unit three speed gearbox with central change, torque tube, helical bevel axle. Transverse leaf front, quarter elliptic rear suspension. This was the fashionable model that wiped out virtually all the other light cars listed in this book, thanks to a combination of "Big car in miniature" qualities and low price. Around 50mph and 50mpg were on the cards. The Seven had four wheel brakes (handbrake on front, footbrake on rear until coupled in July 1930) and gained an electric starter in November 1923, coil ignition and nickelled radiator in late 1928, and ball gearchange in 1929.

Sports models were offered from 1924 and enjoyed remarkable success. The Brooklands Super Sports was available for £265 with a 75mph Brooklands certificate, and in 1928 a supercharged road-going two-seater cost only £225 and was capable of 7000rpm.

Several firms offered distinctive bodywork, such as Gordon England, Mulliner, Avon, Boyd Carpenter and, from 1929, perhaps the most famous of all, Swallow. The car was built overseas (notably 9300 by Dixi in Germany 1927-29) and direct exports from Britain accounted for no less than 7669 in 1929 alone.

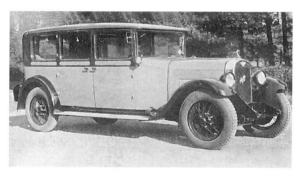

Austin 20/6 "Ranelagh" limousine, 1929.

20/6. 1927-39 (prod: 3018 to end 1930). Chassis 1929 £405, Carlton saloon £560, Ranelagh landaulet or limo £630. S6 SV 3400cc 45-50bhp, single plate clutch, in-unit four speed gearbox with central change, helical bevel axle, semi-elliptic suspension. Six cylinders suited the carriage trade better than the 20/4, which nevertheless refused to die for a couple more years. Although launched in 1926 the 20/6 did not enter quantity production until 1928. In late 1929 the gate change of this and other Austins switched to a ball, and chrome plating and Triplex glass arrived. On test 16-20mpg and 63mph were recorded, with the brakes coming in for criticism (there was no servo and the car weighed 2 tons), though smoothness, the high seating position, silence, torque, and low price, were praised.

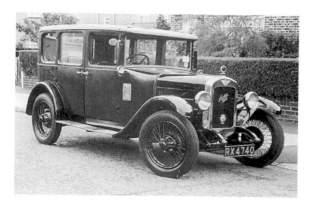

1929 Austin 16 fabric saloon.

SIXTEEN. 1927-36 (prod: 23,107 to end 1930). Chassis 1929 £240, Clifton tourer £305, Burnham or fabric saloon £375. S6 SV 2249cc 15.9hp, single plate clutch, in-unit four speed gearbox, helical bevel axle, semi-elliptic suspension. Like the 20/6 this engine had its timing chain at the rear of the crank to be out of the way of torsional vibration. Figures of 60mph and 23mpg were attained on test and the model gained chrome, Triplex glass and other Austin family updates in late 1929. Zinc strips between the spring leaves and silentbloc bushes in the eyes were earlier improvements, no doubt aided from 1929 by the Smiths shock absorbers. Whilst other models headed towards all-steel bodywork the big Austins remained of composite construction, and you could still have a division in the Iver saloon.

AUTOCRAT

Balsall Heath and Hall Green, Birmingham

This company had its roots in the Birmingham cycle trade and made a typical light car before the Great War. In 1919 it embarked on a series of 10-12hp assembled cars. At first, Coventry Simplex engines were offered, but the bulk of production employed Dorman (240 overhead-valve and side-valve units) and Meadows engines (30 or more). Some of the latter went into a spartan "mile a minute" model.

Autocrat built its own bodywork and the cars were noted for a very high standard of finish. Although the factory closed in 1926, sales of the final cars were undertaken by Calthorpe.

11.9, 12, 12/15, 10/12, 12/24. 1920-21, 1922-23, 1922, 1924, 1924-26 (prod: approx 300). Complete 1920 £600, 1925 £295. Various S4 SV (some OHV Dorman and Meadows) 1500cc-1978cc, cone clutch with three speed gearbox (plate clutch and Meadows four speed on later cars), torque tube,

1920 10/12hp Autocrat two-seater with dickey.

spiral bevel axle, semi-elliptic suspension. Reckoned to be a cut above many of its contemporaries, and some models were unusual in having a detachable hardtop. The sports versions were lowered by 3½ inches and most Autocrats came in dark blue.

1923 Dorman powered Autocrat Occasional Four, restored by Dorman apprentices.

AUTOGEAR

Leeds, Yorkshire

Resembling the Stanhope and Bramham made nearby, the Autogear of 1922-23 had a sidevalve air-cooled vee-twin Blackburne 10hp engine driving the front wheel (which also steered). For £185 one got 7¾cwt of engineering complexity. In 1923 production moved to McLysaght and Douglas in Dublin, where the car was renamed the Leprechân!

The Accellera and Foster car had Autogear variable transmission but the two Autogears appear to have been unconnected. A front wheel drive four wheeler was also built.

AV

Somerset Road, Teddington, Middlesex

Ward and Avey Ltd bought a design from cyclecarist John Carden (see Carden) and commenced production of their Monocar in his former factory in 1919, using rear-mounted air-cooled engines.

Eighty men were employed and output totalled several hundred cars. About 50 tandem two-seater 8hp and 10hp Bicars, introduced in 1920, were also built. These had three speed Sturmey-Archer gearboxes and faired-in JAP or Blackburne engines. There was also a side-by-side two-seater called the Runabout.

AV wisely acquired a Jowett agency when sales of cyclecars collapsed, and was still selling cars long after Jowett itself expired in the 1950s.

An AV Monocar, with serviceman aboard.

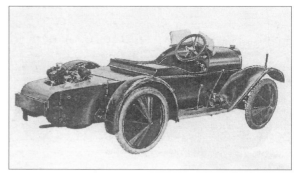

The 1921 "200 mile race" AV Bicar.

An 8hp Blackburne powered Bicar.

MONOCAR. 1919-24 (prod: several 100s). Complete 1920 from £171, 1922 £115. Air-cooled twin-cylinder 5-8hp JAP, Blackburne and occasionally MAG engine in tail, two speed foot operated epicyclic gearbox or Sturmey-Archer three speed and chain drive, quarter-elliptic suspension. The Monocar was only 2' 6" wide and was virtually a glorified four wheel motor cycle, weighing only about a quarter of a ton. Torpedo bodywork was by Thames Valley Pattern Works, in plywood, papier maché or mahogany.

Most were red with black mudguards, or else polished aluminium and blue. Steering was by wire and bobbin on a centre-pivot axle, though stub-axle steering was used on the Bicar.

AVRO

Newton Heath, Manchester

Pioneer flyer and aircraft builder (Sir) Alliott Verdon-Roe had to find other outlets for his factory at the end of the Great War (during which three quarters of all the wood used in aircraft built in Britain was said to have been used by Avro).

There was an exchange of shares with Crossley after the war and Avro became the light car section for a time, making the Harper Runabout, bodywork for several makes of chassis, and the Avro. The latter looked conventional but was actually of integral wood and aluminium construction like an aircraft.

Various engines were offered including a four-cylinder 1330cc sidevalve unit, with three-speed epicyclic gearbox, and about one hundred were built.

Despite the number plate on the 1920 artist's impression there was no connection with AV.

The two-wheeler (with outrigger wheel) is one of several similar prototypes from Sir Alliott – this is his 1927 Mobile with two wheel brakes, 350cc Villiers air-cooled engine, three speed gearbox and worm drive. It was alleged to make wet weather clothes superfluous.

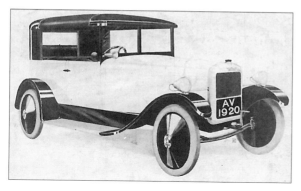

1920 AVRO.

1927 AVRO two-wheeler piloted by Sir Alliot Verdon-Roe.

BABY BLAKE

Croydon, Surrey

A 1922 cyclecar from E G Blake which had a pair of two-stroke engines, each with friction discs instead of flywheels, running in opposite directions. Infinitely variable drive was taken from them by a third disc. Price was £150 but few, if any, were sold.

The 1922 Baby Blake cyclecar.

BAC

Chelsea, London

The British Automotive Co. (its owner Tom Whiting had sold Dodge and Scripps-Booth cars) built prototypes based on the French Mathis but adopted Belgian Peters engines, assembled at Kingston, for its production models of 1922-23. The radiator design was reminiscent of the Lea-Francis and 9.5 and 10.8hp models were built, possibly all with Meadows four speed gearboxes. As chassis number 1025 was used at the start of 1923 it is fair to guess that numbers originally commenced at 1000 and that under fifty cars were built in total. H L Bing, who worked there after a spell with Silver Hawk (he had previously been Works Manager of Iris), believes the figure was closer to 20. A colleague was Bill Watson (later involved with Invicta and Lagonda) who attempted to convert the sidevalve Peters to OHV without success.

A 1923 BAC 10.8hp two-seater with dickey.

BAGULEY

Burton on Trent, Staffordshire

E E Baguley, a locomotive engineer, had started the Ryknield vehicle firm with backing from A Clay of the Bass Brewery. He then designed BSA's first cars and in 1911 returned to Burton to start the firm bearing his name. Only 88 cars were built but the firm continued in the light locomotive and railcar field.

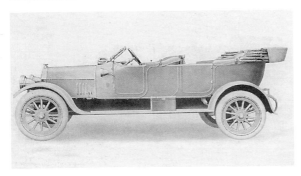

1914 Baguley 15/20.

AE 20/25. 1920 (prod: 5, chassis 1133-37). Choice of bodywork. S4 SV 3½ litres, four speed gearbox, multi-disc clutch. A revival of the 1914 15/20 but with an extra 3mm bore. The car cost £550 in chassis form and had wooden wheels with detachable rims and worm drive.

BAINES

Westbury on Trym, Bristol

A light car that probably never got beyond the prototype stage in 1922.

BARNARD

Whitechapel Road, London E1

St Mark's Engineering Co. built this four wheel cyclecar at the above address in 1921-22. Its unusual feature was a four-in-line 1169cc Henderson air-cooled motor cycle engine, possibly pro-

The Barnard of 1921.

cured as American war surplus. It had a three speed gearbox with no reverse, a multi-disc clutch running in oil and chain drive. For £188 one got the sporting model which, like the £20 cheaper Standard model, had kick-start and a dummy radiator.

BAUGHAN

Harrow, Middlesex; Lower Street, Stroud, Gloucestershire 1921-25

A motor cycle maker that also made four wheel cyclecars between 1920 and 1925 (they continued in some sales lists to 1929). Baughan motor cycle production lasted until 1936 in Stroud (the home town also of Hampton), and Mr Baughan was well known in the motor cycle trialling world as an ACU official and organiser of its International event.

A surviving 1920 Baughan cyclecar

Baughan cyclecars had front-mounted vee-twin 8-10hp Blackburne or JAP engines driving through three speed and reverse Sturmey-Archer gearboxes, and there was final drive by chain.

Each year's models were given a new letter prefix commencing A in 1920, and in 1922 C1 to 874 were listed. If this really represented production then it was drastically reduced soon after the arrival of the Austin Seven.

BAYLISS THOMAS

King's Road, Tyseley, Birmingham

Messrs Bayliss and Thomas were members of the Victorian cycle industry in Coventry whose famous brand name was Excelsior. As this name already existed on a Belgian marque when they entered the car business in Birmingham in 1921 they chose the name Bayliss Thomas (though made by the Excelsior Motor Co., which had in fact just been taken over by the makers of Walkers' ships' fittings and Monarch motor cycles). The first prototypes in 1919 at the Coventry factory (which was to be acquired by Lea Francis) were three-wheelers with air-cooled engines, but production models were conventional 9-13hp four-wheelers with proprietary engines initially by Coventry Simplex and then Meadows. Finish was good and most non-ferrous parts, plus sheet metal, were made in-house. The marque lasted longer than most "assemblers" and was theoretically still available in the early 1930s, though production probably ended in 1929. More than 500 Meadows engines were used, which with other types suggests that well over 1000 cars were built.

A preserved 1925 Bayliss Thomas 12/27.

1923 Bayliss Thomas 8.9hp Junior

9/19, 8.9. 1922-24 (prod: see above). Junior (shown) 1923 £260. S4 OHV 1075cc, own three speed gearbox, cone clutch and Wrigley worm axle, quarter-elliptic suspension. This was the only model that claimed to have Bayliss Thomas's own engine. It was finished in pearl grey with a polished aluminium bonnet.

1925 Bayliss Thomas 13/30 two-seater.

12/27, 13/30. 1925-29 (prod: see above). Complete 1928 £235-255. S4 OHV 1500cc Meadows, own three speed gearbox, Moss spiral bevel axle, semi-elliptic suspension. Front wheel brakes on later versions. Amongst the last cars with a cone clutch in 1929 and still well made. From the mid-1920s most cars had Mulliner bodies. Capacity was stated to be 40 cars per week in 1926, when 10 and 13hp models were also offered.

Bayliss Thomas 10.5hp with Bowden body.

10.5, 10.8, 10/22 (sometimes called 12/22). 1922-24 (prod: see above). Coupé £305, 1922 two-seater £280. S4 SV 1500cc Coventry Simplex, own three speed gearbox, cone clutch, Wrigley worm axle, quarter-elliptic suspension. The Bowden sliding door 10.8 saloon shown weighed only 15cwt complete.

BEAN

Dudley and Tipton, Staffordshire

A Harper Sons and Bean were major components suppliers to the motor industry, with half of the British makers as customers. Bean acquired the pre-war Perry, designed by Tom Conroy, from Willys Overland, and modified it as the Bean 11.9 in 1919. Sales manager B G Panks was recruited from Austin and 2000 cars were planned for 1919-20, followed by 10,000 for the 1920-21 model year. Financial links were established with ABC, Vulcan, Swift and various component suppliers as well as the sales group BMTC. Harper Bean Ltd, as it became known, was capitalised at a colossal £6 million and equipped its former munition shops at Tipton for assembly and its shell shop at Dudley for bodywork.

Moving track assembly lines made a peak 505 chassis in the month of July 1920 but there was financial disarray soon afterwards and the company was reorganised. After that, 80-100 per week were made in 1922 and sales projections were never reached. Larger cars followed in the mid-1920s and steel supplier Hadfields of Sheffield rescued the company in 1926. Car production ended in 1929, but commercials lasted for another two years. Bean then concentrated on its component manufacture once more, and in recent years has returned to car manufacture with the acquisition of Reliant.

The 1923/4 Bean 11.9hp.

11.9, Twelve. 1919-27 (prod: approx 10,000). Chassis falling from £400 to £245. S4 SV 1796cc, cone (later multi-disc) clutch, three speed separate gearbox, spiral bevel axle, semi-elliptic suspension. The Twelve was technically similar to the Fourteen but with smaller engine. Ninety per cent of the parts for these models were said to be produced by Bean. The Twelve was cheaper than typical assembled family cars (it was the lowest priced 11.9 in 1920) but in the end could not compete with Morris or Austin. It was a strong car – even if early ones had fragile china mascots – and typically returned 35mpg.

FOURTEEN, became 14/40 in 1927. 1924-28 (prod: approx 4000). Chassis £325 falling to £245. S4 SV 2.3 litres, in-unit four speed gearbox, multi- or single-plate clutch, bevel axle, two wheel brakes to mid-1920s, semi-elliptic suspension. The 14/40 had Ricardo-designed combustion chambers, separate gearbox and a more rounded radiator. Tough and cheap, this model could do 5-50mph in top gear and consumed petrol at the rate of 26-28mpg. Its chassis was used as the basis of the small Beverley.

18/50. 1926-28 (prod: 500). Chassis £365, complete up to £650. S6 OHV 2692cc Meadows, single-

An early Bean 14, pictured at Dudley in 1924.

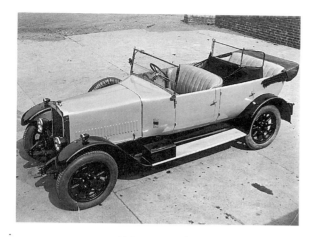

1927 Bean 18/50

plate clutch, in-unit Meadows four speed gearbox, bevel axle, semi-elliptic suspension. The pinnacle of the range, which sometimes had a flat Austin-like radiator and sometimes one resembling a Bentley, both with the company's lion rampant badge.

A high-performance fabric sports saloon, with a duplex Zenith carburettor, capable of 70mph, was offered by dealer Tom Knowles for £595 in late 1928.

The "Hadfield" Bean 14/45.

14/45, 14/70 Sports. 1928-29 (prod: see Fourteen). Tourer £295. S4 SV 2.3 litres, four speed gearbox, right hand change, single dry plate clutch, four wheel servo brakes, worm drive axle. Semi-elliptic front, cantilever rear suspension. These were called Hadfield Beans on account of the firm's new ownership, and with Ricardo turbulent head gave 65mph along with good stopping thanks to a Dewandre servo. The Sports had wire wheels.

Commercials by now accounted for most of Bean's sales and the cars were quietly dropped.

BEDFORD BUICK

see Buick

BEARDMORE

Anniesland, Coatbridge and Paisley, Scotland

At the end of the Great War this vast Scottish engineering and shipbuilding concern became involved with cars, Precision motor cycles and engines (used by several cyclecar makers including Black Prince, Bound and Bow-V-Car), railway locomotives, airships and much else. Its chairman, Sir William Beardmore (Lord Invernairn) also had financial control of Arrol-Johnston and used its Paisley factory to make the new Beardmore taxi.

The importer of Austro-Daimlers, Francis Luther, had introduced this make of aero engine to the firm before the Great War and afterwards became a director of Beardmore Motors Ltd, which had its Light Car Works at Anniesland. G W A Brown (see Arrol Johnston) designed overhead cam engines for Beardmore, and after early teething troubles these gave it an exclusive and sporting clientele. However, Beardmore failed to weather the aftermath of the Wall Street Crash, and the arrival of a new joint MD from Armstrong-Whitworth, who shut all loss-making divisions. Later a separate company continued making the Beardmore taxis from a London factory from the 1930s to the 1960s. Beardmores were sold under the slogan, "A better car is outside the range of practical engineering".

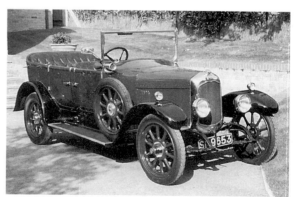

1924 Beardmore 12/30.

11.4, 12/30. 1919-23, 1923-25 (prod: several hundred). S4 chain-driven OHC 1500cc increased in stages to two litres, four speed gearbox, dry plate clutch, spiral bevel axle. Attractive, well made and available as a tourer at a competitive £395 in 1923. A familiar feature of the cars (as opposed to commercial models like taxis) was the forward sloping radiator cap to ease filling. The engines were similar to the Arrol-Johnston Victory but smaller.

14/40, 16/40, 15.6. The latter was available as either a car or the ubiquitous Taxi, which became known as the Hyper model and of which 6000 were in ser-

A Beardmore 15.6hp Taxi.

vice in London in 1928. The 14/40 was new in 1924, to a design by B J Angus-Shaw, and had an aluminium head and block with cast iron liners. The chassis crossmembers ran underneath the frame to double as running board supports. It was technically flawed and was replaced by the 16/40, which lasted to 1929 and had a separate gearbox to the end of production. These models had radiators like the 12/30 unlike the taxi style shown, which itself became flat at the end of the decade. Production of all but the taxis was small.

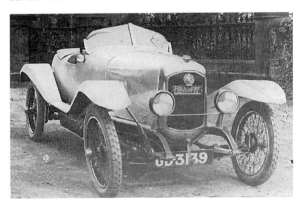

1923 Beardmore 12hp Sports.

SPORTS 12. 1924-26 (prod: n/a). Aluminium-panelled sports skiff £550. S4 OHC 1860cc, single plate clutch, in-unit four speed gearbox, two wheel brakes then four, semi-elliptic suspension. This was virtually the only sports car made in Scotland until recent years and amongst the best looking of all Scottish cars. Designed by A Francis, a 2-litre racing version held the Shelsley Walsh hillclimb record in 1925. All these Sports and Super Sports models came with a Brooklands certificate guaranteeing 70mph. An 11hp Sports was also listed.

BELL

CWS, Chorlton Road, Manchester

The Bell car had been made in Ravensthorpe, Yorkshire, for ten years from 1905. After the Great War 16, 20 and 30hp models were proposed, plus commercial vehicles. In the event the Co-operative Wholesale Society bought the designs and built twenty of the commercials in Manchester in 1919. The 30hp and 16hp cars were listed for 1920 but after that just the 16, which was supplied to CWS officials and presumably to Co-op customers. A 25 with Dorman 4-litre engine was listed in 1922 and the 16/20 became a 15.9 with 2614cc sidevalve Dorman in 1923. Eighty men were employed in the motor department, but presumably most were engaged on Bell lorry and bus chassis, and the ultra-conservative car (a strange contradiction for a Socialist inspired co-operative) was quietly dropped in 1926.

Though there were 550 Co-op branches it seems very unlikely that even that number of vehicles of all types was built.

The CWS had another motor branch making Federal and Federation motor cycles in Tyseley, Birmingham, and in 1922 it offered a three wheel JAP 8hp air-cooled twin powered cyclecar for £150 under the CWS name.

There was an unconnected Bell from Rochester, Kent in 1920 in the shape of a JAP engined cyclecar with a single wheel at the front.

A 1919 or 1920 Bell 16hp, bearing Armagh registration.

BELSIZE & BELSIZE-BRADSHAW

Clayton, Manchester

An old-established firm which employed 1200 men and was building 50 vehicles per week in 1914. After the Great War it offered too many models and made virtually all parts in-house, an expensive process for the small runs actually sold. It also adopted designs like the Bradshaw (see ABC) engine and a 2.5-litre straight eight which were too revolutionary or too expensive for the average buyer.

The company was run by a Receiver from 1923, a year in which production rarely exceeded 20 cars per week, and it was downhill all the way after that to the end in 1925, with debts of £500,000.

Belsize Bradshaw in three-seater form.

A Belsize 15 Tourer.

15, 15/20. 1919-23 (prod: 2-3000). Open, landaulette and coupé 1922 £575-885. S4 SV 2.8 litres, four speed gearbox, cone clutch, helical bevel axle, semi-elliptic suspension. A throw-back to pre-war design with a non-detachable cylinder head, though both brakes were on rear drums rather than the footbrake operating on the transmission. Well made but dull, and expensive to tax as it was rated by the Treasury at 20.8hp.

9hp oil-cooled Belsize Bradshaw coupé at £260.

9 Bradshaw model. 1921-24 (prod: 750-1500). Open 2/3- or 4-seater plus coupé from £210. V2 OHV 1100cc oil-cooled, multi-plate clutch in oil, three speed gearbox, spiral bevel axle, quarter-elliptic suspension. "The no trouble light car" was anything but, and Granville Bradshaw's unconventional engine quickly earned a reputation for frailty, oil leaks and lack of reliability. The extra large sump contained oil that also surrounded the cylinders. A fan cooled the heads and the oil, the latter doubling as lubricant for the steering gear and three speed gearbox. In the end the vagaries of the Nine resulted in a conventional four-cylinder water-cooled 1250cc engine being substituted. This 1924-25 model was called the 10/20 and had the same bore and stroke as the 14/30 and 20/40.

14/30 six-cylinder Belsize.

14/30, 20/40. 1924-mid-'25 (prod: few). Chassis £315, complete from £675. S6 OHV 1875cc, S8 OHV 2496cc, multi-disc clutch, in-unit four speed gearbox, four wheel brakes, semi-elliptic suspension. Beautifully built swansong for Belsize. The straight eight came at the very end and only a handful were built – whatever can the Receiver have been thinking of? Even the Six was an unusual layout for the time.

BENTLEY

Cricklewood, London

W O Bentley, born 1888, sold French DFP cars and improved their performance by substituting aluminium pistons. During the Great War he modified Clerget aero engines at the factories of Gwynne and also Humber. Prototypes of the cars bearing his name were developed in 1919-20 and made available to the public late in 1921. They were amongst the most expensive cars of the era and the playthings of wealthy young motorists. Attempts to break into the carriage trade met with little success and the company consistently lost money despite dazzling racing successes. Millionaire sportsman Woolf Barnato financed Bentley from 1925 until the business was bought by Rolls-Royce in 1931. Its swansong in 1930-31 was the 4-litre and 8-litre models.

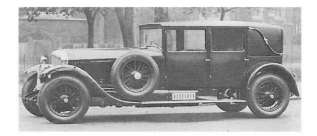

Bentley 6½ litre with Mulliner fabric saloon body.

The ex-Barnato Speed Six, bodied by Gurney Nutting.

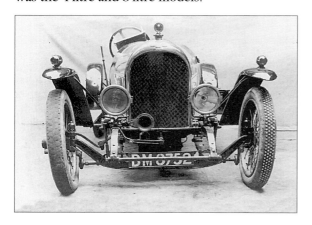

1919-20 Bentley 3 litre, the second car built.

3 LITRE. 1919-29 (prod: 1622). Various sports, tourer and enclosed styles. Chassis 1922 £1050, 1928 £895. S4 OHC 2996cc, four valves per cylinder, twin magneto ignition, cone clutch, separate four speed gearbox with right hand change, spiral bevel axle, semi-elliptic suspension. Initially two wheel brakes but four for 1924. Famous model with different colour radiator badge depending on type: Red Label, short-chassis Speed Model; Blue Label, the early short and then long chassis suitable for formal coachwork; Green Label, denoting one of approximately eighteen 100mph types. 80mm bore and a very long 149mm stroke on an engine derived from 1914 GP ideas gave great lugging ability and a low Treasury Rating of 15.9hp when in reality a minimum of 70bhp was developed. All cars had a five year guarantee. Examples won at Le Mans in 1924 and 1927.

6½ LITRE and SPEED SIX. 1926-30 (prod: 545). Sports and formal types. Standard chassis 1929 £1575. S6 OHC 6597cc, four valves per cylinder,

140bhp or 180bhp as Speed Six, single plate clutch, separate four speed gearbox with right hand change, spiral bevel axle, semi-elliptic suspension. Launched in June 1925 as a luxury rival to Rolls-Royce with a chassis price of £1450, but deliveries did not commence until 1926 and sales were slow. In 1928 a Speed Six version arrived, of which 181 or 182 were built. Some of these also wore handsome enclosed coachwork but others were out-and-out sports cars responsible for victories at Le Mans in 1929 and 1930. The Speed Six was on a shorter chassis and had a higher compression engine with twin SU carburettors rather than a single Smiths. Sadly many chassis have been shortened in later years and replica Le Mans bodywork fitted.

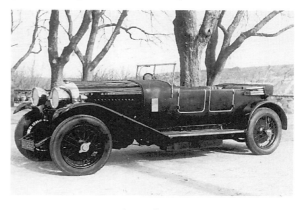

Bentley 4½ litre, 1929

4½ LITRE, SUPERCHARGED 4½ LITRE. 1927-31 (prod: 665, 55). Various open and closed styles plus sports/racing models. Speed chassis 1928-30

£1050, same price as Standard in 1930, when supercharged version cost £1475. S4 OHC 4398cc, four valves per cylinder, 104bhp in standard form, inverted cone clutch then single plate, four speed gearbox with right hand change, spiral bevel axle, semi-elliptic suspension. Sharing the same bore and stroke as the 6½, this was the last four-cylinder Bentley. One gained victory at Le Mans in 1928 but many carried heavy saloon bodywork. Apart from one car delivered in 1929 the supercharged models (55 in total) were all delivered to customers in 1930-31. They were made against the wishes of W O Bentley, and were developed by Bentley team driver Sir Henry Birkin.

A standard car roadtested in 1928 had a top speed of 90mph and a fuel consumption, driven hard, of 16mpg. The driver mentioned perfect driving position, excellent brakes, delightful steering, extraordinary roadholding, and acceleration from 10mph to 80mph in a "rocket like" 18 seconds.

BEVERLEY-BARNES & BEVERLEY

Barnes, London SW18

Fugitives from German aggression in Belgium, Dolphens, Flamand and Lenaerts took over the Eagle cyclecar and Beverley Aeroplane Works in Barnes in 1914 and ultimately employed 1800 Belgian and other refugees making Le Rhône aero engines on the banks of the Thames. Their machine shop expertise subsequently assisted Beardmore, Bentley, Lagonda and probably others such as AC. They employed Andrew Robertson from Talbot as managing director, and in 1923 decided to use their well-equipped works to make luxury cars. All had OHC straight-eight engines and early cars had Belgian or Belgian-inspired Van den Plas bodies. Experts agree that M. Dolphens arranged for the cars to be built by a team of seven men as a sideline to the company's general engineering and that under 20 were built. In 1927-29 over 60 3-litre Meadows engines were bought by the company, probably for use in Invictas that Beverley is believed to have built under contract.

The 5½-litre 30/90 Beverley saloon.

A Beverley 18hp 2½-litre coupé.

Front view of the 2½-litre 20/80 Beverley straight-eight.

STRAIGHT EIGHT. 1923-31 (prod: about 20). Early chassis £750-£850, latterly £650. S8 OHC 4 litres, 4.8 litres, 5.5 litres, DOHC 2.5 litres, four speed gearbox, spiral bevel axle (initially with torque tube), four wheel servo brakes, semi-elliptic suspension. First came 4-litre 90bhp model, of which about six were built with American Warner four speed gearboxes. Then came a 4.8 litre and the 5.5-litre 30/90. Beverley-Barnes became Beverley in 1929 and the 2.5 (sometimes referred to as a 3 litre) appeared at the 1929 and 1930 Motor Shows with twin OHC engine (and option of supercharging) designed by Emile Petit, formerly of Salmson (see GN). This last model was allegedly based on a Bean 14/40 chassis and a few Beverley engines were also utilised by Burney. The last of these interesting and ephemeral cars were sold in 1931, shortly after the death of founder M. Dolphens.

BLACKBURN

Olympia, Leeds, Yorkshire

A well known aircraft maker founded by Robert Blackburn in 1909 and with a seaplane base at Brough near Hull, Blackburn introduced a luxury car in 1919 that was built in small numbers. It also made bodywork on other chassis. Blackburn was financially involved with Jowett after the Second World War.

1920 Blackburn 20hp tourer.

20HP. 1919-25 (prod: under 100). Various bodywork built in-house at £260 on top of £795 chassis price. S4 SV 3160cc bi-bloc (monobloc from 1922) Coventry Simplex, cone clutch, four speed gearbox by Blackburn mounted amidships, torque tube, spiral bevel axle. Semi-elliptic front, cantilever rear suspension. A large, low-built and expensive car with Rolls-Royce shape radiator and artillery wheels. Chassis numbers commenced at 299/300 each year from 1922 to the end and presumably never reached 400.

BLACK PRINCE

Barnard Castle, Co. Durham

A cyclecar built in small numbers by H G Wright and about five colleagues between 1919 and 1924. Single- or twin-cylinder air-cooled two-stroke Precision or Union 2¾hp engines drove through a two speed belt or Albion gear transmission. Construction was largely of seasoned ash, the resilience of which provided the rear suspension!

1919-20 Black Prince cyclecar.

BLERIOT-WHIPPET

Addlestone, Surrey

The French Blériot company under manager Norbert Chereau established a factory at Brooklands and built Blériot aircraft there until 1916. In this year a new factory in Addlestone also run by Chereau began to make SPAD and AVRO aircraft, and the company became Air Navigation and Engineering Co. at the end of the Great War. Just as the French Blériot factory turned to cyclecars so did Air Navigation in 1920 with its Bleriot-Whippet (previously called the Jones-Marchant in 1919 after its designers). The Eric Longden car (see Eric Longden) was also built at Addlestone and after Air Navigation's liquidation in 1928 the factory became the English home of Weymann coachwork. Postwar Morris Minor and Mini designer Alec Issigonis was a Whippet owner and made various improvements to his car.

A roadgoing two-seater Bleriot-Whippet.

Bleriot-Whippet driven by W J Marchant in the JCC 200 Mile Race at Brooklands in 1921.

WHIPPET. 1920-27 (prod: over 50 in 1920, several hundred in total). Open two-seater starting at £275 and falling to £125 in 1924. V2 SV air-cooled 1-litre Blackburne, 9hp Treasury Rating. Initially drive via variable pulley on Zenith Gradua principle, but after two years chain drive and a three speed and reverse gearbox were standardised. A sporty light car from a maker that had several other tenuous connections with makes of car other than Eric Longden. There appears to have been some financial connection with Blackburne through André (see Marlborough), with Gillet and Stevens (which made engines for Blackburne and Invicta), with coachbuilder Salmons, and with aircraft firm Martin and Handasyde, which also built motor cycles 1919-25. See also HP and Cambro.

BOND

Thorncliffe, Brighouse, Yorkshire

Unconnected with the post-Second World War minicars of the same name. F W Bond assembled large cars using an assortment of British and American components between 1922 and 1928. The company also designed a Meadows-engined car for the Australian market which was made in Adelaide 1925 to 1929 and used approximately 25 Meadows engines including three "sixes". Other parts came from the Monarch Motor Co. of Castle Bromwich. It was called the Chic.

To begin with Bond made substantial cars, of the type later espoused by Brocklebank, but in 1927 it offered a lighter sporting type of which one had an Anzani engine and two had 1½-litre Meadows.

Bond's first cars had four-cylinder 14hp side-valve Tylor engines but in 1923 Continental four-cylinder OHV and six-cylinder sidevalve engines powered the 14/40 and 20 models respectively. Both had other American components like Timken axles and Brown-Lipe gearboxes, the larger car with three ratios and the smaller with four. Front wheel brakes were available as an optional extra, and chassis were attractively priced in 1924 at £350 and £375. Chassis numbers started at 102 but very few cars were built, including the three 1½-litre sports models in 1927 referred to above.

This Bond model was called the Chic after its backer Clarence Chick, who is shown sitting to the right of the driver of this 1924 test chassis.

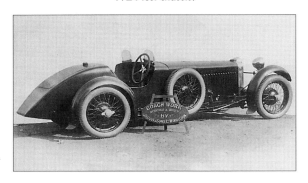

1927 Bond 1½-litre Super Sports with Jarvis body.

BOUND

Southampton

In 1920 Bound Brothers built a diminutive cyclecar with friction drive and a Precision 3½hp engine.

BOWSER

Burley Street, Leeds, Yorkshire

A light car of 1922-23 with a 1-litre 9hp flat-twin Koh–i-noor engine from the maker of the Rob Roy car (the same engine was also used in the Kingsbury). There was shaft drive and a three speed gearbox but the price of £300 far exceeded that of the Austin Seven and sales were minimal. E Bowser, the proprietor, was unconnected with the well-known Bowser fuel pumps.

The Bowser light car.

BOW-V-CAR

Upper Norwood, London SE; Bute Street, Luton, Bedfordshire

Of integral plywood construction, the Bow-V-Car was made by the Plycar Co. and was powered by an air-cooled vee-twin sidevalve Precision 10hp engine with a three speed and reverse Juckes gearbox. There was a multi-disc clutch and final drive by chain. Steering was by cable and bobbin. Only available in 1922-23, the two-seater cost £165.

1922-23 Bow-V-Car.

BRAMHAM

see Stanhope

BRITISH EAGLE

see Hodgson

BRITISH ENSIGN & ENSIGN

Willesden, London NW10

Run by Edward Gillett, a steam commercial vehicle pioneer, Ensign Motors introduced a range of cars and lorries in 1913 and built the latter with Tylor engines at the rate of five per week through much of the Great War.

Afterwards, commercial production, employing over 40 Dorman engines, continued to 1923, but a remarkable luxury car appeared in 1919. This was a financial disaster, but it was joined by a small Ensign assembled car in 1922. Amongst the seven men involved in car production was Harry P Crown, son of J L Crown of Entz magnetic transmission fame (see Crown and Owen). Needless to say, British Ensign built one car as a Crown Ensign or Ensign Magnetic in 1922. The firm was involved with the 1926 Gillett.

The 38.4hp British Ensign EP6.

EP6. 1919-23 (prod: probably 4-6). Tourer and others theoretically available, chassis 1921 £1700. S6 OHC 6.8 litres 38.4hp, aluminium block with steel liners, dry multi-disc clutch, three speed gearbox, spiral bevel axle. A glorious Bentley-like car long before the 6½-litre Bentley had been thought about. The chassis, at £1700 in 1921, was colossally expensive, comparing with the Rolls-Royce 40/50 at £2100. When it and the Entz magnetic-transmission version didn't sell there was even talk of a 13½-litre V12!

11.9HP, 12HP. 1922-23 (prod: 37). 1922 tourer 2-seat £395, 4-seat £415. S4 OHV 1795cc Meadows, cone clutch, separate three speed gearbox, spiral bevel axle. Quarter-elliptic front, cantilever rear suspension. Comfortably sprung and capable of 5-

The British Ensign 11.9hp.

55mph in top gear, this was a well made and competitively priced car whose sales were presumably limited by restricted facilities for production.

BRITISH IMPERIA

Cordwallis Works, Maidenhead, Berkshire

A bit of wishful thinking by GWK, which needed a more conventional car to compensate for its own collapsed sales. Van Roggen of the Belgian Imperia company and Grice of GWK had long been friends and had even invented a G&VR car between them in 1917. The British Imperia was a 10hp car with slide valves but the 40 or so that were sold in 1924-28 were almost certainly Belgian imports. In December 1926 Imperia Motors Ltd had been formed to acquire the GWK business and with its conversion to a Public Company it soon proved to be a financial disaster.

A 10hp British Imperia with saloon body by Weymann.

BRITON

Willenhall Road, Wolverhampton, Staffordshire

Sister make to Star since 1908, Briton specialised in light, high quality cars. After the Great War it made 50 examples of the 14/16 in 1919 and then 10hp and 12hp cars. Following liquidation in 1922, G A Weight continued production until 1928, during which time 600 cars were said to have been sold.

1920 10/12 Briton with wheels reminiscent of Angus-Sanderson. Most later cars had Sankey artillery wheels.

10/12 1919-28, 9.8/10 1921-29 (prod: about 1400). Various bodies, chassis commencing at £325 and ending up at around £130. S4 SV 1373cc, 1743cc, cone clutch, three speed gearbox, semi-elliptic suspension. Britons still had two wheel brakes in 1927, and the 10/12 also retained its cone clutch and separate gearbox to the end, though the 10 was more modern in concept.

BROCKLEBANK

Oozells Street and Adderley Park, Birmingham

"Birmingham's answer to the American challenge" came from Brocklebank and Richards, the latter having apparently worked for Hudson. Though Warner gearboxes and axles and Lockeed brakes (the first hydraulic application in Britain alongside Triumph and Horstman) were American, the engine was built by Brocklebank. Assembly took place in Wolseley's former aero engine sheds under the supervision of Charles Bull from Wolseley, and angular American-inspired saloon bodywork was built by the local firm of Watsons until lighter Weymann type construction arrived.

Brocklebank 15hp.

15HP. 1925-29 (prod: approx 600). Chassis £275, usually supplied as £395 saloon. S6 OHV 2051cc, single dry plate clutch, in-unit three speed gearbox, spiral bevel axle, semi-elliptic suspension. The six was really too small to compete with American cars and performance was very leisurely,

though 70mph was just attainable and a Treasury rating of 15hp made it cheap to tax. Most were exported to the Empire. A Mk II was intended in 1930 (certainly a Meadows six was bought in 1929) but the firm had failed by then, with Brocklebank working for the family garage, Brocks, in London, and Richards getting a lowly job at the Austin factory. A surviving relative, Sir Aubrey Brocklebank, believes that only 350 cars were made.

BROMPTON

Upper St Martins Lane, London WC

This cyclecar probably failed to get beyond the prototype stage but was interesting for its MAG vee-twin driving the front wheels. There was also independent suspension all round.

BSA

Sparkbrook and Small Heath, Birmingham

The famous Birmingham Small Arms Company added cars to its range of products in 1907 with help from E E Baguley (see Baguley) and three years later acquired Daimler. From that time BSA cars were the lighter models at the bottom of the Daimler range and often, like them, used Knight patented sleeve-valve engines. However, the Ten of 1921 was a true light car, as was the three-wheeler that emerged from the BSA Cycles branch at Small Heath in 1929. See also Hammond.

BSA Ten on the Scottish Light Car Trial in 1922, where it was said to be "steady, fast and stood up well".

TEN. 1921-25 (prod: approx 1500 per year at peak – perhaps 4000-5000 in total). Grey or blue two-seater from £230. Air-cooled V2 OHV 1075cc 18bhp Hotchkiss, plate clutch, three speed gearbox, Lanchester silent worm drive, quarter-elliptic suspension. 52mph and 38mpg were possible from this well-made car using the same engine as the Hotchkiss (Coventry) light car. It was unusual to have electric starting in a car of this size.

A surviving 1924 BSA sleeve-valve 14hp.

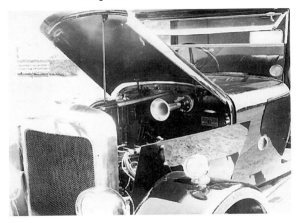

BSA sleeve-valve 16hp, 1926.

Sleeve-valve types. 1923-26 (prod: n/a). Various body styles, chassis from £375. S4 and S6 10-16hp Daimler Knight sleeve valve, plate clutch, Lanchester worm drive, quarter-elliptic suspension at first. The smallest was 1446cc and the largest the equivalent of the Daimler 16/55 with BSA radiator. In 1923-24 there was also a diminutive six of only 1594cc, but all were made in small numbers.

1929 BSA Three Wheeler.

THREE WHEELER. 1929-36 (prod: approx 5200). Sports, family, etc., from £130. V2 OHV 1021cc 9hp, three speed and reverse gearbox, spur-type differential, drive to independently sprung front wheels. After Morris bought Hotchkiss, BSA obtained rights to make the air-cooled motor used in the BSA Ten. It was revised in 9hp form for the F W Hulse-designed three-wheeled "Beezer" of 1929.

BUCKINGHAM

Spon Street and Holyhead Road, Coventry

J F Buckingham, inventor of the incendiary bullet for destroying Zeppelins, made cyclecars from 1913 and competed in them most successfully. Their manufacture was undertaken by the new Alvis concern in 1922-23, although "the motorist's dream" was more of a nightmare to Alvis' sales manager once the Austin Seven had arrived, and possibly only 30 were built by Alvis. See also ABF.

Buckingham 10hp.

10HP. 1920-23 (prod: probably under 100). Open sports £250. V2 air-cooled OHV 1100cc 10hp, cone clutch, two speed with belt and then shaft drive, latterly Moss three speed gearbox with shaft drive to bevel axle with differential, quarter-elliptic suspension. Very few, if any, were sold until Alvis briefly adopted the car. Before the War up to 15 a week had been made. There was coil ignition, hand starting and rack and pinion steering. Standard colour was blue.

BUGATTI

Molsheim, Alsace and Crossley Motors, Gorton, Manchester

Crossley's London agent, Charles Jarrott and Letts, was importer of the renowned Bugattis. As a director of Crossley Motors, William Letts persuaded the Manchester firm to build the popular Type 22 under licence (as did Diatto in Italy and Rabag in

Germany). Two thousand Types 13, 22 and 23 were built between 1920 and 1926 in their homeland, becoming known as Brescias after Type 13s filled the first four places at this venue in 1921. Crossley intended to build 500 but not much more than two dozen were produced. Various explanations have been given for this failure, notably that customers wanted Ettore Bugatti's inspired originals made by his fully trained team.

The 16-valve Bugatti Type 22.

TYPE 22. 1921-22 (prod: engine numbers 1600-1625). Open three-seater £650. S4 OHV 1.5 litres, four valves per cylinder, 40-50bhp, wet multi-plate clutch, four speed gearbox, two wheel brakes. Semi-elliptic front, quarter-elliptic rear suspension. A watch-like car capable of up to 75mph and equally at home in amateur motor sport and fast touring. Several other models of Bugatti were offered, but these were of course the Alsatian originals.

BUICK, BEDFORD BUICK

Flint, Michigan; Old Oak Wharf, Willesden Junction and The Hyde, Hendon, London

The Buick was unmistakably an American car and one of the first constituents of GMC (see Vauxhall). Its founder had, however, been born in Scotland in 1854, and an "All British Bedford" of 1909 turned out, when challenged by the motoring press, to be a Buick chassis with British radiator and coachwork. The Trade Descriptions Act did not apply in those days and henceforth the Willesden cars built from CKD kits became Bedford-Buicks. Though this name largely died out in the Great War it was enough to ensure ready sales in the brief boom afterwards. To avoid punitive tax, cars were sourced from GM's Canadian factory, and from 1925 and the increase in

1927 Buick 25/75 sedan.

McKenna Duties some may have been assembled alongside the more familiar Chevrolets at General Motors' factory at the Hyde, Hendon. Certainly the 1927-30 sedans were described as "London built" though this probably referred to the bodywork.

25/75. 1927-30 (prod: n/a). S6 OHV 4497cc, multi-plate dry clutch, three speed gearbox, torque tube, spiral bevel axle. Semi-elliptic front, cantilever rear suspension. At £495 for a Master Tourer and £398 for the Sedan shown the 25/75 was a great bargain, even if sales were hampered by the Treasury's 30hp rating. Buick engines were used in GMC's Hendon-built commercials, which in 1931 led to the "All British" Bedford commercial range.

BURNEY

Cordwallis Works, Maidenhead, Berkshire

Sir Dennistoun Burney, an airship designer, created Streamline Cars Ltd in 1927 to exploit his experience of aerodynamics. The prototype in 1928 used a front wheel drive Alvis chassis turned

This Burney Streamline, with its dummy radiator, was good for 80mph.

back-to-front (though with front-end steering!), clothed in teardrop-shaped bodywork. Cooling was effected by twin lateral radiators at the rear and there was independent suspension all-round. The 12 production cars of 1929-33 had space frames, hydraulic brakes and independent suspension by transverse leaf springs, and used an assortment of Armstrong-Siddeley, Beverley, Meadows and Lycoming engines.

Top speed was 80mph. This avant garde design was adopted by Crossley in 1933 but soon faded away.

CALCOTT

Far Gosford Street, Coventry

The Calcott family made roller skates and were involved in the cycle and motor cycle industry before hiring A Alderson from Singer (and later with Lea Francis and Cluley) to design their first cars of 1913. These Tens were built to 1917 and then revived after the Great War with the same bore and stroke, continuing in production to the end of 1926, when Singer acquired the factory. This was later used for paint and canvas manufacture and is now a listed 1896 building. At its height Calcott employed 150 workers and made most of its own components, though chassis came from Mechans of Scotstoun. Its car radiators resembled those of Standard's, and its 12/24 model designed by L T Shorter from Humber gave a lot of back axle trouble due to being made on machinery worn out by war work, notably for E H Siddeley. High dividends were paid to shareholders rather than profits being spent on re-equipping the works.

A Calcott 10.5hp in the factory, c1920.

TEN, 10.5, 10/15. 1919-25 (prod: total all Calcotts 1913-26 approx 2500). Various body styles, chassis 1925 £200, four-seat chummy £285. S4 SV 1460cc,

cone clutch, three speed gearbox with right hand change, spiral bevel axle, semi-elliptic suspension. A hangover from 1913 but gradually modernised and Calcott's best seller. The standard colour was mole brown.

The Calcott 13.9hp.

11.9, 12/24, 13.9. 1920-26 (prod: see Ten). Various body styles, chassis starting at £495 and falling to £295. S4 SV 1650cc, 1955cc, 2120cc, cone clutch (single plate on 12/24), three speed gearbox, spiral bevel axle, semi-elliptic suspension. A four speed 'box and helical bevel rear axle arrived on the troublesome 12/24 of 1925-26. An assortment of rather dull but well constructed family cars. Maybe knowledge of the beautiful Calcott daughters, who between them apparently married several times, or playboy Will Calcott, would have spiced up the image!

Calcott 16/50.

16/50 LIGHT SIX. 1925-26 (prod: see Ten). Various body styles from £495 complete. S6 inclined SV 2565cc, single dry plate clutch, separate four speed gearbox, right hand change, helical bevel axle, semi-elliptic suspension. A valiant last try with a 60mph car with four wheel brakes, but by now the firm had run out of money. When R H Colliers bought the goodwill and spares in 1927, after Singer had bought the factory, all creditors were paid in full. The engine was also said to have been supplied to Vulcan.

CALTHORPE

Bordesley Green, Birmingham

Like Autocrat, Calcott, Lea Francis and many others, Calthorpe's roots were in the cycle industry. G W Hands (see also Hands) had introduced Calthorpe cars in 1904 and by the time of the Great War had built up the firm's reputation with attractively sporting cars and the delightful little 10hp Minor. In 1917 the Birmingham works of the Mulliner coachbuilding family was acquired, and in 1920 Calthorpe was turning out 25-50 cars per week from a workforce of 1200. After failing with his own four- and six-cylinder cars, built in Calthorpe's motor cycle factory, George Hands returned to Calthorpe in 1923, but the business collapsed in 1924. Sporadic attempts to revive the marque, including motor show appearances, kept it alive in buyers' guides to 1928, and in 1926 it attempted to sell the remaining Autocrat cars. Both Mulliner coachwork and Calthorpe motor cycles survived the debâcle.

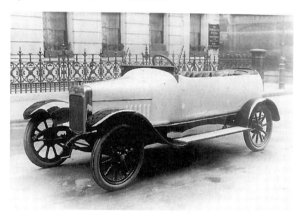

1918/19 Calthorpe 10hp.

1921 Calthorpe 10hp two-seater.

10, 10.4, 10/15, 10/20. 1919-25 (prod: postwar total about 5000 cars). Various body styles, complete 1920 £520, 1925 £235. S4 SV 1328cc, cone clutch,

Moss three speed gearbox, torque tube, spiral bevel axle, quarter-elliptic suspension. A very well made and stylish update of the Minor available in various forms from the 47mph Popular to 60mph sporting types. The Sporting Four had polished aluminium Mulliner bodywork. Sadly all were too expensive to compete with the true mass-producers though Mann, Egerton and then Mebes and Mebes did their best to sell large numbers in the Home Counties.

1925 Calthorpe 12/20.

12/20, 15/45. 1923-26, 1925-26 (prod: see 10). Various body styles, mostly by Mulliner, complete 12/20 £285-425, 15/45 £395. S4 SV 1496cc, S6 OHC 1991cc, four speed gearbox (three on 15/45), spiral bevel axle (Timken on 12/20). The 12/20 was designed by Cecil Davidson, and Hugh Rose was credited with the later improved version known as the H type (he was ex-Sunbeam and later responsible for the high cam Riley and Lea Francis engines). The 12/20 was a well-built car capable of 50mph touring (optimistic according to latterday owner Bill Boddy) advertised as "no mass production this – no experimental car of a mushroom firm". The ohc 15/45, an abortive Hands model of which very few were sold in Calthorpe guise, was a 60mph car and had the same 65 × 100mm bore and stroke as the 10/20. Its six-cylinder engine, like that of Calcott, was tried by Vulcan.

CAMBRO

Northolt, Middlesex

Product of the Central Aircraft Co., this diminutive three-wheeler with single rear wheel drive by a two-cylinder 192cc Economic engine mounted above the wheel had only one speed and weighed 165lbs. It was advertised as the cheapest car in the world at 79 guineas! The name derived from Messrs Cambridge and Broomfield, though it has been suggested that F J Camm, founder of Practical Magazines, did design work (he also worked for ANEC – see Blériot) and maybe lent his name.

The Cambro light car was advertised as the cheapest car in the world at 79 guineas.

CAR

Fishponds, Bristol

Also known as the Cosmos after the Cosmos Engineering Co. which built it, this attractive but unconventional car was the work of Roy Fedden. Fedden had been responsible for Straker-Squire cars and, following the takeover of Cosmos by Bristol Aeroplane Co. in 1920, he went on to design some of the most successful aero engines of all time.

Though a weekly production of two hundred CARs at 200 guineas each was intended, Bristol cancelled the project before more than a few had been built.

The 1919 CAR 11.9hp.

11.9. 1919-20 (prod: possibly only prototypes). Three-cylinder air-cooled radial OHV 1206cc, coil ignition, single plate clutch, in-unit three speed gearbox, torque tube, differential-less axle. Separate single drums for foot and hand brake. One of the many ingenious features of this revolutionary car was its Adams suspension, also used by Douglas, in which centrally mounted coil springs were connected to the axles by long arms with bell cranks.

CARDEN

Teddington, Middlesex and Willesden, North London

John Carden started making cyclecars at his Farnham home in 1913, and in 1919 moved to a factory in Teddington which became the home of the AV based on his design. His next cyclecar was developed at Kennel Ride, Ascot in 1919 and became the Tamplin. It was followed by more rear engined Cardens and, after a 1922 takeover by Arnott and Harrison of Willesden (see Sheret), it became the New Carden.

Carden himself later designed tracked Bren gun carriers and tractors known initially as Carden-Loyd, and was knighted.

The 7hp Carden car.

7HP. 1919-25 (prod: chassis no. 795 reached 1921 and recommenced 101 in 1923, suggesting approx 1000 in total). Side by side two-seater from £100. Rear mounted HO2 TS 700cc, kickstart, multi-disc clutch, two speed gearbox, coil spring suspension . Various versions of this increasingly sophisticated cyclecar were built, but after promising early sales they lost out to mass-produced conventional cars. They were sold with the slogan "No belts, no chains, no frictions", and even King Alfonso of Spain bought one.

CARROW

Newcastle on Tyne and Hanwell, Middlesex

Founded in 1919 by Whitley Bay Motor Co., though production does not seem to have started until the following year, when about ten Dorman engines were acquired. In 1921 the business moved to Hanwell and was associated with Sir Payne Gallwey (see Swallow). Carrows were then described as having their maker's own engine, though it has been suggested that it was in fact a Peters unit of 11.9hp (like the Dorman). Interestingly, a Belgian car called the PM had the same 1820cc capacity (the Peters engine was of Belgian origin, though produced under licence in Britain). The PM's makers, Ateliers Auto-

Mécaniques of Sclessin, are believed to have had financial links with Carrow, and it seems probable that their cars were similar if not identical.

Carrow 11.9hp two-seater.

11.9. 1920-23 (prod: n/a). Various styles, 1922 two-seater £495, saloon coupé £595. S4 SV 1500cc latterly 1821cc, in-unit three speed gearbox, disc clutch, spiral bevel axle. Price reductions of £100 on the two-seater and £150 on the saloon coupé did nothing to boost sales in 1923. The Middlesex versions had quarter-elliptic suspension in place of the previous cantilever type.

CASTLE THREE

Kidderminster, Worcestershire

A garage that had built up an engineering business introduced a high-grade three wheeler in 1919 with the outline of a castle turret around its radiator core. A final effort to launch a four wheeler in 1922 came to nothing after a single prototype had been built.

A 1921 Castle Three.

CASTLE THREE. 1919-22 (prod: approx 350). Two-seater plus dickey. First twelve with S4 SV 1094cc Dorman, then S4 SV 1207cc Peters, in-unit with two speed epicyclic or three speed Moss gearbox, shaft and bevel final drive. Quarter-elliptic front, semi-elliptic rear suspension. This car eschewed the noisy air-cooled engine and chain drive of typi-

The Castle Three chassis.

cal three wheelers but was too heavy for the lower tax normally allowed for this class, and at £225 in 1922 it was far too expensive to succeed.

CENTURY

Euston Road, London NW1

Century Cars Ltd chose this name in 1928-29 in honour of the intended £100 price. Its ephemeral car had a 750cc two-stroke engine and probably never got beyond the prototype stage.

CFB

Upper Norwood, London SE

A 6cwt cyclecar with vee-twin air-cooled 1078cc 9hp engine, friction transmission with final drive by rubber belts, and a reinforced ash frame. It existed in 1920-21 but few were built. CFB stood for C F Beauvais, later to be stylist of Avon bodywork and responsible for attractive work on Standard, Coventry Victor, Crossley and other chassis.

The 9hp CFB two-seater.

CHALLENGE

Golders Green Crescent, London NW4

A spindly four wheel cyclecar project that the promoter was hoping to sell to a larger manufacturer

The Challenge cyclecar.

in late 1919. A cost of £100 for the complete car was mentioned, but whether more than the original prototype were built is uncertain.

CHAMBERS

Cuba Street, then University Street, Belfast

The Chambers brothers had been general engineers since 1897 and had made cars since 1904, brother Jack having also designed the first Vauxhall.

Small premises limited production to one car per week but potential output in University Street after the Great War was ten times that, though it dwindled to only a handful per year and probably amounted to under 50 in the 1920s. Initially Chambers continued to make its own engines but sales were very small and after 1924 Meadows engines were used. Most business by then came from selling other makes of vehicles and production ended in 1927.

12/16 Chambers cabriolet.

12/16. 1919-24 (prod: probably under 50). 1924 chassis £375, saloon £650. S4 SV 2344cc, cone clutch, separate three speed gearbox, torque tube, worm axle. Semi-elliptic front, ¾-elliptic rear suspension. Revival of pre-war design and made alongside a 1972cc 11/15 for much of its life. Sometimes sold as "The only car built in Ireland".

1927 Chambers 18/48. This is the last Chambers to be made and is shown at the Ulster Folk Museum.

18/48. 1925-27 (prod: 9). Various coachwork, chassis £475. S6 OHV 2692cc Meadows, single plate clutch, in-unit four speed Meadows gearbox, torque tube, worm axle. Semi-elliptic front, ¾-elliptic rear suspension. The end of the line, though there were also a couple of four-cylinder Meadows models following a final revival of the pre-war 12/16.

CHARRON-LAYCOCK

Millhouses, Sheffield

The French car firm Charron had British financial backing and an independent British importer, Charron Ltd. Davison Dalziel, the entrepreneur behind it, realised that import duties imposed in 1915 would limit imports after the War and used Charron Ltd to buy Sheffield engineers W S Laycock Ltd so that Charrons could be produced here. A 3-litre model was intended but in the event a 10hp car designed by W F Milward was produced, its first showing being at Olympia in 1919. Two thousand sets of parts were ordered but in the event the well-built but very expensive car sold slowly. Laycock later became well known for garage equipment and Layrub joints. Before the mid-1920s Milward and another employee named Dixon had left for Hampton.

10, 10/25. 1919-28 (prod: about 700). Various styles, tourer 1919 £625, 1928 £350. S4 SV 1460cc, cone clutch, three speed gearbox amidships, spiral bevel axle, semi-elliptic suspension. Stylish and a regular competitor in sporting events, the Charron-Laycock initially had a radiator shape reminiscent of Riley but adopted the shape shown here in 1922. Polished aluminium bonnets were a feature. It has been estimated that around two hundred were assembled from spares by or for London conces-

Charron-Laycock 10hp, c.1922.

sionaires Gower and Lee after the manufacturers were bought by the Birmingham Railway Carriages and Wagon Co. in 1925.

CHATER LEA

Banner Lane, London EC

A prolific supplier of cycle and motor components with a nine-storey factory. It made motor cycles from 1903 to 1936, latterly at the Garden City of Letchworth. A light car introduced in 1913 was briefly revived after the war and virtually all parts including engine were made in-house. See also Gillyard.

An immediately pre-war version of the Chater Lea Ten, with the wicker bodywork that was briefly fashionable.

TEN. 1921-22 (prod: in low hundreds?). Two-seater £350 falling to £300. S4 SV 1315cc, cone clutch, three speed gearbox, worm drive, semi-elliptic suspension. A well equipped 12cwt car with detachable wheels – but it had no chance of success after the Austin 7 arrived.

CHELSEA

Wandsworth, London SW18

A conventional looking coupé with front radiator which was in fact electric powered. A BTH motor was just ahead of the rear axle and the batteries were housed under the bonnet.

Wandsworth Engineering Works built a very small number in 1922.

The Chelsea was electric powered.

CHEVROLET

Old Oak Wharf, Willesden Junction then, from 1923, The Hyde, Hendon, Middlesex

This American constituent of General Motors Corporation had an assembly plant in London from the early 1920s in an effort to circumvent the McKenna import duties. GM had considered buying Citroën and had attempted to acquire Austin in 1925. Soon afterwards it purchased Vauxhall, and then had little need to assemble cars of American origin here. With the arrival of GM's new six-cylinder overhead-valve "cast iron wonder" models in

This Chevrolet 21.7hp sports stone protection in London at the time of the 1926 General Strike.

1929, the Hendon plant concentrated on commercial vehicles (see also Buick) and most Chevrolet cars sold here came from Canada. Bodywork for some of the GM cars came from a branch of Fisher Body Corp., later Fisher and Ludlow.

21.7HP. 1924-27 (prod: under 1000 per year). Various body styles, chassis around £185 (latterly complete two-seater cost the same). S4 OHV 2.8 litres, coil ignition, single dry plate clutch, in-unit three speed gearbox, torque tube, spiral bevel axle, semi-elliptic suspension. A cheap and strong car made from Canadian and local components. There were no front brakes until chassis were imported complete in 1928. Sales were restricted by £22 annual road tax.

CHILTERN

Beale St, Dunstable, Bedfordshire

Made by the Vulcan Motor and Engineering Co. in the Chiltern hills, and connected with the better-known Vulcan of Southport through the multifarious financial involvements of its Managing Director C B Wardman. It has been suggested by former Southport employees that chassis were delivered to Dunstable for fitment of different radiators and bodywork. In 1920 the Southport factory advertised its 12hp Vulcan Chiltern car as "tested on the Chiltern hills".

The Chiltern may have been associated with a firm called Wells Hammond of Dunstable, which bought 98 Dorman engines from June 1919, many of them the sporting OHV type. At any rate one of these appears in Dorman's sales records as being intended for a Vulcan chassis.

In 1926 a garage by the name of Vulcan Motors (London) Ltd existed in Beale Street, Dunstable.

1920 Chiltern 12hp.

12HP. 1919-20 (prod: about 100?). S4 OHV 1.8 litres (Dorman 4KNO), single plate clutch, four speed gearbox attached to torque tube, bevel axle. Semi-elliptic front, cantilever rear suspension. Something of an enigma but presumably a way for Londoner C B Wardman to introduce the Northern Vulcan to the Southern market. See also Eric-Campbell for another Vulcan mystery.

CHRISTCHURCH-CAMPBELL

Christchurch, Hampshire

Only about half a dozen cars (commencing chassis no. 1000) were built by J Campbell (Christchurch) Ltd in 1921-22. They had 10/30 Coventry Simplex engines with spiral bevel axles and gearboxes by Malicet et Blin. The last car was powered by a tuned 11.9hp Dorman unit. Price of the 10/30 was an exorbitant £400.

The Christchurch-Campbell 10hp, 1922.

CHIC

See Bond

CHRYSLER

Kew, Surrey

This new American maker was created from Maxwell and Chalmers in 1924 by Walter P Chrysler, formerly of Buick. A factory was established near Kew Gardens on the Thames in premises first occupied by Maxwell. Here from 1926 partially assembled and CKD kits were put together on production lines. In 1928 Chrysler bought Dodge and the assembly of that company's vehicles was then transferred from Park Royal to Kew.

Chrysler products did not meet the requirement for 65% local content needed for them to be accepted for duty purposes as British cars until 1931, but this was not a problem as the majority were sourced from Canada.

The firm had its own experimental department and machine shop but, of the purely British prototypes tried, only Dodge commercials entered series production.

Chrysler also made the luxury Imperial, and introduced the cheaper Plymouth and De Soto brands in 1928, but few of either were seen in Britain in the vintage period.

1927 Chrysler 62.

60, 62, 65, 66. 1926-30 (prod: UK assembly figures not available). Various body styles, chassis from £312. S6 SV 3209cc 23/75hp, single plate clutch, in-unit three speed gearbox, spiral bevel axle, semi-elliptic suspension. Natural successor to the original Chrysler and with a slightly less pronounced version of its "bullnose" radiator. Like the pioneering original it had Lockheed hydraulic brakes, and wood or wire wheels were available.

Broadly similar four-cylinder cars were available as 50, 52, and 58 (1926), 50 (1927), and 52 (1928).

Chrysler Imperial 80 with Dietrich owner/driver convertible sedan body.

IMPERIAL 80. 1926-30 (prod: n/a). Various body styles, 1926 saloon £1068. S6 SV 4740cc then 5080cc 29/95hp, plate clutch, three speed gearbox, spiral bevel axle. Chrysler's luxury offering nearly landed it with a lawsuit from General motors on account of the Vauxhall-like bonnet flutes. Several sold here had English coachwork. The 80 meant 80mph, though with 112bhp in 1928 it allegedly became the first "cheap" American car to exceed 100mph.

A 1929 Hoyal bodied Chrysler 75 sportsman's coupé.

70, 72, 75, 77. 1926-30 (prod: n/a). Various body styles, chassis from £400. Engine S6 SV 3.5-4.5 litres, plate clutch, three speed gearbox, spiral bevel axle. Three engine sizes were available and the type designation was shown in figures on the lamp/badge bar. For 1929 the car received a narrow ribbon radiator which was widely copied.

1930 Chrysler 77.

CITROËN

Slough, Bucks.

A new French car was launched in 1919 by André Citroën, a branch of whose gear firm already existed in London. His cheap mass-produced cars sold well in Britain (3000 in 1923) and the re-imposition of 33⅓% McKenna duties in mid-1925 after a year's respite persuaded Citroën to establish a factory here. It had the largest area under one roof of any motor plant in Britain at the time and utilised the 60-acre site of a former munitions factory which prior to Citroën had been a sales headquarters for war surplus vehicles. A car was being built every ten minutes in 1927, and all steel bodywork was, as with Morris, built under Budd licence. The British-built types are outlined below.

An all British Citroën 11.4hp tourer.

11.4. 1926-28 (prod: n/a). Various body styles, four-door saloon in grey-blue or fawn from £190 in 1926 (£210 with four wheel brakes). S4 SV 1453cc, single dry plate clutch, in-unit three speed gearbox, bevel axle. Semi-elliptic front, quarter-elliptic rear suspension. Imported from France where it was known as the B2 from 1922, and then assembled here based on the broadly similar B10 and B12. The all steel saloon bodies were jig-built at Slough from imported pressings.

Citroën 12/24 saloon.

12/24. 1926-29 (prod: up to 400 per day in France). Various saloons, tourer and coupés from £178. S4 SV 1538cc, in-unit three speed gearbox, chevron (as in the Citroën badge) bevel axle, Gleason semi-elliptic suspension. This was based on the French B14 and like other models used Michelin low pressure "comfort" tyres. Saloons were sold in Britain as "the world's supreme closed car value at the price" (£225), and all had four wheel brakes and cellulose paintwork.

The 1929 Citroën "Safety de Luxe" 2½-litre saloon.

13/30 and 2½ LITRE. 1929-31 (prod: approx 200,000 in France). Various body styles, chassis from £150 and £190. S4 and S6 SV 1628cc and 2442cc, in-unit dry plate clutch and three speed gearbox, chevron bevel axle, semi-elliptic suspension. These had vacuum-assisted four wheel braking and first appeared in French form as the C4 and C6 with common bore and stroke of 72 × 100mm at the 1928 Paris show. The 2½ had "Six" in script on its radiator and was Citroën's first six-cylinder model – it was rare in Britain despite undercutting the Morris Oxford.

CLEMENT-TALBOT
See Talbot

CLULEY

Wells Street, Coventry, Warwickshire.

Yet another of the Midland bicycle makers that turned to motors, first with two- and three-wheelers and then in 1921 full-size cars. In fact its origins lay in cloth machinery, and it returned to this field when car production ended in 1928, soon adding aero engineering. In more recent times Clarke, Cluley and Co. have been involved with gear production for Westland helicopters.

10, 10/20. 1921-26 (prod: possibly 2000). Various body styles, tourer £525 falling to £225 at end. S4 SV 1200cc, 1300cc, cone clutch, three speed gearbox, spiral bevel axle, semi-elliptic suspension. A nicely made car with monobloc engine and virtually everything built in-house. It was designed by A Alderson, ex-Calcott and Lea Francis. There was also a pair-cast 12 in 1922-24, and a monobloc six-cylinder 15.7hp in the following year which probably never entered series production. (See over for photograph.)

1927 Cluley 14/50.

14/30, 14/50. 1925-29 (prod: approx 50 14/50). Various body styles, chassis from £275. Cluley S4 SV 1944cc (14/30), Meadows S4 OHV 2120cc (14/50), cone clutch, separate Meadows four speed gearbox (14/30), in-unit four speed gearbox (14/50), spiral bevel axle, semi-elliptic suspension. The 14/30 was designed by E Farebrother (ex-Windsor) and was joined a year later by the more expensive Meadows engined model. It is thought that none of the cheaper model were sold, though evidence is elusive.

CLYDE

Queen Street, Leicester

In 30 years 1901-30 G H Waite and his garage employees assembled about 250 cars, plus many more bicycles and motor cycles. After the Great

Cluley 10hp, c1923.

War Humber and other agencies kept the firm afloat but a few loyal customers still specified Clydes. The range consisted of a two-cylinder 8hp model allegedly powered by Waite's own engine with three speed rear-axle gearbox, and a few larger Coventry Simplex and Dorman powered models with Waite's own three speed gearbox and some, if not all, with Wrigley axles. Chassis numbers started at 4350 in 1919 and had reached 5050

in 1923, though this presumably included motor cycles. The final cars were the 11/19 of 1928 and its successor, the 11/24 of 1929.

CLYNO

Pelham Street, Wolverhampton

A large scale producer of motor cycles which gained its name from an inclined pulley variable transmission. Clyno planned a light OHV car in 1918 designed by C van Eugen, ex-Daimler and ABC, but when this failed to materialise he departed for Swift (and later Lea Francis and Riley). Another departure from the 1000 strong workforce was Henry Meadows, to make his famous proprietary engines nearby.

By 1922 a limited company with £100,000 capital had been formed by Frank Smith, and a Coventry Climax engined car designed by A G Booth was mass-produced. Sales boomed, eventually reaching 12,000 per year, thanks in part to the efforts of sales director and motor cycle racing personality Jimmy Cocker.

The firm over-extended itself with a new fac-

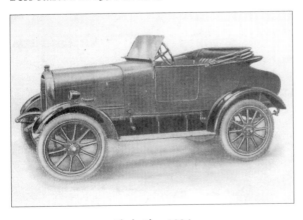

Clyde 8hp, 1924.

tory at nearby Bushbury (now home of Britool adjoining Goodyear tyres) in 1927, and a cut-throat price battle with Morris combined with the loss of Rootes as its distributors led to bankruptcy in 1929 after something like 40,000 cars had been sold.

The spares were bought by R H Collier and Co. of Birmingham, who built a few more cars and discovered a prototype straight-eight Clyno in the works. Designer A G Booth departed to AJS, which had acquired some Clyno patents for its own small car, and he was later responsible for the Singer Le Mans. Frank Smith went to Star as works manager.

The Clyno 10.8hp Family Model, 1923.

10.8, 11, 11.9. 1922-28 (prod: 18,500 in 1926-27, suggesting total of about 35,000). Various body styles, chassis £220 at beginning, complete tourer £152 at end. S4 SV 1368cc Coventry Climax, cone clutch, separate three speed gearbox, initially no differential, quarter-elliptic suspension, later semi-elliptic front. A combination of low price, good specification and pleasant driving characteristics made this Clyno's staple product. 623 were made in 1922 and the 1926 peak was 11,149. The 1923 Family Model shown cost £238, making it exceedingly competitive with the Morris Oxford. Good four wheel brakes were standardised in 1926, and steering and economy came in for favourable comment.

The Clyno 12/28 saloon.

12, 13, 12/28. 1924-28 (prod: approx 8000). Various body styles, chassis starting at £215. S4 SV 1496cc, cone clutch, separate three speed gearbox,

torque tube, spiral bevel axle, four wheel brakes. Semi-elliptic front, quarter-elliptic rear suspension. Clever marketing put this 50mph car in a class above its 11.9hp Treasury rating, and at £250 for a four-door saloon in 1925 it was a tremendous bargain. These models had Clyno's own gearbox and engine though Moss axles seem to have been used in most models. The increase in capacity over the 10.8 model was achieved by means of a 3mm increase in bore size.

A Clyno 12/35.

12/35. 1927-29 (prod: approx 2000). Various body styles commencing at £157. S4 SV 1593cc, cone clutch, separate three speed gearbox, torque tube, spiral bevel axle. Semi-elliptic front, quarter-elliptic rear suspension. Clyno's own engine was under the bonnet again but now there was a more distinctive radiator style. Also designed by A G Both, this 11.98hp-rated model was made alongside the 9 at Bushbury. It matched the price of the larger 14/28 Morris and usually had locally built Hayward fabric bodywork. Unusually for a cheap car it had a 12-volt electric system (unlike the 6-volt 9).

9hp Clyno fabric saloon.

9. 1927-29 (prod: approx 300). Fabric saloon £160, Century four-seater tourer £145 dropping to £112.10s. S4 SV 951cc, plate clutch, in-unit three

speed gearbox, spiral-bevel axle. Semi-elliptic front, quarter-elliptic rear suspension. Like the 12/35 the make or break 9 was launched at the 1927 London Motor Show. Though cheap it was perhaps a little too spartan, and it was out on its own with no competitive Morris Minor when production started in March 1928. The factory closed in August 1929, the Century being unkindly known to many as the Cemetery, though the name had been intended to reflect £100 for which it had been hoped to sell the car.

COMET

London WC1

In 1921 the Preston Autocar Co. Ltd made a 10hp four-cylinder sporting two-seater with four speed gearbox and shaft drive. It was pricey at £600 and may not have got beyond the prototype stage.

1921 Comet 10hp.

CONSTANTINESCO

Grosvenor Gardens and Wilton Road, London SW1

The fertile brain of Georges Constantinesco, who became a British subject in 1916, designed the ferro-concrete parliament building in his native Roumania and perfected the interrupter firing mechanism on Allied Great War fighter planes. Sonics were his pet subject, and he invented a sonic torque converter which was allied in 1922 to a Sheffield Simplex chassis powered by a small Singer engine. He also tried a similar system with a railway locomotive.

In 1924 a 350cc Blackburne-engined prototype car was built using GN components, and in 1925 Constantinesco Torque Convertors was formed and a two-cylinder water-cooled 500cc two-stroke car was built in France. The torque converters (which lay between the cylinders) were made in Wilton Road and the clutchless, gearless (except

The Constantinesco Car had a 500cc twin mated to a clutchless, gearless transmission.

to provide reverse) chassis probably arrived from Paris. A few of the 35mph/35mpg cars appear to have been sold at £250 in 1927.

COLTMAN

Loughborough, Leicestershire

Built at the Midland Iron Works in Loughborough, this was a traditional 20hp car introduced in 1907 of which the final two (chassis numbers 628/629) were produced in 1920 (none were said to have been made 1912-19). It had a four-cylinder 25.8hp Treasury rating engine with four speed gearbox and bevel drive.

COOPER

Ampthill Road, Bedford and Lythall's, Coventry

Current in Bedford 1919-20 and revived in Coventry in 1922 by theatre and garage owner S H Newsome (who married into the family of the makers of Calcott cars). Newsome drove Coopers (nothing to do with the post-World War Two variety) and a variant called the Warwick at Brooklands, and was later a rally driver and SS Jaguar promoter.

The 1923 Cooper.

In its first incarnation the Cooper had a three-cylinder 11hp air-cooled engine which probably got no further than the prototype stage. The production cars in Coventry used Coventry Climax engines and Moss gearboxes.

MODEL F. 1923 (prod: first in 1923 was chassis 70 and few were built). Various body styles from £235 two-seater to £300 coupé, S4 SV 1368cc Coventry Climax, cone clutch, three speed gearbox, two wheel brakes, spiral bevel axle, semi-elliptic suspension. "The car that is built to an ideal" in fact had very similar specifications to the far cheaper Clyno 10.8 and was doomed from the outset.

CORONA

Tollington Park, London N4

Made by the Meteor Manufacturing Co., which appears to have had no connection with the producers of the Meteorite cars, the Corona was current from 1920 to 1923 and used a different engine each year. Bore and stroke of the first two years' 12hp models was 65 × 110mm, and then came a 65 × 115mm 8hp flat twin (shown). The early fours were said to be by Bovier, whilst in 1923 a 63 × 100mm (1247cc) 10hp had a sidevalve Coventry Climax with right hand change, three speed gearbox, cone clutch and worm axle. The 1923 chassis price was £260.

Corona two-seater.

COSMOS
See Car

COVENTRY PREMIER

Coventry, Warwickshire

A bicycle firm, founded in 1875, which had William Hillman as one of its original partners and which by the turn of the century boasted that it was "the largest cycle manufactory in the World".

The Premier Cycle Co. added motor cycles to its products in 1908, and a four wheeled cyclecar in 1912. In 1914 Premier became Coventry Premier, and Works Manager, G W A Brown of Talbot fame, designed an advanced four wheeled, four-cylinder light car which was extensively tested in prototype form during the Great War. However, by the end of hostilities fashion had changed in favour of a three wheeled cyclecar, totally different to the previous design, and therefore almost certainly not attributable to Brown, who had moved to Arrol Johnston in 1917. Early in 1921 Singer acquired Coventry Premier and worked on a four wheeled replacement of the three wheeler which was introduced in September 1921, by which time three wheeler stocks were still being slowly sold off. For 1923 a cheaper version of the Singer Ten was badge engineered as a Coventry Premier, and that marked the end of the firm. Singer also used the Coventry Premier name on their bicycles into the late 1920s.

Coventry Premier 8hp three-wheeler.

8 HP SUPER RUNABOUT. 1919-23 (prod: 500 three wheelers, 1200 four wheelers). Two-seater, both models acquiring dickey seats in latter production, approx £250. V2 1056cc water-cooled 8hp, shaft drive to rear mounted three speed and reverse gearbox, with final drive by enclosed chain on three wheelers, quarter-elliptic suspension. Not quite as luxurious as a Castle Three, but a cut above typical cyclecars. The four wheeler was similar mechanically, but the gearbox was mounted in unit with rear axle. The final four wheeler in 1923 was a £241 version of the £294 OHV Singer Ten.

COVENTRY VICTOR

Coventry, Warwickshire

Morton and Weaver made horizontally opposed engines from 1904 and one powered the first monoplane to leave the ground in Britain in 1906. The engines, which became Coventry Victors in 1911, were supplied to numerous cyclecar makers including Grahame-White. In 1919 W A Weaver designed a light car but it was motor cycles for sidecar work that actually went into production. Then, in 1926, following the gradual loss of its light car clients, Coventry Victor launched a three wheeler which, with an update in 1933 by C F Beauvais (see CFB), lasted to 1938. Surviving Coventry Victor registration records run into thousands, though many reveal vehicles with van bodywork as replacements for trade sidecar outfits. Chassis numbers in 1930 ran from 3200 to 5000 (the latter possibly the total since 1926) so 1800 vehicles were probably produced that year. They reached 12,500 in 1936.

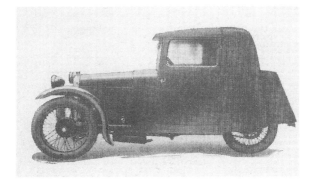

Coventry Victor three-wheeler Coupé.

STANDARD, SPORTS, DE LUXE, PARCELCAR. 1926-33 (prod: see above). Two-seater with optional small dickey starting at 95 guineas and falling to £75 in early 1930s. HO2 SV 688cc then 749cc 7hp (OHV 7.5hp in Sports), two speed chain transmission, initially rear wheel brake only, quarter-elliptic suspension. Principal rival to Morgan and BSA long after most rivals had expired. Victor Oil Engines existed from 1932 but though engines were tried on Jowetts there is no evidence that Coventry Victor cars were diesel pioneers!

CREWFORD

See Ford

CROSSLEY

Gorton, Manchester

After supplying thousands of vehicles and aero engines for the war effort Crossley settled down to making 45 cars per week for the civilian market. They were high-grade machines, though the firm also had more prosaic involvements with Willys-Overland and Avro, as well as Saunderson tractors and, later, AJS cars and the Burney Streamline. At the other end of the scale, in the early 1920s it also

Crossley 25/30 laundaulette, c1920.

built a couple of dozen Bugattis. To begin with, civilian versions of Crossley's respected 25/30 Staff cars were reconditioned or built new, but then came more modern types with, at the end of the decade, a model using an engine that Crossley also supplied to Lagonda. Buses and military vehicles became another speciality. The total postwar output to the end of car production in 1937 was 13,200 (of which 3000 were produced in the 1930s). Chief engineer throughout the vintage period was Cecil Bianchi, who in 1929 moved to Bean, though he was ably assisted by T Wishart.

25/30. 1919-25 (prod: nearly 10,000 including other models to 1925). Various body styles, chassis £950 1919, £725 1923. Pair-cast S4 SV 4536cc, cone clutch, right hand change, four speed gearbox, spiral bevel rear axle, detachable wire wheels. Semi-elliptic front, ¾-elliptic rear suspension. Designed by A W Reeves (see Enfield-Allday) well before the Great War (in which, as the 20/25, it was standardised as the Royal Flying Corps Squadron four-seater), it was revived afterwards to be a Royal favourite – the Prince of Wales used 12 on an Indian tour in 1921, and the Kings of Spain and Siam as well as Prince Hirohito favoured the type. Ironically, war surplus versions were popular with small bus operators.

Crossley 19.6hp.

19.6, 20/70. 1920-26, 1923-26 (prod: 1100). Various body styles, chassis commencing at £1085 and falling to £710. **S4 SV 3705cc, cone clutch, four speed gearbox, spiral bevel axle, four wheel brakes available from 1924, semi-elliptic suspension.** A detachable cylinder head spelled modernity though there was still a transmission brake. The 20/70 was a 75mph version for less formal coachwork. The 19.6 was another favourite with the Prince of Wales, and in 1923 one was the first ever to succeed in a 20,000 mile RAC trial. The 20/70 was described by *The Motor* as "One of the best cars ever produced in England" and it must have been one of the last thoroughbred sports cars with side valves.

The same engine was used in military six-wheelers, Kegresse half tracks and a special grouse moor six-wheeler for Royal use.

Crossley 14hp, 1925.

12/14, 14. 1923-27 (prod: 5600). Tourer £475 1923, £395 1924 and 1925. S4 SV 2388cc (15.6hp Treasury rating), single dry plate clutch, three speed centre change gearbox, spiral bevel axle. Four wheel brakes in last two years, semi-elliptic suspension. Crossley's up-market popular model (compared with Willys-Overland, Crossley's cheaper offerings). Described by *The Autocar* as staunch, comfortable and economical (28-30mpg and 54mph top speed with a very flexible engine). No wonder Belsize down the road threw in the towel soon after this model arrived. In 1925 the new 14 came with attractive bodywork and extra equipment including a rear blind to overcome dazzle. Like the cheaper Armstrong-Siddeleys it featured a different, flatter radiator.

18/50 Six, 20.9. 1925-27, 1928-37 (prod: 1700). Various body styles, tourer £675 1926. S6 OHV 2692cc, 3198cc, single plate clutch, in-unit four speed gearbox, right hand change, spiral bevel axle, semi-elliptic suspension. New at the Olympia show in 1925, the 18/50 had Crossley's first overhead-valve and first six-cylinder engine. Despite achieving an average of 48.5mph for 24 hours at Sitges and

The Crossley Six enclosed limousine.

The Crossley Sports 2 litre had a maximum speed of 77mph.

despite the model's commendable smoothness, there was a demand for more power, answered by an increase in bore from 69mm to 75mm for 1928 onwards.

The 15.7hp Crossley Six fabric saloon, 1928.

15.7 Six. 1928-34 (prod: 1700). Various body styles, Shelsley fabric saloon £550, limousine £595. S6 OHV 1991cc 45bhp, single plate clutch, four speed gearbox, right hand change, spiral bevel axle, semi-elliptic suspension. Being smaller and lighter than its 20.9 sister, this model had similar 60mph performance but was more economical (25mpg touring consumption). As usual owners spoke of fine top gear performance, though it had one of the easiest crash gearboxes on which to change ratio. Still hand made, without conveyor lines, and Crossley built most of its own coachwork.

Sports 2 litre. 1929-31 (prod: included with 15.7). Open two-seater £625, chassis £475. Specification as 15.7 but higher power output. A beautifully made classic British sports car, though testers complained of engine harshness in early cars before a crankshaft damper was fitted. 77mph and 21mpg

were available. The same Crossley twin-carburettor engine was used by Lagonda in its 16/80 model.

CROUCH

Cook Street, Coventry

The Crouch family made about 400 three and four wheel Carettes before the Great War. They revived the model afterwards as the 8hp, making virtually all of it, and a more conventional successor, in-house. After that engines were bought in from British Anzani, Coventry Climax and Dorman, though most bodies were built by Crouch after earlier using Carbodies. Peak production from the 400 workforce was about 25 cars per week, but as competition increased it fell back rapidly. Total output to the end of 1927 was quoted as high as 3000 cars but 2000, including pre-war, seems more likely. The demise of the firm was attributed to an Australian export venture that went wrong.

John Crouch, who had originally worked for Daimler, returned there and was joined by his son, who was to be responsible for the DB18 sports and later was in charge of bus sales.

The 8hp Crouch two-seater tourer.

8, 8/18. 1919-23 (prod: approx 1500). Sold only as a complete two-seater in Royal Blue at £235-285. V2 OHV water-cooled 1022cc (1248cc 8/18), cone clutch, three speed gearbox, chain drive on 8, shaft and bevel on 8/18 of 1922-23, quarter-elliptic suspension (duplex at front). Increasingly modernised version of the 1913 four-wheel Carette with virtually all parts except the BTH magneto, Cox Atmos carburettor and Miller lighting set made by Crouch. 30-35mpg from a very quiet and refined engine with legendary lugging ability.

The engine in the 8hp model was mounted transversely amidships but was moved to the front on the 8/18.

Alfred Moss's Anzani engined Crouch 12 at Brooklands.

12/24, 12/30. 1923, 1924-27 (prod: approx 800). Various body styles, chassis from about £250. S4 SV 1496cc British Anzani 30bhp (up to 45bhp tuned), cone clutch, three speed gearbox amidships, torque tube, spiral bevel axle, four wheel brakes on late cars, quarter-elliptic suspension (duplex at front). Well built and with a Brooklands pedigree thanks to Stirling Moss's father Alfred, who sold Crouch cars in London. The Sports (later Super Sports) model was guaranteed to do 60mph – 90mph with streamlining and without wings.

1924 models bore the names Classic for the two-seater and Magnetic for the four-seater, both at £295. Magnetic was plainly a trendy word at the time, even for cars without Entz magnetic transmission!

1924 Crouch 10hp four-seater.

10. 1923-24 (prod: about 60). Economic four-seater £225, Climatic two-seater £235, in usual Crouch Royal Blue or maroon. S4 SV 1196cc fixed head Dorman, cone clutch, three speed gearbox, torque tube, spiral bevel axle, quarter-elliptic suspension (duplex at front). This was the four-cylinder replacement for the old vee-twins. Moss "The Crouch Enthusiast" sold it with a free warranty for one year.

Crouch 11/27 semi-coupé with Coventry Climax engine, 1926-27.

11/27. 1926-27 (prod: about 100). Chassis from £180, semi-coupé (shown) £220. Quorn saloon also on 12/30. S4 SV 1368cc Coventry Climax, cone clutch, three speed gearbox, torque tube, spiral bevel axle, quarter-elliptic suspension (duplex at front). This was a cheaper and somewhat slower (55mph) companion model to the British Anzani types. As usual it was well engineered and built, but one of a dying breed that had little tangible to offer to distinguish it from cheaper mass-produced cars.

CROWN ENSIGN & CROWN MAGNETIC

High Holborn, London WC

Harry Crown (see British Ensign) interested his father, J L Crown, in the British Ensign HP6 model as a potential user of his Entz magnetic transmission, a frictionless variable system with high power loss invented by Justus B Entz whilst working for an American battery firm. Crown had sole non-American rights in the system as used on the battleship *New Mexico*, and put it to use in the American Owen and then Crown Magnetic cars of 1914-22.

The Crown Magnetic sold in Britain in 1920 was the latter Buda 6.8 litre engined machine, but in 1921 perhaps ten Minerva sleeve-valve 30/50hp engined cars (allegedly on Berliet chassis) were assembled by the J L Crown Motor Co. Ltd, followed by at any rate one Crown Ensign with HP6 engine in 1922.

Whether the American Owen had any connec-

A 1921 Crown Magnetic.

tion with the cars supposedly sold under the name of Owen and Orleans from Comeragh Road, West Kensington, is not clear.

Another mystery is the Magnetic offered by the Magnetic Car Co. Ltd of Callow Street, Chelsea and Lime Street EC2. This existed in buyers' guides from 1921 to 1926, starting with Burt McCollum four-cylinder sleeve-valve engines as used by Argyll and built by Greenwood and Batley, then a mysterious 5228cc eight and an assortment of OHV sizes of up to 3.9 litres. All used Entz transmission so were probably an offshoot of the J L Crown affair! A 2.6-litre four was listed in 1923 in a chassis costing a formidable £750, or £950 as a five-seat tourer. General Ironside was a satisfied user.

CUBITT

Southern Works, Aylesbury, Buckinghamshire

A subsidiary of civil engineers Holland, Hannen and Cubitt Ltd, which had built Osborne House for Queen Victoria, numerous munitions and aircraft factories (at one of which Constantinesco's interrupter gears had been made), and even the Cenotaph. The firm had experience of mass production and plenty of financial resources, and made an American-inspired postwar car on the 28 acre site of one of its munitions factories. By 1921 it was turning out 60 cars per week with a workforce peaking at 1000. Senior staff had previous experience with Daimler, Decauville, Humber, Renault, Ford and Arrol-Johnston. Bodywork came from the premises of the Iris car firm across the road. Production of 5000 cars a year was intended but when this was not achieved the modest profit of the first year gave way to massive losses. S F Edge (see AC) was brought in and works director J S Napier (ex-managing director of Arrol-Johnston

and still on the board of AC) designed a rather sleeker replacement model. Edge used surplus capacity to make Anzani-based engines plus bodywork for AC, but Cubitt ended in late 1925.

A 1925 Cubitt 16/20

16/20. 1920-25 (prod: approx 3000). Chassis £420 falling to £270 at end. S4 SV 2815cc, cone clutch, four speed separate gearbox, worm axle. Semi-elliptic front, cantilever rear suspension. Ideal for the colonies, being heavy, high-built and strong. Performance was rather pedestrian though very flexible due to the 140mm stroke (80mm bore) of the Cubitt built monobloc, detachable head engine with coil ignition. In 1926 all Cubitt's stock of parts was with Elephant Motors in London. Early models had a distinctive scalloped pattern below the radiator but after Edge took over this vanished, and a different shape radiator was used on a better-looking car.

CWS

Tyseley, Birmingham

As well as making Bell cars the Co-op movement built Federal and Federation motor cycles in Birmingham from 1919 to 1937. In 1922 it unveiled a three-wheeler with single rear wheel driven by a JAP vee-twin 8hp air-cooled engine via a three speed and reverse gearbox and Renolds chain. At £150 it did not last long against the £165 Austin Seven. It came with lamps, tools, windscreen and horn – but an extra £3.15s was required for the hood!

The CWS Three Wheeler

Daimler Light 30 vee-screen saloon outside Watkins and Doncaster.

DAIMLER

Sandy Lane, Radford, Coventry, Warwickshire

Founded in 1896 as a licensee of the German company of the same name, Coventry Daimler soon became one of the most British of all Coventry firms, despite in 1909 adopting the American C Y Knight's design for a double sleeve valve engine. In 1910 BSA purchased a Daimler and not surprisingly their cars developed close links. G T Smith Clark, who became chief engineer at Alvis in 1922, was involved with the early postwar Daimlers and then came the legendary L H Pomeroy (see Vauxhall) who, after designing the Double-Six, became Daimler's managing director in 1929.

Daimlers were expensive luxury cars, typically with seven-bearing crankshafts, the firm's own multi-jet carburettors, cast iron and from the mid-1920s steel sleeve valves, and in-house bodywork built on subframes for attachment to the chassis via rubber cushions (this method speeded up production with outside coachbuilders too). On the subject of production, chassis numbers were not made known to the likes of Motor Records Ltd, and a very complex model range – thirteen different chassis and nine standard body styles in 1924 alone – makes it difficult to produce more than the following simplified listing of types. The problem is exacerbated by Daimler's records having been destroyed in the Blitz. One school of thought

has typical annual production in the 1920s being 2500 to 3000 whilst others say it went as high as 8000. The firm certainly built about 3500 vehicles in 1911 so following wartime expansion the upper figure is feasible.

The company has several parallels with Armstrong-Siddeley (which interestingly averaged about 2500 cars p.a.) and in 1930 began to offer pre-selector gearboxes made by this near neighbour.

A 1921 Daimler "Light Thirty" coupé saloon.

30, 45. 1919-25 (prod: n/a). 1923 chassis £850, £1275, limousine £2000. S6 sleeve-valve 4962cc, 7413cc, cone clutch (disc after 1922), four speed gearbox with right hand change, underslung worm axle. Semi-elliptic front, ¾-elliptic rear sus-

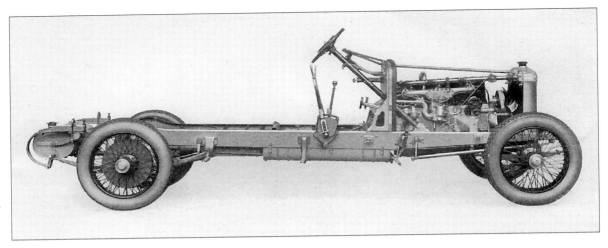

The 45hp Daimler "Special" chassis.

pension. Staid and sumptuous carriages revived from pre-war days. The 45, which developed 80bhp, had silver-plated fittings. Around 250 assorted models were run by Daimler Hire Ltd in London in 1921 alone – six-seaters cost £1.5s for an evening between 6pm and midnight as long as mileage was limited to 25. Daimlers marked the height of conservatism and tradition with their "Silent Knight" sleeve-valve engines. The 45 was sometimes billed as the Special, and the Standard Thirty was also available as the shorter wheelbase Light Thirty, distinguished by its invisible radiator filler cap. A few 8500cc 57hp replicas of George V's 1924 official car were also made.

Daimler 20hp two-seater, 1921.

12, 16, 20, 21. 1921-24 (prod: n/a). 1923 £880-£1375 complete. S6 (20 S4) sleeve-valve 1542cc, 2167cc, 3308cc, 3021cc, disc clutch, four speed gearbox with right hand change (three speed centre change later on 16), underslung worm axle, semi-elliptic suspension. These were more suitable for owner drivers (once they had got used to the traditional push-on handbrake). The 21 was good for 23mpg and 50mph, all in uncanny silence. Like their big sisters these models featured BSA detachable wire wheels, which helped to make all of them look surprisingly delicate despite the formal coachwork found on most.

The four-cylinder 20, effectively two thirds of a 30, was a marketing mistake in 1921-22 (all other 1920s Daimlers being sixes or twelves) and was replaced by the monobloc 21. The 12 was the same as the BSA (see BSA) but with the famous fluted radiator evolved from the finned header tank of early days.

35hp Daimler chassis fitted with a Windover Pullman limousine body.

35, 35/120. 1924-32 (prod: 800 quoted but more claimed). Chassis 1924 £900, 1930 £975. S6 sleeve-valve 5764cc, single plate clutch, separate four speed gearbox with central change, underslung worm axle, semi-elliptic suspension. Launched at Olympia in late 1923 and fitted with four wheel brakes from the outset (vacuum servo assisted from mid-1926). Alloy pistons and lighter steel sleeves permitted 3000rpm (4000rpm on test) and 30mph in top involved a leisurely 1060rpm. Despite Daimler having no formal connection with Lanchester cars until 1931, the 35/120 had a Lanchester vibration damper and the usual Lanchester worm drive (F W Lanchester was a consulting engineer to Daimler throughout the 1920s). The noisiest part of this impressive car was said to be its speedo drive and the engine was also used in Daimler bus and coach chassis.

Daimler Double-Six 50hp saloon, 1926.

A rare Hoyal-bodied sports version of the 1929 Daimler Double-Six 30hp, capable of 85mph.

DOUBLE-SIX 50, DOUBLE-SIX 30. 1926-30, 1928-30 (prod: under 500). 50 chassis £1950 1927/1929, 30 chassis £1000 1929. V12 sleeve-valve 7136cc, 3744cc, single plate clutch, separate four speed gearbox with central change, underslung worm axle, semi-elliptic suspension. Cheaper than the 40-50 Rolls-Royce, the 30 and 50 were Europe's first production V12s. The snag was their colossal weight (even the shortest 50 chassis weighted 38cwt) though 80mph was on the cards. Each bank of cylinders had its own cooling, carburettor and dual ignition systems, and naturally there were four-wheel servo brakes. The Double-Six was a tour de force that became frighteningly expensive to maintain in later life. The bigger model could climb Birdlip Hill in top gear in impressive silence.

1928 Daimler 25/85 with Stratton-Instone Special saloon body.

16/55, 20/70, 25/85. 1926-30 (prod: possibly 7000). 1926 16 chassis £490, 1929 20 fabric saloon £695. S6 sleeve valve 1872cc, 2650cc, 3568cc, twin plate clutch on 16/55, single plate on others, four speed (three on 16) gearbox with central change, underslung worm axle, semi-elliptic suspension.

Appropriate for the well-heeled family motorist, though still often bodied in highly traditional style. The 1928 Stratton-Instone Special saloon shown had a division so that a chauffeur could be used on formal occasions.

The 16 could do 60mph and about 28mpg, and the 20 model 60mph and about 20mpg. The 25/85 was closely related to the 35/120 and 20/70 whilst the 16/55 differed in having an in-unit gearbox (with only three forward ratios).

DANDY

Hart Street and Moss Lane, Southport, Lancashire

Listed from 1922 to 1925, this was an 8hp three wheeler with a JAP air-cooled sidevalve twin of 988cc capacity, a three speed gearbox and chain drive. It weighed a quarter of a ton, cost £135 and could be folded to fit through a 2'8" doorway. Elias Sumner, the maker, may have had some connection with the Sumner blacksmithing and engineering family which had started the famous commercial vehicle factory at nearby Leyland.

The Dandy folding three wheeler.

DARRACQ

See Talbot

DAWSON

Priory Street, Coventry, Warwickshire

A J Dawson had been apprenticed to the GWR at Wolverhampton and had worked for BTH, Daimler and Hillman. After a spell with Hotchkiss he returned to Hillman as Works Manager to develop the postwar 11hp model, but before it appeared he left to start his own car factory with a car made almost entirely in-house. After this venture failed the factory was acquired by Triumph for its new car and he moved to Australia.

The 11-12hp Dawson car.

11-12HP. 1919-21 (prod: 65). 2/3 seater £750, coupé £820, saloon £995. S4 OHC 1795cc, cone clutch, three speed gearbox, bevel axle, semi-elliptic suspension. Its overhead cam engine and very high price were the most notable features of the Dawson. The engine was an early user of aluminium pistons and big end bearings were of die-cast white metal. A distinctive feature was the bulldog radiator badge.

DAY & DAYTON

See Day-Leeds

DAY-LEEDS

Ellerby Lane, Leeds, Yorkshire

Makers of packing machines and bacon slicers, Job Day and Sons added motor cycles to their products and then, in 1913, light cars. Some were powered by Turner engines but the company made its own engines from 1915. Design was attributed to W L Adams, who had created a V12 Laxtonia aero engine during the war and was afterwards involved with the Mendip car.

The Day-Leeds 10hp.

A Day car from Chas Day Mfg of Shoreditch and Stebbing Street, London W11, in 1922 never got beyond the prototype stage and may have been intended to be marketed under the name of Dayton.

10HP. 1919-24 (prod: about 300). Sold complete with grey-painted bodywork by Lockwood and Clarkson at £500 falling to £225. S4 SV 1267cc fixed head monobloc, cone clutch, three speed separate gearbox, torque tube, spiral bevel axle, semi-elliptic suspension. A typically over priced, hand built postwar offering wiped out by the mass-produced competition.

DEEMSTER

Victoria Road, Acton, London W3

The Ogston Motor Co. of Deemster Works was situated near to the Napier factory and manned by several ex-Napier staff including the chief draughtsman, J N Ogston. Its first car of 1914 was based on the former Wilkinson (made by the Wilkinson sword and razor blade firm). Deemster (which means judge or umpire) was revived in new premises in Victoria Road in 1919. Deemsters gained a good reputation in competitive hill climbs and Kaye Don drove one at Brooklands. The pre-war Demeester from France was unconnected.

A Deemster 10hp, c1920.

10, 12. 1919-23, 1922-24 (prod: chassis numbers ran from 580 in 1919 to 680 in 1920 and thereafter to over 4125 but annual output probably never exceeded the 100 suggested by 1919's figures). Various open two- and four-seaters, chassis £475 falling to £240. S4 SV 1086cc (own 10hp), 1496cc

(12hp British Anzani), cone clutch (until dry single plate on final 12hp), three speed gearbox, spiral bevel axle. Semi-elliptic front, quarter-elliptic rear suspension. Sporty looking light car of which about seven were bought in 1923 to be turned into the first Frazer-Nash cars. The £315 "Popular" model of 1923 had no speedometer so testers found it difficult to produce acceleration figures. It was however said to be lively and to give an average 32mpg.

DEREK

West Norwood, London SE27

Puzzlingly, buyers' guides spoke of Derek Motors of Invicta Works (no connection with Invicta cars) using Chapuis Dornier and its own engines, yet the bore and stroke quoted for the latter (63 × 100mm) were the same as the Meadows OHV 1247cc engines with matching three speed gearboxes it is known to have bought.

Derek "Standard" two-seater, 1925.

9/20 and 10/25. 1925-26 (prod: first year chassis numbers said to be up to 197 but presumably far fewer sold as only four Meadows engines were used). Complete cars in blue or red £168-£325. S4 SV 1018cc (Chapuis Dornier 9/20) or OHV 1247cc (Meadows 10/25), cone clutch, three speed in-unit gearbox, spiral bevel axle, quarter-elliptic suspension. 1925 was very late for an undistinguished assembled car to break into the market and failure soon followed. The Meadows cars were similar in specification to Bayliss-Thomas or Lea Francis.

DE SOTO

Kew, Surrey

A cheaper brand of Chrysler assembled at Kew from Canadian parts and often with British bodywork. Its 26.4hp car introduced in 1930 for the 1931 season was the cheapest with eight cylinders. Chassis prices started at £295 but the brand

The De Soto 'OW' 21/60.

then disappeared from the British market until later in the decade.

OW. 1928-30 (prod: n/a). Various bodies often by Hoyal, chassis £240. S6 OHV 2748cc 21/60hp, single plate clutch, three speed gearbox, spiral bevel axle, four wheel hydraulic brakes, semi-elliptic suspension. Cheap and cheerful American-type transport, offering flexibility and 60mph, that didn't do as well here as the price would suggest on account of its £22-a-year road tax.

DL & DLM

Toll Street, Motherwell, Lanarkshire

The DL Motor Manufacturing Co. Ltd, originally known as W Guthrie and Co. and Dalziel (hence DL) motor manufacturing – William Guthrie had worked for Argyll – introduced 8 and 10/12hp four-cylinder cars in 1913 and revived them for a year after the war. DLM became involved with Wallace (Glasgow) Ltd in the production of the three wheel drive Glasgow tractor, which was soon knocked out by the far cheaper Fordson. Only two cars were made after the war, one saloon and one tourer.

A 1920 DL 11.9hp tourer.

DODGE

Stevenage Wharf, Fulham, London SW6, Park
Royal NW10 and Kew, Surrey

This familiar American manufacturer was, like
Bean, initially a mass producer of motor components. It turned to complete cars in 1914 and by
1920 was second in sales terms only to Ford in its
homeland.

Early British involvement was limited to locally
produced bodywork but the Park Royal factory
was opened to allow a greater degree of assembly
after the re-imposition of McKenna Duty in July
1925. Dodge was acquired by Chrysler in 1928 and
later moved to Kew, which became home to the
all-British Dodge commercial vehicles of the early
1930s.

1927 Dodge 24hp.

**17/24 and 24. 1923-27 (prod: n/a). Various body-
work, chassis from £245. S4 SV 3.6 litres, three
speed gearbox, spiral bevel axle. Four wheel
brakes, single plate clutch and coil in place of
magneto ignition on later examples. Semi-elliptic
suspension.** As usual it was The £-a-horsepower tax
that held back sales against the typical British 7-12hp
cars of the time.

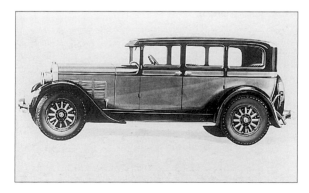

1928 Dodge Victory Six.

**SIX (Standard, Victory Senior and New). 1927-30
(prod: n/a). Various bodies, chassis from £285.
Commenced with 25hp engine then S6 SV 3391cc**

**27hp, single plate clutch, in-unit three speed gear-
box, spiral bevel axle, semi-elliptic suspension.**
Chrysler quickly killed off Dodge's fours (only to
reintroduced new ones in 1931 for Europe), but
which of the sixes it actually built at Kew is difficult
to ascertain. The Victory Six was widely advertised
in Britain but seems to have had an American-built
pressed steel sedan body that gave a low roofline
thanks to the lack of sills. The Park Royal factory was
still in use in late 1928 and from Kew for 1931 a
British Tax 19.8hp model was introduced.

The Dodge Eight.

**EIGHT. 1930-33, (prod: n/a UK but under 20,000
US). Various styles, chassis £435. S8 SV 3616cc
26.45hp, dry plate clutch, in-unit three speed gearbox, spiral bevel axle, semi-elliptic suspension.**
Introduced in July 1930 as a luxury model suitable
for limousine and landaulette coachwork. A very
similar but cheaper version was offered as a De Soto.
The Dodge Ram (actually a Rocky Mountain goat)
mascot arrived in 1930 for the '31 season.

DOUGLAS

Kingswood, Bristol

Douglas was famous for flat-twin motor cycles, of
which thousands were in use in the Great War. Its
1070cc light car of 1913 was revived after the war

The 10.5hp Douglas two-seater.

Douglas 10.5hp chassis.

with enlarged engine for a couple of years. The factory has been used by the makers of Westinghouse brakes since motor cycle production ended in 1956.

10.5. 1920-22 (prod: a few 100s). Chassis £460, two-seater £500. HO2 1224cc water-cooled, cone clutch, three speed gearbox, bevel axle. A refined and expensive light car with Adams AFS helical rear suspension (as on CAR) though with conventional semi-elliptics at front.

DUNALASTAIR

Birkin Avenue, Nottingham

Like Derek, another late recruit to the field of expensive hand-assembled cars. Also like others, it had no particularly distinguishing features so its existence was brief.

14. 1925-26 (prod: 3 or 4). Only supplied with coachwork, tourer cheapest at £500. S4 OHV 2120cc Meadows, cone clutch, in-unit Meadows four speed gearbox, spiral bevel axle, semi-elliptic suspension. A chassis frame from Mechins of Scotstoun and hand buffed leather seem to have been the Dunalastair's principal claims to fame. Surprisingly it had no front wheel brakes, though OHV and four speeds were in its favour.

DUNKLEY

Bradford Street, Birmingham

Offered by a pram firm that had made sporadic attempts at car manufacture since 1896. Dunkley had made the Alvechurch cyclecar, named after its Alvechurch Works, shortly before the Great War but afterwards concentrated on motorised transport for babies. Dunkley's Pramotor of 1923-25 came in a variety of sizes up to the 135 guinea model 20 shown. Various engines of up to 750cc with one or two gears were unleashed on power-crazed nannies.

The 135-guinea Dunkley Pramotor Model 20.

DUPLEX

Trafford Park, Manchester

Made by an ephemeral producer of lorries at premises adjoining those where the Ford T was made. The Duplex had two banks of four parallel cylinders, each pair sharing a combustion chamber and firing simultaneously, though one was slightly in advance of the other to balance out any roughness. The 1479cc engine had a single crankshaft and sleeve valves: the inlets in one bank of cylinders and the exhausts in the other. It was started by a hand lever in the passenger compartment. The cone clutch and three-speed gearbox were in-unit with the engine, which developed an impressive 33bhp at 3000rpm. Presumably it was a technical disaster as it was replaced by a Coventry Simplex engined model in 1920. "The world's smallest eight" was rated by its makers at 10hp though its RAC rating was 15.6hp.

The 10-20hp Duplex four-seater.

10, 10/20. 1919, 1920-21 (prod: chassis numbers 101-200 for 10, possibly including 10/20). Chassis £425. 10 described above. 10/20 Coventry Simplex S4 SV 1498cc, cone clutch, three speed gearbox, spiral bevel axle, quarter-elliptic suspension. After the bizarre came the bog standard, though the 10 was revived again in the final year when teething troubles were hopefully overcome.

ECONOMIC

Wells Street, London W1

Lived up to its name in 1920-21 with a £60 asking price for a two wicker seated three-wheeler (single front wheel) weighing 150lbs. A 165cc horizontally opposed air-cooled two-stroke twin drove via two speed and reverse friction discs to a chain wheel on the back axle. There was a conventional steering wheel and no springs – the ash frame and

1921 Economic three-wheeler.

pneumatic motor cycle tyres providing some resilience.

The firm also made a £28.10s motor cycle with the same engine and American designed friction transmission.

EDMOND

Lee Green, London SE

A very basic £198 cyclecar made 1920-21 by the Shand Motor and Engineering Co. Curiously the sole sales outlet was Central England Motors of Temple Street, Birmingham. The Edmond was powered by an air-cooled Coventry Victor 689cc twin with three speed gearbox and only the nearside rear wheel was driven. It was built at the same North Star Works as the North Star. Sir J F Payne-Gallwey Brown & Co. Ltd (see Swallow) acquired the business.

1921 Edmond 5/7hp cyclecar.

EDMUND

Chester, Cheshire

A motor cycle maker current 1907-24 which used various proprietary engines including JAP and Blackburne, and made a few cyclecars in 1920 with two-cylinder engines and shaft drive.

ELMO

Hertford Street, London W1

An old established maker of electric cars, initially under the names British Electromobile, BEC and Powerful. Sales were small and in the teens most went into its own hire fleet. A brief revival in 1919-20 was with an 8/12hp bonneted limousine, bodied by Gill of Paddington, which could be charged, stored and maintained at the makers' premises. It cost a prohibitive £1050 plus £250 for battery and £42 for tyres.

A 1919 Elmo electric limousine laudaulette by Gill.

EMMS

Walsgrave Road, Coventry

Made 1922-23 and starting at chassis number 106, very few of these Coventry Climax 9.8hp and

The EMMS Light Car.

10.8hp light cars were sold. They were of 1247cc and 1368cc capacity and had cone clutches, three speed gearboxes, worm drive and quarter-elliptic suspension. The smaller car was finished in corn-flower blue and the larger in polished aluminium. Prices started at £230 for an open two-seater.

EMSCOTE

Warwick

A light car, made in the Emscote Works in the Warwick suburb of that name, which was unusual in having in-unit engine and gearbox. 500 engines and gearboxes were ordered from DMK Marendaz, who built 260 before very slow sales led to cancellation of the order. Emscote was run by Marlowe, a former works manager at Standard, and Seelhaft, who had worked with Marendaz at Siddeley-Deasy. With the failure of Emscote, Marendaz and Seelhaft went into partnership on the Marseal car.

1920 Emscote two-seater demonstrates its front suspension.

8/10, 11.9. 1920-21 (prod: under 260). Frameless-construction two-seater £250. V2 JAP or four-cylinder Alpha, single plate clutch, three speed gearbox, bevel drive to one rear wheel. Transverse front spring with pivoting axle. Unsuccessful commercially, but with a number of interesting features, and significant for launching Marendaz into car manufacture. He was a friend of de Freville, whose engines helped to make the Alvis 10/30 a reality.

ENFIELD-ALLDAY

Sparkbrook, then Small Heath, Birmingham

The motor interests of Enfield Autocar and Alldays & Onions were merged in December 1918. A C Bertelli (ex-Grahame-White) was works manager whilst A W Reeves from Crossley was in charge of design. Their first offerings were the revolutionary Bullet and a sleeve-valve 15hp six (discontinued in late 1919), followed by more conventional machines – all beautifully made but expensive.

Highly developed versions of the 10/20 with twin overhead inlet valves and front wheel brakes were raced by Bertelli in 1921-22 and he then left to make sports and racing cars (see R & B and Aston-Martin). Enfield-Allday's output was small – no more than 100, according to an ex-employee (who moved to Lea Francis) interviewed by Michael Sedgwick in 1960. The Company staggered from one financial disaster to another and finally succumbed early in 1926.

The Enfield-Allday Bullet chassis, showing the air-cooled radial engine.

BULLET. 1919-20 (prod: about 5). Air-cooled radial five cylinder 1247cc sleeve-valve 20.5bhp at 2500rpm, single plate clutch, three speed gearbox, helical bevel axle, transverse cantilever suspension. This extraordinary vehicle with tubular lattice frame and three-seat cloverleaf bodywork mounted on tubular outriggers was offered at £295, but was found to be uneconomic below £550, at which price there were no takers. A W Reeves was so taken with it that he considered making it himself as the Reeves Radial.

10/20 and 10/30, 12/30. 1920-26, 1923-24 (prod: about 100). Chassis from £380, various styles including 10/30 sport, two- and 2 + 2-seater £475-£625, sports saloon £795. S4 SV 1488cc, 12/30 bigger bore 1757cc. 10s had cone clutch and three speed gearbox, 12/30 plate clutch and four speeds. Semi-elliptic front, cantilever rear suspension. Advertised as the "car de luxe" these were certainly attractive but very expensive. There were only ten agents around the British Isles in 1922 and sales after that date were very infrequent, despite Bertelli's prowess on the race track.

ENSIGN
See British Ensign

Enfield-Allday 10/20 two-seater.

An Eric-Campbell 10hp two seater.

ERIC-CAMPBELL

Claremont Road, Cricklewood, N London;
Durdan Road, Southall, Middlesex

Made initially in part of a Handley-Page aircraft factory for H Eric Orr-Ewing and Noel Campbell Macklin of Silver Hawk and Invicta (Orr-Ewing married Macklin's ex-wife). The Silver Hawk being a competition version of the Eric-Campbell built at Macklin's home, where he had also developed the Eric-Campbell and in particular two racers for the 1919 Targa Florio. The prototype was based on a Swift chassis with Coventry Simplex engine.

Production stopped in 1920-21 but was revived by Vulcan Iron and Metal Works (1918) Ltd at

The 1924 Eric-Campbell saloon sold for £450.

Southall in 1922. What connection this firm had with Vulcan of Southport is unclear, though in 1922 it also sold the 10hp Vulcan. A Receiver was appointed in January 1926 and that marked the end of the Eric-Campbell.

10.5, 10/22. 1919-24 (prod: possibly as many as 500). From £215 in 1923 for Everyman's model. S4 SV 1498cc 23bhp Coventry Simplex, cone clutch, three speed Moss gearbox, spiral bevel axle. Semi-elliptic front, cantilever rear suspension. Unlike most assembled light cars this one was actually intended for aspiring sportsmen and had the benefit of high-lift camshafts, drilled piston skirts and lightened reciprocating parts to enable 60mph to be exceeded and 55mph to be guaranteed. There was also an 8/20 model (60 × 95 bore and stroke) in 1924-25, and a 69 × 100 11.9 in 1925-26, the latter with British Anzani engine.

ERIC LONGDEN

Addlestone, Surrey

Eric Longden was an Australian steeplechase jockey who after a serious injury came to London and started a theatrical agency. He enjoyed motor cycle preparation and racing at Brooklands, and in 1919-20 started assembling light cars (probably with Coventry Simplex engines and Moss gearboxes) in a building adjoining what is now Foyles bookshop in Charing Cross Road. The Air Navigation and Engineering Co. (see Bleriot-Whippet) acquired the business in 1922 and output settled down to JAP and Alpha engined sports cars resembling GNs.

ANEC also made Martin and Handasyde aircraft and gliders, and went into liquidation in 1927, soon after which the premises were used by Weymann Coachworks.

The V-twin Eric Longden light car, Southsea speed trials 1922/3 .

1923 Eric Longden all-aluminium saloon.

8, 10 and 11. 1921-22, 1922-27 (prod: chassis numbers from 113 to over 2000 but far fewer built). Various engines including JAP V2 SV 8hp and OHV 10hp, then Alpha S4 SV 1320cc, cone clutch amidships, three speed gearbox, spiral bevel axle with no differential, quarter-elliptic suspension. Specification seems to have varied and for example in 1923 included a 9hp 1088cc model. Amateurs often used the cars for racing and hill climbing.

ERSKINE
See Studebaker

ESSEX
See Hudson

EURICAR

Parkfield Street, Manchester

J V and E G Eurich planned a three-wheeler with single rear wheel and choice of rear mounted air-cooled engines. It had a retractable metal hood and hydraulic braking without friction (no details were released!). Production did not materialise in 1929-30.

The Euricar with its metal hood erected.

FERGUS
See OD

FIAT

Wembley, Middlesex and Crayford, Kent

This Italian firm was represented in Britain by D'Arcy Baker's Fiat Motors Ltd from 1903 to his death in 1932. The McKenna duties forced some assembly projects on the company as early as 1924, but the first major attempt was in 1928 with the 520, assembled at the Vickers plant in Crayford that had previously produced the Stellite. Some 1-litre 509A models were also made there using British wheels, tyres, springs, instruments, bodywork and probably lamps.

In 1930 either the Wembley or Acton Fiat premises assembled a few 1438cc 514 models with British components including Dellaney Gallay radiators. The Galloway car was heavily influenced by the earlier 501.

520. 1927-29 (prod: 20,996 including Italy). Chassis £250, tourer £315, saloon £375, coupé £395. S6 SV 2234cc 46bhp, single plate clutch, in-unit four speed gearbox, spiral bevel axle, semi-elliptic suspension, four-wheel brakes. This was the first Fiat built with left hand drive in Italy so it made sense for RHD versions to be built in Britain in 1928-29 after McKenna duty had been re-imposed. It was a long-lasting American-inspired car with coil ignition.

Fiat 520, c1929.

FLYING SCOTSMAN

See Scotsman

FORD

Trafford Park, Manchester; Cork, Ireland; Dagenham, Essex

The ultra-strong, cheap and sensible Model T arrived in America in 1908. It was not the first car to be mass produced but its eighteen year production run of between 15 and 16 millions made it the most widely sold car in the first half of the century. The brass age type lasted to late 1916, after which black painted pressed steel replaced the brass radiator shell.

An assembly plant was opened at Trafford Park in 1911 with North American parts sent to it via the Manchester Ship Canal. In the 1920s most parts came from Cork, Ireland, a site purchased in 1917 to make tractors.

Including imports, 41% of all vehicles registered for British road use in 1919 were Fords, though in 1924 Morris actually outsold the Model T for the first time. Numerous specialists made customised versions of the Model T. In some cases, including the Crewford from Caledonian Road, North London or the Aeroford from Bayswater, London

The 1921 Crewford, a converted Ford Model T.

Rear of the 1921 Crewford.

The Maiflower coupé, another Model T conversion.

W2, they had fancy bodywork and altered radiator shapes. The Goodyear from Manchester had a tuned engine and lowered chassis, whilst the Bishop from Brighton was made specifically as a trials car, with overhead valve conversion, front wheel brakes and an AC-shaped radiator. The Maiflower from Gloucester was another with a lowered frame and more sporting appearance. See also Whitehead.

MODEL T. 1913-27 (prod: UK approx 80,000 cars 1919-27). Chassis 1919 £170, 1921 £250, lowest in 1924 at £85 (£110 for a complete two-seater). S4 SV 2896cc 20hp, in-unit epicyclic two speed and reverse gearbox, torque tube, bevel axle, transverse semi-elliptic suspension front and rear, two wheel brakes. The Model T had by far the largest production in Britain in the 1920s if all the commercial derivatives are included (these considerably outnumbered the cars). In the 1919-21 period Ford's output was 33,600 cars compared with Morris's 5280, but the latter soon reversed the situation. The Model T was the vehicle that introduced the greatest number of people to motoring and, with its pedal-operated epicyclic gears, it was one of the easiest to drive. The butt of numerous music hall jokes and the immortal Tin Lizzie of the movies.

MODEL A, AF. 1928-31 (prod: UK 14,516). Chassis from £140. S4 SV 3285cc 40bhp, 2043cc 28bhp, dry multi-disc clutch, in-unit three speed gearbox, torque tube, transverse semi-elliptic springs front and rear, four wheel brakes. After months of speculation when Ford abandoned the T, the first A models produced traffic stopping crowds. A conventional "crash" gearbox replaced the T's epicyclic arrangement. The Model A was a thoroughly conventional, strong and reliable car, first built for Britain at Cork and Trafford Park (the Dagenham

The Ford Model T.

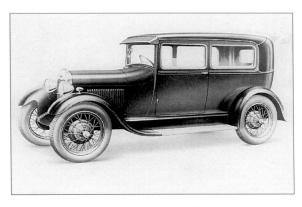

1929 Model A Ford.

complex did not open until October 1st 1931). The
14.9hp AF (smaller bore, same stroke) was a special
variant for Britain to save on horsepower tax and
outsold the 3.3 version.

FORSTER

Grosvenor Road, Richmond, Surrey

A very brief 1922 revival of the 1913-16 Globe
designed by E H Forster. The original variety was
made concurrently in France and by Tuke and Bell
in Tottenham and used JAP, Anzani or Aster
engines. Due to lack of finance it may not have
progressed beyond the pilot stage in its second
incarnation as a 1.4-litre 7hp (10hp RAC) light car
costing £225 complete. E H may be a misprint for
J H Forster, designer of the Sphinx car in France
which was sold in Britain in 1923 as the Anglo
Sphinx.

Forster chassis, with lengthways flat twin and belt drive.

FOSTER

Letchworth, Hertfordshire

Pyrometer manufacturer C E Foster of Foster
Instruments invented a variable friction
"Autogear" that was unusual in having a governor
to give it "automatic" changes (though a clutch
had to be disengaged to return it to "low speed and
neutral"). A E Bowyer-Lowe from Phoenix helped
to perfect the system in six prototypes powered
by Bovier, Coventry Victor and possibly other
engines. A 7hp Coventry Victor flat-twin powered
version took part in the 1922 London-Edinburgh
trial and a sales price of £150 per car was costed
on batches of one hundred. To avoid confusion
with Autogears of Leeds the Autogear Foster was
also known as the Accellera, but it seems unlikely
that series production ever commenced.

The original prototype of the 1920-21 Foster – the Pup.

FRAZER NASH

London Road, Kingston-upon-Thames, Surrey to
1929, then London Road, Isleworth, Middlesex

Upon leaving GN, Archibald Frazer-Nash founded
Frazer-Nash Limited in 1922. Initially he offered
OHV conversions for Rovers and also modified
about twelve GN chassis obtained from his old
company. A single car was produced under his
own name, fitted with a French manufactured
Ruby engine and Rudge Whitworth wire wheels.
At the same time an agreement was entered into
with the Deemster company to sell its shaft driven
Anzani engined cars with a Frazer Nash designed
body and radiator as a Frazer Nash, but only five or
six vehicles were sold.

   The first production Frazer Nash was manufactured in 1924. It was a 1½-litre overhead-valve Plus-
Power engined car, the chassis owing a great deal
to GN, and it was, of course, chain driven. The
body was available as a two-seater, three-seater or
a Super Sports. Seventeen cars were sold. Frazer
Nash model names were always confusing, being
determined by the chassis specification rather

than the body type. Considerable trouble was taken to leave behind the cyclecar image, but at the same time light weight was essential because of the low powered proprietary engines available at the time.

The Plus-Power engine company went into liquidation in 1925, and after considering a 12/50 Alvis engine Frazer Nash standardised the light and tunable sidevalve 1½-litre Anzani unit.

Financial difficulties struck the company in 1927 and the assets were acquired by H J Aldington, who continued under the name AFN Limited. Considerable redesign of the Frazer Nash car was undertaken. As the Anzani engine was no longer available the Meadows 1½-litre unit was adopted and considerably redesigned. The new management by the Aldington family was to see the firm safely through the 1930s, culminating in their involvement with BMW.

1926 Frazer Nash standard Fast Tourer.

11.9HP SPORTS. 1925-30 (prod: 165 to end 1930). Two-seater 1925 from £275, three-seater 1929 from £398. S4 SV (OHV from 1929) 1496cc, dry plate clutch, separate three speed (four from 1927) chain transmission, quarter-elliptic suspension. The initial 1924 model is outlined above. The later Fast Tourer and the Super Sports were the most popular Anzani engined types. The light and simple chain and dog system for swapping ratios (with no

differential) was a GN cyclecar idea that lasted long after the arrival of cheap and more conventional sports cars like the MG. Four wheel brakes were adopted in the mid-1920s and 139 cars were built with Anzani engines, the peak years being 49 cars in 1925 and 42 in 1926. 75-80mph and 35-40mpg were attainable.

In 1928 the "new type" Super Sports appeared, with no running boards, a lower chassis and a wide front axle giving the familiar Frazer Nash crab-track appearance. 100mph supercharged versions with 80bhp were also built from late 1927, and from 1929 the 63bhp OHV Meadows engine was offered, 29 having been used by the end of 1931.

The four wheel drive French of 1923.

FRENCH

Motor Engineering Works, London

In 1923 a four wheel drive car to the design of a Belgian named Hollé was built in London. It employed an Anzani engine with Wrigley gearbox and had a separate propshaft to each wheel centre. Series production did not follow, though in 1926 Vulcan built some larger Holverta vehicles on the same principles.

Four wheel drive vehicles had been built since the earliest years of the century but did not become widespread until the 1940s.

GALLOWAY

Tongland, Kirkcudbright, Scotland; Heathhall, Dumfries, Scotland

Sister make to Arrol-Johnston that used up some of the metal wasted in the A-J Victory, the Galloway surfaced in 1921 in a wartime aero engine factory run by Dorothée, daughter of T C Pullinger, with a largely female workforce. The car was designed by T C Pullinger and was based on the Fiat 501. In 1922 surplus capacity at Arrol-Johnston caused Galloway Motors to move into its factory at Heathhall, where it carried on for a time after the Aster merger of 1927. Its original ferro-concrete factory is now a chicken farm.

Galloway 10/20.

10/20. 1920-25 (prod: chassis numbers ran from 1 to 1842 at the start of 1925). Various body styles, chassis 1922 £375, complete car 1925 £265-£325. S4 SV 1460cc, cone clutch, three speed later four speed gearbox, central change, torque tube, spiral bevel axle. Semi-elliptic front, quarter-elliptic rear suspension. Two 10/20s took part in the 1922 RSAC 6 days trial and were amongst only five cars which completed the course without mishap. They were described as "well-sprung, and not fast but steady – the Scots know what is needed".

The Galloway 12hp.

12, 12/30, 12/50. 1925-29 (prod: chassis numbers 045 to 370 in first year. Complete £280-£398 initially. S4 OHV 1669cc, cone then plate clutch, four speed gearbox, torque tube, spiral bevel axle, four wheel brakes on later cars. Semi-elliptic front, quarter-elliptic rear suspension. Arrol-Johnston made the block and many other components. The saloon came in brown, crimson or lake. Final versions in the Arrol-Aster range resembled a scaled down 15/40 with a "family" radiator shell.

GB

Wilton Mews, Grosvenor Place, London SW1

As such cramped coach-house premises suggest, the three-wheeled cyclecar of George Baetz had little chance of volume sales, even at the projected £120 chassis price. A Coventry Victor sidevalve 668cc opposed twin drove the rear wheels via a Sturmey-Archer three speed gearbox and Chater Lea worm axle. The normal model was a unitary construction 550lbs two-seater listed 1922-24, chassis numbers commencing B106 in 1923.

GERALD

Birmingham

Offered in 1920, this cyclecar had an 8hp water-cooled JAP engine powering the solid rear axle by belt via a chain-driven countershaft.

The 1920 Gerald cyclecar.

GIBBONS

Station Road, Chadwell Heath, Essex

E R Gibbons made a series of light cars between 1921 and 1926 which featured offside mounted engines by Precision, Coventry Victor or, latterly, air-cooled 998cc Blackburne. There was belt drive to each rear wheel – high ratio to nearside, low to offside, though a conventional Sturmey-Archer three speed and reverse gearbox was used with chain drive on the 1925-26 cars. Two- and four-seaters were offered at prices from £80 for the 3½hp Precision powered model, and plywood played a large part in the integral construction.

Chassis numbers started at 100 in 1921 and at 500 in 1925 and this illustration from an advertisement in an un-dated modelling and electrical magazine speaks of over 1000 under construction. For 25p one received plans and could then buy finished or unmachined parts from Gibbons.

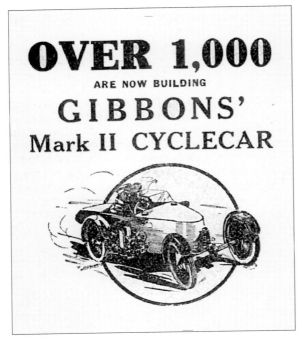

The Gibbons Mark II Cyclecar.

GILCHRIST

Orchard Drive, Giffnock and Govan, Scotland

Sam Gilchrist had worked in New Zealand before returning to take up a post with the makers of Caledon commercial vehicles (run by the Tainsh family, ex-Argyll). In 1920 he introduced a 12hp car powered by an overhead-valve version of the Coventry Hotchkiss engine used by Morris and containing "no finer materials grown, forged,

rolled, moulded or drawn".

After the first car or two had been assembled in the garage of his home at Giffnock, production was transferred to Govan, though Sam Gilchrist still personally tested every vehicle sold. The firm folded when Gilchrist's brother-in-law had to withdraw his financial support to keep his colliery going after crippling strikes.

1923 Gilchrist 11.9hp tourer.

11.9. 1920-23 (prod: about 20). Various bodies by Sim and Wilson of Cathcart including "Tourer" on chassis falling from £500 to £400. S4 OHV 1550cc 28bhp, wet multi-plate cork clutch, in-unit three speed gearbox, torque tube, worm axle. Semi-elliptic front, cantilever rear suspension. A car with such a similar specification to Morris (albeit with OHV) stood no chance against falling Morris prices. Nevertheless it had several well-conceived features like instruments mounted on the gearbox for ease of body fitment, and a cast aluminium radiator on an in-built chassis crossmember.

GILLETT

Hawthorn Road, Willesden Green, London NW10

Edmond Gillett ran British Ensign and in 1926 introduced a car of his own name from Ensign's old address. It was aimed at the market for a very cheap £100 car and unlike cyclecars was not particularly skimped in specification terms (even if £3 extra was needed for nickel plating).

8HP. 1926-27 (production: 25). Two-seater £100. S4 OHV 1020cc, multi-plate clutch, three speed gearbox, spiral bevel axle, quarter-elliptic suspension. Gillett seems to have made most parts including the engine in-house, and probably found the car

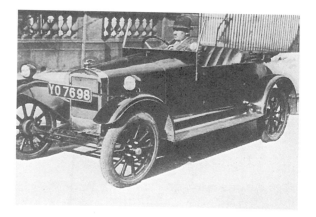

1926 Gillett 8hp two-seater.

unprofitable to make. OHV was a nice touch and four wheel brakes were theoretically available. Electric starting and coil ignition were other features.

GILLYARD

Barkerend Road, Bradford, Yorkshire

The Chater Lea cyclecar introduced in 1912 was discontinued early in the Great War. In 1920 *The Autocar* announced that it was to be revived by E Gillyard of Barkerend Engineering with a two-cylinder 8hp 961cc engine, multi-plate clutch and chain drive. It seems unlikely that this happened, despite a listed price of £225 for a complete two-seater, and in the event the Chater Lea itself was briefly revived. The 9hp Gillyard reported by *The Autocar* in a 1919 hillclimb may have been a prototype or an updated pre-war car.

9hp Gillyard at a hill climb late in 1919.

GLOVER

Woodhouse Lane, Leeds, Yorkshire

This was a typical American assembled car outside the scope of British vintage cars except that it was

allegedly designed in Britain for the British market. It was claimed not to be someone else's car simply badged and sold by Glover's Motors Ltd, and the American maker was said to have made no other car than the 2262cc four-cylinder sidevalve Glover (principally for the UK market). Whatever the truth, very few were sold.

GN

East Hill, Wandsworth, London SW18

Founded by Godfrey and Nash in 1910, GN was well into its stride by 1919. The largest of the cyclecar manufacturers, GN was notable in having the car produced under licence by Salmson in Paris, and about 1600 were sold in France. New premises capable of a peak 55 cars per week were acquired at East Hill from the importer of Grégoire cars and the works manager was John Bell from Talbot. The cars were comparatively inexpensive to buy and run, and their performance from a 1086cc vee-twin engine was considerable, if noisy. The novel form of transmission was to stand the test of time, and actually remained little changed from its introduction in 1910 until the last chain-driven Frazer Nash of 1939. 1921 and 1922 were the golden years for GN, but then the more conventional light car began to be introduced by the quantity manufacturers. GN countered by producing a Rover-like "family" car for 1923. This had four-cylinder DFP, Anzani or Chapuis-Dornier 1100cc engines and shaft drive, but retained a solid rear axle. It was not a success and the company ceased production in 1925. In protest at the Rover 8 crib Nash left in 1922 followed by Godfrey, the former founding Frazer Nash and the latter much later involved with HRG.

STANDARD. 1919-25 (prod: approx. 4000). 1922 tourer £225, 1923 four-seater (4-cylinder) £255. V2 IOE air-cooled 1100cc, single plate clutch, shaft drive to bevel cross shaft, thence via different chains for four ratios to a solid rear axle, quarter-

Ron Godfrey's own 1921 GN sports model.

elliptic suspension. With its doorless body, vee dummy radiator and all-up weight of 6½cwt this was the archetypal GN of the years 1919-24, and its Salmson derivative was virtually identical. Then, from 1923, came the water-cooled four-cylinder OHV 1100cc version, with shaft drive to a spiral bevel axle, which was also offered with the vee-twin. Sporting Vitesse and Légère vee-twins were offered and were successfully raced, an OHC vee-twin Akela engine being used in some. Frazer Nash's own Kim I was the fastest cyclecar in the world in 1920. For GN owners a box of all the spares likely to be needed in an emergency was available for £2!

GNOME (and NOMAD)

Elysium Place, London SW6

Sold from premises in the New King's Road long before it became fashionable, this was an attempt at a £75, but rapidly £100, "real car" (£99-9s-9d to be exact). Unfortunately there was little real about it apart from appearance. Its 27 × 4.40 Dunlop tyres provided all the suspension thanks to inflation at only 6psi. The integral body and chassis were of steel and plywood and the engine lived in unit with the back axle. The bonnet detached (sometimes when running!) to give access to a luggage compartment.

The 3½hp single-cylinder Gnome.

3½HP. 1925-26 (prod: few – chassis numbers started at 101 in 1925 and at 126 in 1926). Rear-mounted single-cylinder TS Villiers 343cc 8.25bhp with forced draught cooling, friction drive (four forward and reverse segments). The Gnome name (nothing to do with motor cycle maker Gnome and Rhône) was used in 1925-26 and then changed briefly to the £100 Nomad with its electric starting. 40mph and 50mpg were said to be achievable. Described in the press as "one of the best proportioned miniatures that has ever been produced".

GOODYEAR

See Ford

GRAHAME-WHITE

London Aerodrome, Hendon NW9

A well-known early sportsman in speedboats and aeroplanes, Claude Grahame-White gave flying lessons at his 300-acre airfield from 1913. After the war his extensive premises made furniture, bodywork, cyclecars and aircraft. Works manager was A C Bertelli (see Enfield-Allday and Aston-Martin).

The Buckboard was little more than a go-kart, but more substantial were 3.5hp and 5.7hp single- and twin-cylinder cyclecars and a shortlived 10hp conventional car. All his efforts came to nought, though the factory was also used for the final throes of Angus-Sanderson.

The gates into Grahame-White's premises are still visible on the perimeter of the present RAF Museum at Hendon.

Grahame-White Buckboard.

BUCKBOARD. 1920-24 (prod: chassis numbers commenced at 100 in 1922, 250 in 1923 and 376 in 1924, suggesting a total of several 100s). Complete two-seater approx £100. Single-cylinder air-cooled 3hp, kick start, plate clutch, two speed gearbox, chain drive. Similar to American contraptions of the type, like the Briggs and Stratton Flyer, it had an unsprung ash frame and could carry two passengers on sprung seats at 25-30mph with 70mpg economy and "easily climb any main road hill".

The Grahame-White "Wonder Car", c1923

CYCLECAR, WONDER CAR and 7HP. 1920-24 (prod: see Buckboard). Chassis £160 (£245 for twin) falling to £50 for complete car. Single cylinder TS air-cooled 348cc 3.5hp Precision or 685cc 7hp twin. Transmission as on Buckboard though twin had friction drive. Both had quarter-elliptic suspension. This was a slightly more car-like version of the Buckboard looking quite sporting as the 8'1" wheelbase 7hp but very cramped in its 6'4½" 3.5hp versions. Several hundred engines were allegedly supplied by Coventry Victor, presumably intended for the twin, though as this was only listed 1920-21 it seems unlikely that many were sold.

The 10hp Grahame-White.

10.2HP. 1920 (prod: possibly only 3). Complete coupé or tourer £417. S4 SV Dorman 1094cc, other specifications uncertain but believed to include cone clutch and three speed gearbox. This very obscure model carried attractive Grahame-White coachwork. Only three engines appear in the Dorman records, all in late 1919.

GRICE

Cordwallis Works, Maidenhead, Berkshire

This was one of Arthur Grice of GWK's lost causes (see also Unit). It was a single front wheeled three-wheeler experimented with in 1925-7 but never produced in quantity despite, or perhaps because

1927 Grice three-wheeler.

of, a price of only £90. In contrast with Grice's usual preoccupation with friction drive it had a three speed gearbox. Power came from a rear mounted 680cc JAP air-cooled vee-twin, and there were coil springs all round and individual brakes on each wheel.

GUILDFORD

Guildford, Surrey

Griffith's Engineering Works developed an 8hp Blackburne vee-twin engined cyclecar in 1920, but wisely chose not to market it. Attempts to find a

buyer for the whole project appear to have failed, though it is conceivable that the car was briefly built under another name.

GUY

Fallings Park, Wolverhampton, Staffordshire

Service Manager of Humber and then works manager at Sunbeam, Sidney Guy started to make commercial vehicles under his own name in 1914. After building aero engines in the Great War, as well as Tylor engines and Maudslay gearboxes, Guy developed a V8 car in 1919 (when Vulcan was

The Guildford Miniature car.

Guy 20hp chassis, showing the V8 engine.

Guy 20hp, c1920.

experimenting with the same car engine configuration for the first time in Britain). Guy's V8 was designed by R H Rose from Sunbeam (later at Crossley, Lea Francis, etc.).

After a couple of years a variety of other models were added but commercial vehicle sales then started to improve following the postwar slump and Guy abandoned cars in 1924. However, its takeover of Star in 1928 brought it briefly back into the field.

20HP. 1919-23 (prod: approx 25). Various bodies (some built in-house) on chassis starting at £1475 and falling to £875. 90° V8 inclined SV 4072cc 25.7hp Treasury rating, cone clutch, four speed gearbox, spiral bevel axle, semi-elliptic suspension. Britain's first production V8. The chassis had automatic lubrication activated by turning the steering wheel to the extreme right. There were detachable heads, aluminium pistons which could be withdrawn after undoing the big ends through covers in the crankcase, and waterways on the outside of the main castings. The horizontal valves were said to give the advantages of OHV with easier maintenance.

The 1923 Guy 13/36.

FOUR-CYLINDER MODELS. 1922-24 (prod: approx 110). Chassis £395. Specification for 13/36: S4 inclined SV 1954cc, cone clutch, in-unit four speed gearbox, spiral bevel axle, semi-elliptic suspension. In 1922 11.9, 15.9 and 16.9hp Treasury rating engines were offered, all with a common stroke of 114mm, though some of the engines were not by Guy but by Coventry Climax. All disappeared in 1923 to be replaced late that year by the cheaper 13/36. It had automatic chassis lubrication and an aluminium cylinder head with inclined side valves worked direct from L-shaped rockers. This was one of the first British cars with four wheel brakes.

GWALIA

Gwalia Works, Cardiff

Cars from Wales have always been a rarity but in 1922 Stanfield Ltd built an interesting example

A 1922 Gwalia 9hp with cloverleaf body.

with all parts but the engine allegedly made locally. The engine was a 9hp Alpha from Coventry, mated to a three speed gearbox. The most unusual feature of the design was suspension by coil springs and bell-cranks. An open three-seater cost a competitive £250 but availability scarcely lasted one year.

GWK

Cordwallis Works, Maidenhead, Berkshire

Grice, Wood and Keiller had made over a thousand of their twin-cylinder, rear engined, friction drive cars between 1911 and 1915. These were revived after the war and joined by a model F with front mounted four-cylinder engine, but the firm never regained its light car reputation and liquidation followed in 1922. Wood and Keiller left but the inventive Grice, who had been working elsewhere on his Unit cars, returned to make sporadic attempts to find a niche for GWK well into the 1920s. He was involved with the abortive Grice and British Imperia cars (GWK becoming Imperia Cars Ltd in December 1926 for the purpose, with Van Roggen of the Belgian firm running it) as well as several shortlived GWK variants. He did research work on the French Lafitte and Galba as well as the bargain basement Waverley.

A final attempt with a new GWK took place in 1930-31 but by then the factory site was being shared with Burney's experiments on streamlined cars. The best known subsequent occupant of what later became immortalised as the "Jam Factory" in Lord Montagu's *Lost Causes of Motoring* (researched by Michael Sedgwick) was Marendaz.

REAR ENGINED MODELS: E 1918-19, J 1922, G 1930 (prod: nearly 200). Two-seater £210 falling to theoretical £100. Twin-cylinder 9.8hp Coventry Simplex plus 74 with Dorman engines in 1919 (G model S4 SV 1370cc Coventry Climax). Engine across frame, at right angles to drive shaft, with

The Type E rear-engined GWK.

friction disc driven by flywheel. The E shown was a continuation of the pre-war type whilst the J was modified with a longer bonnet and similar appearance to the front engined models. These models were very successful in the long distance trials that were such a feature of enthusiastic motoring at the time. Friction discs were good for 10,000 miles. The G, with punt frame bodywork, barely entered production.

Surviving 1921 Type H GWK belonging to Rev. L C Stead.

FRONT ENGINED MODELS: F 1919-21, H 1921-26 (prod: approx 1700). Complete 1924 200-255 Guineas. S4 SV 1370cc Coventry Climax (plus one Dorman MV in July 1922), shaft drive to friction disc at rear which drove axle tube to reduction gearing in hub. Four wheel brakes (10 guineas) in 1924. Like the rear engined cars, these were sold under the slogan "a gear for every grade". Richard Twelvetrees, later well known as a motoring writer, was joint London agent.

GWYNNE

Church Wharf, Chiswick, London W

This pump making firm had built aero engines (some in collaboration with W O Bentley) during the Great War and engines for the Albert car afterwards. When the Albert's backers got into difficulty Gwynne rescued the firm in 1920 and made Gwynne-Alberts. Its own cars were based on Elizalde's design for the Spanish Victoria, of which about a thousand were made 1919-23. Neville Gwynne had seen one of these returning from war

The Gwynne 8hp (left).

service through Spain, but his version was delayed by the 1919-20 moulders' strike, and then it lost out to Morris, Clyno and the other mass producers in the small car boom. The Service Motor Co. of Great Portland Street were distributors though latterly Sydney G Cummings of Fulham Road took on the difficult task.

Nevertheless, because of the support of its other engineering involvements, and its ability to make all parts, Gwynne lasted longer than most, its premises being bought in 1929 by building and haulage specialists Willments, who continued to supply Cummings for a time. The pump side of the business had been sold to Foster of Lincoln in 1926. Latterly French Salmson cars were sold from adjoining premises, all of which had been Thornycroft's factory in Victorian times.

8HP and 8/24. 1922-28 (prod: approx 2250). Various styles on chassis falling from £385 to approx £250. S4 OHV 850cc, cone clutch, separate three speed gearbox, torque tube, bevel axle, semi-elliptic suspension. A lively little engine made this a likable sporting car, some being sold in 60/70mph

Brooklands form. In 1924 a Gwynne won the RAC Six Days Small Car Trial. The engines were also used in fire pumps in much the same way as surplus Coventry Climax units for Clyno, etc., were used up. A Receiver was appointed in 1923 and output of 8hp types after that was only a handful per week.

Gwynne 10hp.

10. 1927-30 (prod: approx 600). Tourer £220 1927, chassis £175 1928. S4 OHV 1247cc, similar specification to 8. An extra one and a half feet in the wheelbase and increased torque made this a more suitable four-seater, particularly when supplied as an enclosed London, Chiswick or England saloon. Sold as the "car of unusually fine quality". Lots of the saloons were of Weymann type construction, which reduced their life expectancy. Three 10s survive in the Antipodes and eight 8s (there are 17 of the latter confirmed to exist in Britain).

14. See Albert 14GA. (Known as Gwynne 14GA 1923-30).

HADFIELD BEAN

See Bean

HALL

Tonbridge, Kent

A prototype forward control town car was built in 1918-19 but series production did not follow. The only known survivor has a Talbot radiator, Studebaker back axle and 20.6hp flat-eight engine built in H E Hall and Company's own workshops.

HAMILTON

Compton Works, Wickford, Essex

A vee-twin 1090cc sidevalve air-cooled 9hp Precision engine powered this two-seater with circular "radiator" current from 1920 to 1925. In 1920 chassis numbers ran from 50 to 59 and the chassis price was £150, which was the same price as the complete car in 1924. Transmission was by friction discs and chain.

HAMMOND

North Finchley, London N

An 11/22 car was made in 1919-20 by former Arrol-Johnston employees and embodied several features of that company's abortive Victory model (as, allegedly, did the Phoenix). It had a 150mm stroke and 69mm bore, giving it a large capacity (2.25 litres) for its low 11.9hp Treasury Rating. Its four gears, worm drive and cantilever rear springs were above-average features. Plans were made by the Whitworth Engineering Co. Ltd to mass produce it in a former aircraft factory but either finance or performance were lacking and few cars were built. The car also seems to have been offered under the Whitworth name in 1921, and a letter dated 4/4/1922 exists to show that Mr Hammond of The Red House, Florence Road, Ealing was endeavouring to sell rights to a new

8.25 model to BSA. He was presumably unsuccessful, though features may have been incorporated in the BSA Ten.

The Hammond 11/22.

HAMPTON

Dudbridge, Stroud, Gloucestershire

Hampton lasted longer than most other producers of 100-300 cars per year, despite frequent financial setbacks and changes of constitution. It owed its name to Hampton-in-Arden, where it commenced in 1911, but in 1919 part of a large iron foundry in the industrialised rural community of Stroud was acquired with finance from a local wool merchant. Hampton was an active participant in trials and a frequent competitor in the local Nailsworth Ladder hill climb.

Assembled cars using Dorman and Meadows engines saw the firm through the 1920s, though its brief survival into the next decade was based on German Rohr components.

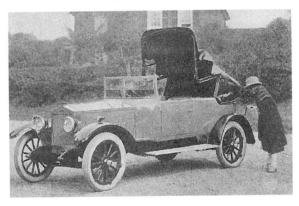

Hampton 11.9hp, 1921.

9.8, 10/16 and 11.9. 1919-22 (prod: approx 350). Initially complete two-seater (bodywork made in-house) £520 in dark biscuit or lavender. S4 OHV 1496cc or 1795cc Dorman, cone clutch, three speed gearbox, bevel drive. Semi-elliptic front,

semi- or ¾-elliptic rear. Widely used in competitive trials and designed by William Paddon, founder of the firm. He resigned with the next spate of financial problems in 1924 and Major Griffith Jones helped Works Manager W F Millward and G Dixon (who had both been with Charron-Laycock) to take control, along with Hampton's sales manager J W Leno (son of music hall artist Dan Leno). Millward raced a largely standard Hampton in the Brooklands 200 Mile Race.

The 1924 Hampton 9/21 Junior.

1926 Hampton Twelve, with front wheel brakes a £20 extra.

9/21, 10, 11/35, 14, 12/40. 1923-31 (prod: approx 500). Typical tourer price £500 falling to £315. Various S4 OHV Meadows mostly 1496cc, plate or multi-disc in oil clutch, four speed gearbox, spiral bevel axle, semi-elliptic suspension except ¾-elliptic rear on early cars. Hampton's backers were known as Stroud Motor Manufacturing Co. through much of this period, and then as Hampton Cars (London) Ltd in honour of some short-lived city backing from a Fyffes banana shipper in 1927. Superchargers, friction cone "gear" boxes and Hodgson rear suspension were tried on some late 12/40s, and some late Twelves were said to have Hampton's own engine, but this seems unlikely.

20, STRAIGHT 8. 1929-30, 1930-33 (prod: probably under 100). Tourer £450, saloon £495. S6 OHV 2931cc Meadows, S8 OHV 2262cc Rohr, plate clutch, four speed gearbox with right hand

The Hampton Straight Eight used a Rohr 2262cc engine.

change, spiral bevel axle, semi-elliptic suspension. A six of uncertain origin had been listed as the 15/45 for 1928 but the 20 used the same flexible engine, with twin Zenith carburettors, as Invicta, Bean 6, Whitlock and others. The straight eight, with its Empire and Sportsman variants, used a Rohr 2262cc engine and in some cases an independently sprung frame from the same German supplier. One hundred engines and 50 chassis were ordered but it seems unlikely that more than a few were delivered. The firm was reorganised as the Safety Suspension Car Co. using an enlarged Rohr engine but few, if any, of "the eighth wonder of the world" were built. The surviving car shown is one built specially with Rohr engine by partner Millward when he was ousted in the firm's penultimate reorganisation.

HANDS

Barn Street, Birmingham

George Hands ran Calthorpe and in 1922 used its motor cycle factory to assemble a Dorman engined car. After two years he abandoned the project, though not before developing an overhead cam six-cylinder Hands, of which a few may have been built before becoming a short-lived Calthorpe model.

Hands also owned a garage and the Palace Hotel in Torquay.

9.8, 10/20, 11/22. 1922-24 (prod: approx 150). Chassis 1924 £176-315. S4 SV 1100cc then 1360cc Dorman, Wrigley three speed in-unit gearbox, cone clutch, Wrigley spiral bevel axle, quarter-elliptic suspension. Built initially by the Minstrel and Rea Cycle Co., which became the Calthorpe Motor Cycle Co. (with the telegraphic address of Crank!), a firm that lasted to 1938. Dorman records

The 1922 Hands 10/20 two-seater cost 260 guineas and was said to tour at 40mph and 38mpg.

The Hands 11/22 coupé was dearer, at 330 guineas.

show the purchase of roughly 153 engines, though the OHC six appears to have been built in-house with gearbox and rear axle coming from Moss.

HARISCOTT

Wellington Road, Undercliffe, Bradford, Yorkshire

A 60mph sportscar listed in 1920-21 with Coventry Simplex sidevalve 1.5-litre engine and four-speed gearbox. Harrison, Scott and Co. was responsible. A more modest touring model was also offered.

Four-seater Hariscott.

HARPER

Gorse Hill, Stretford and Avro Works, Newton Heath, Manchester.

The Harper Runabout was a glorified three-wheel motor scooter invented by R O Harper (formerly works manager of Newton and Bennett) and made by aircraft and Avro car firm A V Roe and Co. Ltd, at that time financially associated with Crossley. It had a 269cc Villiers air-cooled single-cylinder two-stroke engine and three forward speeds (no reverse), with cone clutch and chain drive. There were quarter-elliptic springs all round and one of the earliest applications of disc brakes on the rear wheels. It had handlebar steering and came as a two-seater in blue with primrose lining. Offered 1921-26, its price fell from £100 to 77 guineas. Chassis numbers in 1922 were 201 to 349 so it seems unlikely that more than 500 were sold in total.

The Harper Runabout.

HATTON-McEVOY

Leaper Street, Derby

This remarkable 9.7-litre six-cylinder car was announced in 1929 but few, if any, were built. There were four valves per cylinder worked by only six pushrods on each side of the block. 260bhp was said to be developed at 3000rpm. It is conceivable that some parts were shared with the Double Six Daimler as Pomeroy was involved with both projects. Michael McEvoy was well known in connection with Zoller supercharging, whilst Fred Hatton had worked for the motor cycle firm New Hudson. Lavish catalogues for the abortive car were printed.

HE

Wolsey Road, Caversham, Berkshire

HE stood for Herbert Engineering, the Herbert in question being Herbert Merton, who had employed 500 men on aero engine repairs (and possibly production) during the Great War. The firm entered the car business in 1919 with a design from R J Sully and soon gained a sporting reputation for its very expensive and stylish cars. Many had "Dutch Clog" style bodywork by Morgan of Leighton Buzzard built on aircraft principles with wire bracing.

Six-cylinder models were available from 1927 but finances were precarious after a hiatus in 1924, and HE succumbed to the depression in 1931. Its premises on the Thames were then acquired by Thornycroft for marine engine work.

The 14/20hp HE.

13/20, 14/20, 14/40, 14/50. 1919-23 and 1926-28 (production: 500). Chassis approx £600. S4 SV 1800cc increased to 2120cc in 1920, 30/35bhp, dry plate clutch, four speed gearbox, overhead worm drive. Semi-elliptic suspension except early cars with underslung ¾-elliptic rear suspension. Virtually everything but bodywork was made in HE's well-equipped works. The 65mph 14/40 was one rung below a Bentley and, at least to begin with, had few other British competitors. Wire wheels were soon standardised and a complicated system of four wheel brakes was fitted from 1923. The 14/50 in 1926 (when a complete four-seater cost £695) was sold with a five year guarantee and the exhortation "If you don't buy an HE, buy another British make".

An HE 2 litre whilst owned by the late Bunty Scott Moncrieff.

2 LITRE. 1923-25 (prod: n/a). Chassis from £450, two-seater sports initially same price. S4 SV 1981cc, multi-disc clutch, mid-mounted four speed gearbox, torque tube, worm drive. Semi-elliptic front, ¾-elliptic rear suspension. Most had an aluminium cylinder head (detachable, but still with valve caps). The 2 litre came in various states of tune and was known initially as the 13/30, followed in 1924 by the 13/35 and 13/45 and then the 13/40. An early racing version had four valves per cylinder.

The HE Six fabric saloon.

16/55, 16/60 1927-31 and 13/35 1929-31 (prod: 61 plus 12 13/35). Chassis £590 falling to £525, fabric saloon built by HE 1928 £850, £545 on 13/35. S6 SV 2290cc (1622cc 13/35), multi-disc clutch, mid-mounted four speed gearbox, spiral bevel axle, torque tube (not 13/35), semi-elliptic suspension (quarter-elliptic 13/35), four wheel brakes, servo available. Available with magneto or coil ignition and a traditional right-hand gearchange, these models came with HE's remarkable five-year guarantee. One fitment was a gear synchroniser dial to match revs to road speed. The 2.3-litre cars averaged 24mpg and 50mph and could reach 30mph from a standstill in 5 seconds. Their top speed was 70mph – the little car was just about capable of 65mph but don't ask about acceleration unless it was fitted with a Cozette supercharger.

HENRY

Oxted, Surrey

Listed only in 1920, the Henry was an American-inspired car using lots of Transatlantic components like a Lycoming 19.6hp four-cylinder engine, a centre change three speed gearbox, Detroit axle and Borg and Beck clutch. The whole vehicle may have come from America, though its designer was said to be Geoffrey Henry, who had been developing the car for several years in England and who, with E L Tessier, acquired the Oxted Motor Co. Ltd in 1920 to sell (and build?) the car. E L Tessier is believed to have been related to the makers of BAT motor cycles.

1920 Henry 19.6hp tourer.

HERON

Strode Park, Herne, Kent

The Heron came from the same stable as the Westcar, which itself had originated in the motor house of a large country estate. The heron was a heraldic device used by Herne Bay District Council. Whilst the Westcar was a conventional assembled car the Heron of 1924-26 bristled with curious features. At first a tubular frame was used, with a 998cc Ruby engine from France, a Moss gearbox and belt or chain drive. A subsequent model had a transverse mid-mounted Dorman 11.9hp unit driving the back axle by chain. The last type had a front-mounted 1368cc Coventry Climax 11hp engine with three-speed gearbox in a chassisless car built of stitched Consuta plywood (by the makers of Saunders-Roe seaplanes) under Australian Marks-Moir patents. Very few were produced and the Marks-Moir original shown, which was made largely from British components in Sydney by Marks Motor Construction Co., did little better in 1923-24.

HFG

Broadfield Road, Heeley, Sheffield, Yorkshire

Made, or at any rate sold, by a company called C Portass and Son Ltd, the HFG was relatively conventional until one looked under the bonnet and saw a fore and aft mounted air-cooled twin on the nearside. Friction disc and shaft drive were on the offside.

10HP. 1920-21 (prod: n/a). Two-seater £325. HO2 air-cooled OHV 1244cc 24bhp, friction transmission, shaft drive to bevel axle. Quarter-elliptic front, cantilever rear suspension. The dummy radiator and Goodyear wavy disc wheels gave a "real" car look but eccentricities like pedal and ratchet starting frightened customers away. The HFG slogan was "made like an aeroplane", but there was little evidence of this!

The Marks-Moir from which the Heron evolved.

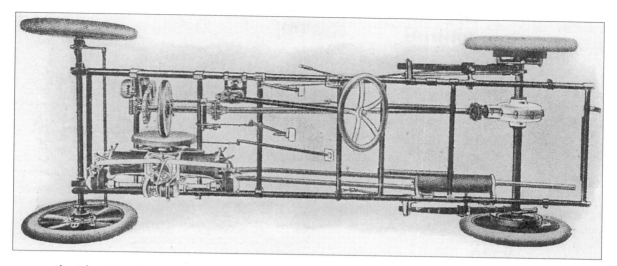

The 10hp HFG and its extraordinary layout.

worm then spiral bevel axle, semi-elliptic suspension. Usually painted blue or grey, this was a well liked model evolved from Dawson's design for a Peace car. Aluminium pistons and crankcase and splash and pump lubrication were features. (See over for photograph.)

HILLMAN

Pinley, Coventry, Warwickshire

One of the early motor manufacturing firms with roots in the bicycle trade, Hillman had become one of the larger manufacturers by the time of the Great War, with 450 of A J Dawson's Nine built in 1914. Dawson evolved this into the Hillman Peace model of 1917 and left to make the Dawson car. Founder William Hillman died in 1921 and his sons-in-law Black and Wilks ran the firm successfully. The 14 became the staple model in the mid 1920s. In 1927 the factory was greatly enlarged and the Rootes brothers acquired distribution rights, having failed to buy Clyno. Humber bought Hillman in late 1928, Black and Wilks leaving to run Standard (Wilks later transferred to Rover). Rootes then built up a controlling interest and rationalised the Humber-Hillman ranges.

The Hillman 10hp Super Sports, 1921.

11HP. 1919-25 (prod: approx 4500). Chassis 1919 £345, 1925 £240. Various styles (several by Vanden Plas). S4 SV 1592cc (initially fixed head) 20bhp, cone clutch, three speed central-change gearbox,

10HP SUPER SPORTS. 1920-22 (prod: 100-200). Two-seater £590. S4 SV 1496cc 28bhp at 2800rpm,

Hillman 11hp.

cone clutch, three speed gearbox, bevel axle, semi-elliptic suspension. A smaller-bore version of the 11 to create a 1.5-litre race contender. The 1921 GP des Voiturettes version is shown, but all had pointed radiators and external copper exhaust pipes and were capable of 4000rpm thanks to lightened reciprocating parts and drilled pistons. One of the first sports cars from a quantity producer and capable of 65mph in standard form and 30mpg touring. Raymond Mays began his racing career with one.

14hp Hillman Segrave coupé, 1928.

14. 1925-30 (prod: approx 11,000). Early saloon initially £345 when Austin 12 £455. S4 SV 1954cc 35bhp, single dry plate clutch, in-unit four speed gearbox with right hand change, spiral bevel axle, semi-elliptic suspension, four wheel brakes. An instant success for "the car that costs less than it should" thanks to above average fittings, good quality and plenty of space. 1500 were made in the first year and 4000 in 1928, when the new factory came on-stream. The Rootes "family look" with shallow, chromed radiator surround was applied in 1929. Various styles were offered including the Segrave coupé, the Husky tourer, and the Safety Saloon with Dewandre servo, safety glass, etc.

20 STRAIGHT EIGHT. 1928-31 (prod: about 3000). Various styles, chassis £365, Safety Saloon £485. S8 OHV 2618cc 58bhp, dry plate clutch, in-unit four speed gearbox, spiral bevel axle, semi-elliptic suspension, servo brakes. Rootes' answer to American cars in traditional British export markets was launched at the 1928 London Motor Show. It was good for 0-50mph in 23 seconds, a 70mph top speed and 18mpg touring consumption. However, big end troubles brought a bad reputation and the 60-a-week

Hillman Straight Eight.

alleged production for 1929 was presumably not maintained. Yet the 20 easily outsold Sunbeam, Lanchester and other British straight eights.

HODGSON

Moortown, Leeds; Whitehall Road, Leeds, Yorkshire

Harry Hodgson was an instructor in automobile driving and engineering and a keen amateur racer. He developed a sports car with a British Anzani 1½ litre sidevalve engine and Meadows four speed gearbox of which about 8 were made in 1924-25. These were known as 12/40 models and there was a Super Sports version guaranteed to do 80mph. Four years later Mr Hodgson built five British Eagles of similar specification before returning to his theoretical work, designing a suspension system for Hampton and racing a Brooklands Riley.

The Hodgson 12/40.

HORNSTED

Bishopsgate, London EC2

This was in fact the German Moll sold by racing driver Capt L G Hornsted in 1922. It was made in

Chemnitz and had an OHV 1539cc engine, cone clutch, four speed gearbox, bevel axle, and suspension that was semi-elliptic at the front and double quarter-elliptic at the rear. 55mph and 35mpg were publicised and the open four seater cost £325.

1922 Hornsted.

HORSTMAN

James Street West, Bath, Somerset

Sidney Horstmann (the Germanic second "n" was dropped as a result of the Great War) was from a clock-making family. His light car of 1914 had all manner of eccentricities, most of which were revived after the war. His cars had a sporting flair, though at least one was fitted with a saloon body in 1920.

Financial problems in 1921 saw the end of the firm's own engines, which utilised parts from Lister of Dursley. In 1925 Horstman built one of the first British cars with Lockheed hydraulic brakes, having first tried mechanical four wheel brakes on its 1921 racing cars. About 1500 cars of all types were built between 1914 and the end in 1929. Horstmans often featured friction dampers and Sidney Horstman built a special coil-sprung car in 1928, features of which were used in his work on tracked vehicle suspension in the 1930s.

A Horstman 10.4hp.

10.4. 1919-21 (prod: about 200). Tourer and saloons £350-575. S4 1327cc 20bhp, horizontal valves operated by rockers pivoting on side of block, plate clutch (some wood lined), three speed gearbox in-unit with back axle, cantilever suspension. The front part of the chassis was an aluminium casting carrying the radiator, controls, suspension and engine (it also acted as sump). Starting was by a pedal acting on an Archimedes screw. Ride was unusually good for a small car, as was the standard of weather protection provided (including properly fitting sidescreens).

The 1921-22 Horstman Super Sports.

10.5. 1921-22 (prod: about 60). 1498cc S4 SV Coventry Simplex, plate clutch, three speed gearbox, bevel axle, cantilever suspension. This model retained the Horstman kick starter and was sold at a similar price to the 10.4 despite lower production costs. Several different Horstman chassis provided the basis of sports cars after May 1921, with tuned engines guaranteed to provide 60mph. Shown is one with an early use of siamesed driving lamps. A 9/20 with OHV Coventry Climax engine was offered in 1923-24.

12/30hp Horstman, 1923.

11.9 and 12/30. 1923-29 (prod: about 500 to 1925, thereafter less). Various styles on chassis at around £300. S4 SV 1496cc British Anzani, single plate clutch, in-unit four speed gearbox from 1925, torque tube and spiral bevel axle, cantilever suspension, hydraulic four wheel brakes from 1925. "The car that passes you" was capable of 60mph and better handling than most. In 1923 it was offered as the first British light car to be supercharged. The Horstmann kick starter departed with the arrival of the four speed gearbox in 1925. In 1927-28 there was also a Hayes engined 9/25 with rear axle gearbox, whilst some earlier sporting types had Plus-Power engines, as used by Frazer Nash. Spray painting was another Horstman innovation in late 1925.

HOTCHKISS

Coventry, Warwickshire

A branch of the Paris-based but English-run car and gun firm was established in Coventry when Paris was threatened with German control. Coventry Hotchkiss turned out 40,000 weapons and then turned swords to ploughshares with its engines for BSA, Gilchrist, Morris and others. It had sufficient capacity to make cars too: a prototype with a Morris chassis, a BSA type 1100cc vee-twin engine and a three speed gearbox was built in 1920 and tried out in an MCC Trial. Presumably the other customers were not happy about this development and in any event Morris grew rapidly in importance to the firm, finally acquiring it in 1923. A Hotchkiss employee, A J Wilde, became chief engineer at Standard in the later 1920s.

HP

Board School Road, Woking, Surrey

Current 1926-28, these three-wheel £65 cyclecars turned up some years after such ideas had gone out of fashion, and took records at nearly 50mph at Brooklands in 1927. JAP 500cc singles with three speed Sturmey-Archer gearboxes and chain drive were standard, though more exhilarating motor cycle units were also available. About 40 HP (Hilton-Pacey) cyclecars were sold, Hilton-Pacey Motors also listing the availability of Bleriot-Whippet spares.

1927 HP three-wheeler.

HUDSON

Great West Road, London W4

Most of the success of this American firm in Britain could be attributed to the Essex, developed in 1918. Not only did the Essex sound British but it had a decidedly European specification, with a relatively small 18.2hp four-cylinder engine, and a low price – a saloon (called a Coach) could be bought for £295 in 1924. Essex was the pioneer of cheap sedans in America in 1921 and offered all with left or right hand drive.

Hudson concentrated on sixes (Herbert Austin was a devotee) and Essex offered a 16.5hp, soon 17.3hp, six from 1924 from premises in Acton Vale, W3. The McKenna import duties imposed again from mid-1925 encouraged an increased use of British assembly and bodywork, and a large modern factory was opened on the Great West Road (Hudson Essex Motors of Great Britain Ltd having existed since September 1922). Here a £2 million body plant contained dozens of hydraulic presses able to form all body components, which after assembly were Belco spray painted – moving tracks being a feature of the plant.

A vintage-period peak of 300,000 cars was made in America in 1929, of which about 50,000 were exported in complete or CKD form. A Canadian factory opened in 1932, which presumably supplied duty free components to Hudson Essex Motors Ltd in London.

ESSEX SIX. Introduced 1924 (prod: UK n/a). Coach £295 steadily reduced to £235 1930. S6 SV 2374cc 17.3hp (initially 16.5hp), multi-disc wet clutch, in-unit three speed gearbox, spiral bevel axle, semi-elliptic suspension, two wheel brakes until optional four wheel brakes in 1927. The cheapest six-cylinder saloon in Britain, soon getting less angular radiator and bodywork and, from 1930, a ribbon radiator shell. This was the machine that probably most helped to kill the open tourer, and 80 per cent of Essex production is estimated to have been the Coach. The wire wheels on this 1926 car were a £15 extra. The Hudson Essex distributor in Slough, Fullbrook, Bell and Co., offered a £295 landaulette version of the Coach in 1925.

Hudson Great Eight, 1930.

1926 Hudson Essex Six.

HUDSON GREAT EIGHT. 1929-31 (prod: UK n/a). Various styles, chassis from £295. S8 SV 3504cc 24hp, single disc wet clutch, in-unit three speed gearbox, spiral bevel axle, semi-elliptic suspension. Earlier Hudsons had looked similar to Essex but for 1930 this slim radiator style was adopted. All 1920s Hudsons had been Sixes, and by the end of the decade nine out of ten had sedan bodywork. The straight-eight engine (which speedily grew to 4.2 litres) carried on in production to 1952 and was to be a feature of the Railton and the Brough Superior.

HUMBER

Humber Road, Coventry, Warwickshire

A pioneer bicycle and then car manufacturer which was second only to Wolseley in car sales by 1913 and which employed a workforce of 2324 in 1920. It was a very conservatively run company (Chairman Lieut. Col. J A Cole presided over most of the teens and twenties), despite having been one of the few major players to try cyclecars. Front wheel brakes were avoided on some models right up to 1927 because Cole distrusted them. On the other hand the cars' traditional looks, high quality finish and fittings (particularly weather equipment) and competitive pricing made them a middle class favourite.

In 1925 Humber acquired commercial vehicle maker Commer and in late 1928 added its Coventry neighbour Hillman. From then on the Rootes Brothers built up control of the new group (60% of the shares by 1931) and launched it into the world market with the help of Capt. Irving's designs. Total Humber production 1919-30 inclusive was almost 33,000 cars, and motor cycles were also made to 1930.

The 10hp Humber tourer.

10. 1919-21 (prod: 2302). Various styles, chassis £525. S4 SV monobloc 1398cc 19bhp at 2000rpm, cone clutch, four speed gearbox with right hand change, bevel axle, semi-elliptic suspension.

Revival of an excellent product introduced in 1914 with relatively modern features for the time, like the monobloc engine with detachable cylinder head. Another revival of an established model was the 14 of 1919, of which around 100 were built, plus one or two of the old 11hp.

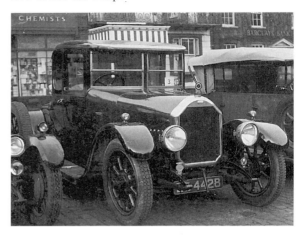

1923 Humber 15.9hp saloon-coupé.

15.9. 1919-25 (prod: approx 2500). Chassis 1921 from £525, 1924 £530. S4 SV (IOE from 1922) 2815cc, cone clutch, separate four speed gearbox, bevel axle, semi-elliptic suspension. The shortlived postwar version of the 14 grew into the 15.9 by dint of an 80mm instead of 75mm bore, but retained the same antiquated 140mm long stroke with fixed cylinder head. In 1922 it gained a detachable head with inlet over exhaust valves. Like most Humbers of the time the standard paint finish was mole.

The Humber 11.4hp saloon.

11.4, 12/25. 1921-25, 1924-27 (prod: 5500, 3000). Various styles, chassis £370. S4 SV (IOE from 1922) 1743cc, 1795cc, cone clutch, in-unit four speed gearbox with right hand change, spiral bevel axle, semi-elliptic suspension. This was an updated and bored-out version of the 10hp initially called the Improved Ten. The IOE engine fitted from late 1922 was to have valve gear that would remain a Humber feature right through to the depressing reversion to side valves in 1933. Styling was reminiscent of a miniature version of the 15.9. The 11.4, Humber's most successful vintage model, developed into the 12/25, which had the option of front wheel brakes from 1925.

1923 Humber 8hp.

8 (called 8/18 for 1925/6). 1923-26 (prod: 2400). Often sold as Chummy for £250. S4 IOE 985cc, cone clutch, in-unit three speed gearbox with right hand change, spiral bevel axle. Semi-elliptic front, quarter-elliptic rear suspension. The Humber Light Car was much more a big car in miniature than the old Humberette cyclecar and was an early user of coil ignition. Well equipped and weighing little more than half a ton the car offered good performance and was regularly used in trials.

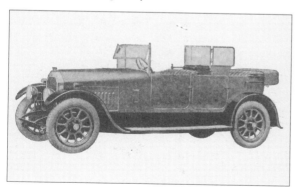

1926 Humber 15/40 five-seater.

15/40. 1924-28 (prod: 1100). Tourer 1926 £645. S4 IOE 2815cc 44bhp, cone clutch, separate four speed gearbox, spiral bevel axle, semi-elliptic suspension. This was an updated version of the 15.9 with the option of front wheel brakes (Perrot system). It had the new feature of most contemporary models in which the sidescreens of the open cars were stowed in the doors. A 58mph top speed and 18mpg touring consumption were recorded in an independent test in 1925, where the retention of a transmission brake was noted.

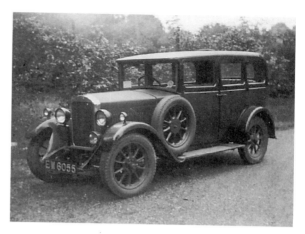

1929 Humber 9/28.

9/20, 9/28. 1925-29, 1928-30 (prod: 3450, 1250). Various styles, chassis from £220. S4 IOE 1056cc, cone clutch, in-unit three speed gearbox, spiral bevel axle, semi-elliptic suspension. An enlarged chassis and engine for the old 8, with front wheel brakes from early in 1927. Lower gearing made it just about capable of carrying saloon bodywork. The 9/28 had a more modern appearance with slim radiator, and an improved engine with coil ignition and full pressure lubrication.

Humber 14/40.

14/40. 1926-29 (prod: 2240). Saloon/coupé £575, tourer £440. S4 IOE 2050cc, specification as 20/55 below. This car used what was effectively two thirds of its larger sister's engine to create a good quality medium priced car. Humber made a particular feature of the weather equipment on the tourer, claiming that it could be turned into a weathertight cosy limousine in two minutes. The sidescreens could now be wound like conventional windows.

Humber 20/55 six-cylinder lundaulette, late 1927.

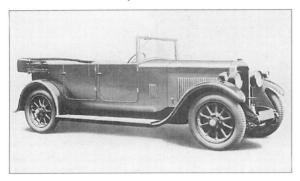

The Humber 20/65 tourer, 1929. Note the change in radiator shape from the model above.

20/55, 20/65. 1926-29, 1928-30 (prod: approx 525, 320). 1928 tourer £675, long saloon £860. S6 IOE 3075cc, cone clutch (single plate from late 1927), four speed gearbox, spiral bevel axle, semi-elliptic suspension. Humber's first six since veteran days and its top of the range model. The steeply sloping shoulders of the radiator gave way to a more rounded top for 1929 on this and other Humbers. With performance improved the 20/65 often returned only 12-14mpg, and it still featured magneto ignition. Dewandre servo brakes were added for 1928.

The Humber 16/50 Sports Coupé.

16/50. 1928-32 (prod: approx 8200). Chassis from £315, sports coupé shown £515. S6 IOE 2100cc, single plate clutch, in-unit four speed gearbox, **spiral bevel axle, semi-elliptic suspension.** The 16/50 was intended as a replacement for the 14/40, which however lasted a little longer. Ancient features included right hand change, but in other respects the car was modern, with a Zenith horizontal twin carburettor (later Stromberg), coil ignition, a seven-bearing crankshaft (with full pressure lubrication – as on all models but the 9 since 1928) and single-pane windscreen (unlike the vee arrangement that typified so many earlier Humbers.) In 1930 guise it looked just like a Snipe and had the same steering wheel centre horn button, which when pulled activated the engine starter.

1930 Humber Snipe.

23.8 SNIPE and PULLMAN. 1929-32 (prod: 4036 and 904 Pullmans). Various styles, chassis from £370. S6 IOE 3.5 litres, single dry plate clutch, in-unit four speed gearbox with right-hand change, spiral bevel axle, semi-elliptic suspension. With a 10 foot wheelbase this was a Snipe, and with 11 foot wheelbase it was a Pullman. 75mph was possible even with quite formal coachwork, and touring consumption could be as good as 20mpg. Bendix Duo-Servo brakes were specified. Humber still built much of the bodywork though Thrupp and Maberly became important. These competitively priced models gave Rootes something to counter American rivals and could be supplied with left hand drive.

IMPERIA

See British Imperia

INVICTA

The Fairmile, Cobham, Surrey

After creating the Eric Campbell and then the Silver Hawk, Noel Campbell Macklin built five larger cars in the garage of his home, The Fairmile at Cobham, the first in 1924 using a 2-litre Coventry Simplex engine in a Bayliss Thomas chassis. In 1925 production started at The Fairmile, and 2½-litre Meadows engines and other proprietary parts were used "to embody the best points of the world's best cars". The essence of these, and of subsequent larger types, was extreme flexibility, making them largely "top gear" cars, allied with sporting appeal and attractive style (the rivets down the bonnet became a virtual trademark). Finance for the project came from two members of the Lyle sugar refining family and from Earl Fitzwilliam (see Sheffield Simplex), who handled London sales, eventually acquring the business in 1933 and attempting a revival with cars built in Chelsea.

Violet Cordery (Macklin's sister-in-law) used Invictas for all manner of endurance runs and gained the Dewar Trophy twice. Donald Healey won his class in the Monte Carlo Rally in a 4½ in 1930 and gained outright victory in 1931. Despite these and many other achievements the market for such exotic cars was small, and under 1000 cars had been sold by the time Invicta expired late in 1933, the factory becoming home to Railton. Many early Invictas were subcontracted to the makers of the Beverley-Barnes car, who in 1927-29 were involved with over sixty 3 litres.

1927 Invicta 3 litre chassis with "Surbico" saloon body.

2½ LITRE, 3 LITRE. 1925-26, 1926-29 (prod: approx 200). Various coachbuilders used chassis commencing at £595 and reaching £895 in 1928. S6 OHV Meadows 2.5 litres 17.7hp, 2.97 litres 19.5hp (latter with dual ignition), dry plate clutch, in-unit four speed Meadows gearbox with right hand change, spiral bevel axle, semi-elliptic suspension. Lots of the bodies for these came from Surbiton Coach and Motor Works, a Surbico saloon of 1927 being shown. Other familiar names were Cadogan, Vanden Plas and Carbodies. 70mph and 25mpg

30,000 MILES AT 61.5 M.P.H.
ON BROOKLANDS TRACK
A TRIUMPH OF RELIABILITY & ENDURANCE

The Cordery sisters with their 4½-litre Invicta.

were attainable with the 3 litre, and top gear could be used from a virtual standstill.

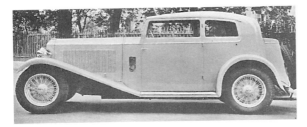

An Invicta 4½ litre coupé.

4½ LITRE. 1928-34 (prod: approx 500). Various styles on long and short chassis from £985. S6 OHV Meadows 4467cc 29.1hp, single plate clutch, in-unit four speed gearbox with right hand change, spiral bevel axle, semi-elliptic suspension. Like earlier models this finely balanced and well mannered car was designed by William Watson and came to include the luxury NLC costing £1800 as a saloon, the high chassis Type-A and the ultra desirable 100mph low chassis Type-S.

Macklin liked steam cars and the 4½ came close to a Doble he had used in terms of flexibility. Until 1933, when Lagonda adopted the engine, Invicta was the principal user of the 4½-litre Meadows. Two copies of the very straightforward instruction book came with each car so one could be kept clean. The horn button starting was similar to Humber.

IRIS

Aylesbury, Buckinghamshire

This firm started as a gear cutting and car repair business before making cars from 1905. The designer was M de Havilland, of the soon-to-be-famous aeronautics family, and production took place at Willesden Green, London N. The Managing Director from 1909 was also involved with the Bifurcated Rivet Co. in Aylesbury, and Iris assembly was undertaken there (opposite what was to become the home of Cubitt cars, for whom bodywork was built in the Iris factory).

After the Great War the works manager was H L Bing, who then worked for Silver Hawk and BAC.

15, 25 and 35hp models were listed until the mid-

An Iris 15hp in Brooklands trim.

1920s but very few were sold, and in the scrap drive of the Second World War eight complete cars, and parts for dozens more, were destroyed.

15HP, 25HP, 35HP. 1919-26 (prod: n/a). Chassis initially £385-£770 falling to £350-£700. S4 SV 2.3 litres, 4.8 litres, 6 litres, cone clutch, three speed gearbox, bevel axle. The 15 (shown in Brooklands trim) had a monobloc engine, the others pair-cast cylinders. It seems that pre-war components were used, though from 1920 there was the option of the latest detachable wheels in place of the fixed wooden variety. The Iris service department was prepared to build cars to order, and one was used by the Bifurcated Rivet Co. well into the 1930s.

JAPPIC

Wimbledon, London SW19

A cyclecar with JAP 350cc kick-start engines designed and raced by H M Walters in 1925. It was intended for sporting competition and had quarter-elliptic suspension, a three speed gearbox and chain drive. Overall weight was less than 4cwt. It took an International Class J record at 70mph, and coachbuilder Jarvis of Wimbledon considered making roadgoing replicas at £150 apiece, but nothing seems to have come of this.

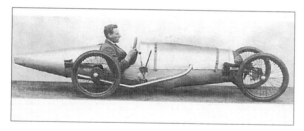

The JAP-engined Jappic, 1925.

JB

Great Crosshall Street, Liverpool

This family car with 13.9hp Meadows engine never progressed beyond the prototype stage in 1926. JB stood for Jones, Burton and Co. Ltd.

JEWEL

Bowland Street, Bradford, Yorkshire

John E Wood (the J.E.W. of Jewel) made two-cylinder Coventry Simplex or Precision powered cyclecars from 1921 and soon offered a 9hp four-cylinder Alpha engined car at £220 complete. From 1922 he used Meadows engines, but output from his tiny premises in Bradford was very small, and included bodywork as well. Cars were still available in the 1930s and latterly Jewel made caravans. He also did contract machining for Jowett cars and for the Bristol crawler tractor that came under the Jowett family wing in the 1930s.

1923 Alpha engined Jewel.

9/21. 1922-33 (prod: 12 to 1927). £230-£295 in 1926 depending on body. S4 OHV 1247cc Meadows, cone clutch, in-unit three speed Meadows gearbox, Moss spiral bevel axle. Quarter-elliptic front, duplex quarter-elliptic rear suspension (like Citroën and Waverley). Jewel used the same engines as were bought in large quantities by Seabrook, Hampton, Lea Francis and Bayliss Thomas. A friction drive Alpha engined car was also offered in 1922 and from 1928 a 12hp car was listed.

JL

East Dulwich, London SE

A E Creese built this sporting light car in 1921, powered by a 1½-litre four-cylinder Decolange engine. The streamlined bodywork was made from plywood.

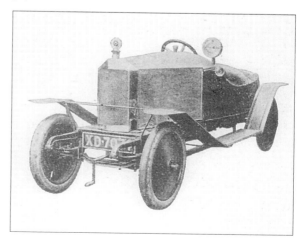

JL Light Ten, 1921.

JOWETT

Bradford Road, Idle, Bradford, Yorkshire

The famous Jowett horizontal twin had been made
since 1904 and about 150 cars so equipped were
built up to the reorganisation of the company as
Jowett Cars Ltd in 1920.

The firm was family run until a public share
flotation in 1935 and produced basically one
gradually evolving model – a very frugal family car
which gained a great reputation for slogging
reliability. This was nurtured by Gladney Haigh's
homespun advertising campaign, which gradually
converted Jowett from a local make like Jewel to a
nationally known one which made a prewar peak
of 3134 vehicles in 1934. Our period ends with the
factory being destroyed by fire in September 1930.

**8HP, 7HP. 1919-20, 1921-25 (prod: approx 6000).
Chassis £180 1921, £125 1925. HO2 SV water-
cooled 800cc (a 6.4hp called an 8hp), 907cc
16.5bhp, cone clutch, three speed gearbox (initially Wrigley), spiral bevel axle, semi-elliptic suspension.** Jowett made its first attempt at a London
Motor Show appearance in 1921, and from 1923
offered the Long Four with increased wheelbase for

four-seat bodywork. 50mph and 50mpg were attainable.

A saloon was offered from 1925, surely one of the
smallest full four-seaters of the time yet capable of
tackling all the most feared "freak hills".

Jowett 7/17 Black Prince.

**7/17. 1926-30 (prod: approx 11,100). 1930 chassis
£111, saloon from £158. HO2 SV 907cc 16.5bhp,
cone clutch (early version) then plate clutch with
in-unit three speed gearbox, spiral bevel axle,
semi-elliptic suspension.** The 7/17 was first offered
in 1925 and differed very little from earlier models

Jowett 7hp two-seater.

though now with coil ignition. A penny-a-mile (when 240 pence made £1) total running cost was advertised in the late 1920s, when increasing numbers of chassis were fitted with saloon bodies. A 60mph sports model was available in 1928, and from 1929 most Jowetts had front wheel brakes.

JUNIOR SPORTS

Torrens St, London EC1

This sporting two- or three-seater was offered by the Aluminium and General Foundry Co. in 1920-21 but whether it was actually built in the City of London is open to conjecture. It had a Moss gearbox, shaft drive and Ford T front and back axles, with a Belgian origin but British built Peters four-cylinder engine. Suspension was quarter-elliptic and price £315.

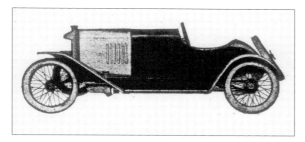

The Junior Sports, 1921.

KINGSBURY

Kingsbury Aerodrome, London NW9

This was yet another attempt to make light cars in a factory formerly occupied on aircraft war work (when, with Storey, it was involved with Le Rhône aero engines). Kingsbury Engineering also made motor scooters and 250-350cc motor cycles (the former being developed in conjunction with Storey) and had 800 workers in 1919 and 8800 sq ft of factories. (See also Sterling.)

In 1923 the factory became home to the British capitalised Vanden Plas coachworks, the origin of which had been in Brussels in 1870. Vanden Plas became an Austin subsidiary in 1946.

JUNIOR. 1919-22 (prod: n/a but 5000 orders were taken initially). Chassis from £230, two-seater from £295. HO2 1021cc 8.95hp 14bhp water-cooled Koh-i-Noor, cone clutch, in-unit three speed gearbox, bevel axle, quarter-elliptic suspension. The engine and gearbox in-unit with pedals and levers came from Kennedy Motor Co., makers of the Rob Roy car. The whole outfit was neat and well designed but scarcely survived the brief initial post-

The Kingsbury Junior two-seater.

war boom. Directors of the firm included the machine tool making Barningham family, and Warwick Wright, the racing driver and motor dealer. A liquidator was appointed in May 1921 but stock continued to be sold into 1922.

KRC

King Street, Hammersmith, London W6

Initially offered by the National Cab Co. (1922) Ltd and then by White, Holmes and Co. Ltd of Down Place and King Street, the KRC was an attractive sporting car of which one ran (briefly) in the 1922 Brooklands 200 mile race.

Initially built in 1922 with Blackburne 10hp 1098cc water-cooled sidevalve or overhead-valve twins, it was then offered with four-cylinder power until the end of production in 1924. These models had Coventry Climax or Janvier 7.5hp or 8.9hp engines and Meadows four speed gearboxes. The early twins had Wrigley rear axles without differentials.

The KRC takes a rest at Brooklands.

LAD

Rustic Walk, Lower Bourne, Farnham, Surrey

This was a version of a 1913-14 LAD cyclecar initially made by Oakleigh Motor Co. of West

Dulwich. In its first incarnation it had been a very simple rear engined single-seater with single gears. In 1923-26 L.A.D. Productions Ltd revived the vehicle with a 350cc 2.75hp engine and a price of £75. A 5/7hp twin-cylinder version was also available briefly in 1923 at £125.

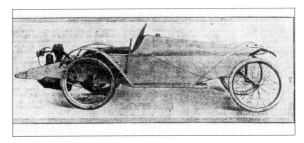

The 1913 LAD, revived in 1923.

LAGONDA

Near Staines Bridge, Staines, Middlesex

Founded by Wilbur Gunn, who died in 1920, Lagonda made about half its 1920-40 cars in the first five years of the 1920s. About 700 cars per year were made in the early 1920s, falling to 400 per annum later in the decade. Just about everything including nuts and bolts was made in-house, and the firm employed 500-800 workers through these successful years. After specialising in light cars the technically highly important 14/60 marked a clever change in direction towards the sporting and luxury market. A larger engined car followed, and in the 1930s Lagonda employed the legendary W O Bentley. It joined forces with Aston-Martin in the 1940s.

11 1913-16, 1919-21 and 11.9 1920-23 (prod: about 6000 including approx 200 to 1916). Coupé 335 guineas 1919, £495 1921. S4 IOE 1099cc (11hp), 1421cc 22bhp (11.9hp), cone clutch, in-unit three speed gearbox, spiral bevel axle (worm on some two-seaters). Transverse front, quarter-elliptic rear suspension. The 11 started as a very advanced pre-war car with unitary construction, in-unit monobloc engine/gearbox and the first known fly-off handbrake. The postwar type (initially with "bull-nose" shape radiator) was very similar except that electric lighting then starting were standardised, and

The 1919 Lagonda 11hp works demo coupé.

Lagonda 11.9hp, 1920-21.

a larger crankshaft was specified. Nickel plating, initially just on the radiator, soon spread to other parts. Output was running at 15 per week in late 1920 and 25 per week in April 1923, when the 11.9 with separate block and aluminium crankcase was developed (though there was still trough and dipper lubrication). Sold under the slogan "the best British light car", several were used with success in competition, notably by Bill Oates.

Lagonda 12/24 saloon, 1924.

12, 12/24. 1923-26 (prod: see 11hp). Complete from £330 initially, £295 in 1926. S4 IOE 1421cc 24bhp, cone then in 1924 plate clutch, in-unit three speed gearbox, torque tube, spiral bevel axle. Transverse front, quarter-elliptic rear suspension. This was a modernised version of the 11.9, with a new block casting with improved waterways, and enclosed valve gear including an aluminium cover over inlet valves operated by rockers in line with the crankshaft. In 1924 front wheel brakes could be fitted on assembly for £10. 50mph and 35mpg were quoted but the lack of a fourth gear

came in for criticism. Tourers had sidescreens in door pockets like Humber.

The 1926 Lagonda 14/60 semi-sports touring car was priced at £590.

14/60, 2 LITRE SPEED MODEL. 1925-31 (prod: approx 1440). Chassis from £450 1927, £495 1930. S4 OHV 1954cc, dry plate clutch, amidships-mounted four speed gearbox with right hand change, spiral bevel axle, semi-elliptic suspension. Gone were the unitary origins of Wilbur Gunn's old models. The new engine designer was Arthur Davidson from Lea Francis whilst the chassis, made now of conventional channel, was the work of A E Masters. The engine at last had a detachable cylinder head with hemispherical combustion chambers, and had high-mounted camshafts working the valves at 90 degrees (they did not have to be disturbed when removing the head). Initially output was 60bhp, increased for the 2 litre Speed Model from late 1927 and again in 1930 when a supercharged version (costing £775 as a tourer) had a top speed of 90mph. High and low chassis versions were built.

16/65. 1926-30 (prod: possibly 250). Chassis £570, saloons from £845. S6 OHV 2389cc soon increased to 2692cc, dry plate clutch, amidships mounted four speed gearbox, spiral bevel axle, semi-elliptic suspension. Using another Davidson designed engine, but far duller than the 14/60 in its original form, this was really for the carriage trade and used a lengthened 14/60 chassis. Lagonda was unusual in building most of its own bodywork, in the case of this model often under Weymann flexible construction licence with fabric covering. (See over.)

The Lagonda 3 litre.

1927 Lagonda 16/65: the only known survivor, owned by David Howard.

3 LITRE. 1928-34 (prod: approx 570). Various styles on chassis starting at £650 (£835 for "special"). S6 OHV 2931cc, plate clutch, four speed amidships mounted gearbox, spiral bevel axle, semi-elliptic suspension. Although the 3 litre shared a common cylinder bore with the 2 litre virtually nothing was interchangeable – the engine was more closely related to the 16/65. There was the usual Lagonda right hand change with third/top nearest the driver, and though this model was at first considered a conservative and formal car all this was to change from late 1929 with the "special" Low Chassis sports versions, developed from racing experience with 3- and 2-litre types.

LANCHESTER

Armourer Mills, Montgomery Street, Birmingham

High-grade products from 1895 pioneers. All had mid-mounted engines with semi forward control driving positions until the 1914 Sporting Forty. This, and the postwar Forty developed from it (with an entirely new OHC engine), continued the Lanchester traditions of worm drive and easy-change epicyclic transmission. Virtually all cars had

Lanchester's own coachwork built on cast aluminium formers. As at Rolls-Royce, the one model policy soon had to be expanded to include a car in the 20hp class and Lanchester saw out the decade to the tune of a magnificent straight eight before falling into the arms of BSA-Daimler in 1931 when its bank called in a modest overdraft. All had the Lanchester "trademark" of the radiator header tank sight glass. Dr Frederick Lanchester (his brother George designed the Forty) was a great consulting engineer and worked for Wolseley and Daimler (from 1909) and many others in this capacity in the 1920s. Lots of cars in the period used Lanchester's crankshaft vibration damper patents and Star also used its four wheel braking system.

FORTY. 1919-31 (prod: 392). Chassis £2200 1919, £1800 1930. S6 OHC 6178cc 105bhp, single dry plate clutch, three speed epicyclic gearbox, torque tube, worm axle. Semi-elliptic front, cantilever rear suspension. This astounding car was in series production until 1929 and available to special order for a couple of years after that. Owners included Prince Chichibu of Japan, the Duke of York, Indian cricketer Ranji (the Sahib of Nawanagar) and the Maharajah of Alwar, who mounted his state coach on one geared to 55mph! There were two racing ver-

1928 Lanchester Forty limousine.

The straight eight Lanchester Thirty.

sions, one of which took numerous international records in 1924 including 400km at 157km/h, and in 1927-31 there were even 39 six-wheel armoured car chassis. Four wheel servo brakes were adopted in 1924, prior to which chauffeurs had been deemed expert enough to manage without them.

sis lubrication, plus shock absorbers at the front. The springs were retained by trunnions in oil boxes. Very smooth and flexible performance to 80mph from one of the very few large non-sporting British straight eights. Humber was another advocate.

LA RAPIDE

London SW

Not French as its name suggested but a 1920 cyclecar with its 8hp air-cooled JAP engine bolted to outriggers on the offside. Just one of the rear wheels was driven by belt, from a Sturmey-Archer three speed gearbox driven by chain.

The Lanchester Twenty One.

TWENTY ONE. 1923-31 (prod: 735). Chassis approx £1000. S6 OHC 2.93 litres (3.3 for 1925 onwards, when it was sometimes known as Twenty Three), single plate clutch, in-unit four speed gearbox with right hand change, torque tube, worm axle. Semi-elliptic front, cantilever rear suspension. Effectively a scaled-down Forty with detachable cylinder head and four wheel servo brakes as a later option. George Lanchester had wanted to retain epicyclic transmission but settled for sliding mesh to give four ratios within realistic space and cost. An excellent car priced to undercut the Rolls Twenty and good for over 60mph.

THIRTY. 1929-32 (prod: 126). Chassis £1325, various styles including fabric saloon. S8 OHC 4.4 litres nearly 100bhp, single plate clutch, in-unit four speed gearbox, torque-tube, worm axle. Semi-elliptic front, cantilever rear suspension. Similar to a 21 with two more cylinders and a ten-bearing crankshaft. The bulkhead was built as part of the Duralumin body frame and there was grouped chas-

1920 La Rapide cyclecar.

LAUNCESTON

Willesden Junction, London NW

Offered only in 1920, at £330, was this assembled flat-twin 12/20hp car with stylish four-seat open touring bodywork.

Launceston 12/20 four-seater, 1919.

LAURENCE-JACKSON

Wolverhampton, Staffordshire

So obscure was this 1920 JAP 8/10hp vee-twin two-seater with friction transmission and chain drive, offered at £295, that it doesn't even stagger into J Boulton's 1976 book *Powered Vehicles made in the Black Country*.

The Laurence-Jackson light car.

LEA FRANCIS

Lower Ford Street, Coventry, Warwickshire

The Coventry pioneer had such a highly complex history in the 1920s that it caused even that great historian Michael Sedgwick to exclaim in his research notes "Oh God". Luckily Barrie Price's excellent book *Lea Francis Story* sorts most of it out in detail, and by lumping most of the Meadows engine types together I shall attempt to simplify the range.

The era started with Lea Francis building a 14hp in-house. This was not a success and thereafter the company became one of the most successful "assemblers". C B Wardman, managing director of Vulcan, was also chairman of Lea Francis for six years, and there were various joint projects. L T Delaney became a Lea Francis director and was to be the force behind the firm's competition successes. From a production of around 1000 cars per year at its peak, the company's profits collapsed, and Wardman left in 1928. Only 290 cars were made in 1920, despite several well publicised racing successes, and R H Lea (a relation of the Lea of Worcester Sauce fame) left when a Receiver was appointed in 1931 (G H Francis had left in 1924 to work for Skefco bearings). The firm then struggled on with Meadows engined cars and its own 2-litre

OHC six until 1936, after which a change of ownership brought new designs.

1922 Lea Francis Twelve tourer.

1923 Lea Francis 8.9hp two-seater coupé.

11.9 TWELVE 1920-22, 8.9 NINE 1922-23 (prod: approx 100). Twelve £700 falling to £395, Nine £235 for two-seater. S4 SV 2 litres, 1.07 litres, cone clutch, four speed gearbox (three speed on Nine), spur gear differential, semi-elliptic suspension (quarter-elliptic at rear on Nine). The Twelve was the design of Arthur Alderson (ex-Singer and Calcott and soon to design the first Cluley and Triumph cars) and it arrived just too late to catch the brief over-priced postwar sales boom. Capable of 50mph, it was well made but had no particularly distinctive features, and despite parts for a large batch having been produced only about a dozen were sold. Chief engineer Charles Van Eugen (appointed 1922, ex-Clyno, Swift, Daimler, ABC and Briton) refined the Nine, which bore the first recognisable angular Leaf radiator. Prototypes had Coventry Victor and Bradshaw (oil-cooled) twins, but his version had a Coventry Simplex four-cylinder unit and Meadows gearbox. A new works manager also arrived – he was H E Tatlow from Ruston-Hornsby. A fourteen version of the Twelve with 2.3-litre engine was also briefly listed for 1923.

1925 Lea Francis 12hp tourer.

EARLY 10-12HP MODELS. 1923-30 (prod: approx 2350). S4 OHV 1247cc, 1496cc Meadows, mostly cone clutch with three or four speed Meadows gearbox, spur gear differential axle. Semi-elliptic front, quarter-elliptic rear suspension. A bewildering assortment of models alphabetically listed from D to O were offered from as little as £210 for a two-seater in 1925 (the C had been the Coventry Simplex engined car). All were nicely made and attractive, with above average performance. Chairman C B Wardman had a company that was associated with the British Motor Trading Corporation, selling arm

of, amongst others, Bean, Vulcan, Swift and ABC, and he handled London sales. About 50 British Anzani engines were used in the N models of 1926 and there was also a Leaf radiatored Vulcan Kirkstone with Meadows or Anzani engine, of which about 70 found customers in 1926.

Lea Francis 12/40 sports tourer, 1927.

TYPE P, U, V, W. 1927-32 (prod: approx 1700). Open car from £325. S4 OHV 1496cc 37.5bhp Meadows, single plate clutch (except cone clutch on first 40 P types), four speed gearbox with right hand change, spiral bevel axle, semi-elliptic suspension. These were much the same as before in appearance but there was a wider chassis from 1927 with improved rear axle, less fierce clutches, and

14/40 Lea Francis of 1927, with Cross & Ellis body.

four wheel brakes (some with servos). Typical hp designations were 10, 12/22, 12/40 and 12/50. Over 60mph and a lively performance were hallmarks of these spirited cars.

14/40 (LFS) 1927/8, 2 LITRE 16/60 and 16/70 1930-36 (prod: approx 350, 67). Chassis from £345, £450. S6 DOHC 1696cc 45bhp Vulcan, S6 OHC 1991cc 60/70bhp, plate clutch, four speed gearbox, spiral bevel axle, semi-elliptic suspension. The 1696cc engine was designed by A O Lord (see Loyd-Lord), the 1991cc unit by Charles Van Eugen. The 14/40 had insuperable teething troubles which greatly damaged the prospects of the 2-litre (which gained the name Ace of Spades on account of the appearance of the engine from the front). A 14/40 is shown on the previous page.

1½ LITRE SUPERCHARGED TYPE S. 1928-31 (prod: approx 185). Chassis from £450, saloon £575. S4 OHV 1496cc Meadows, Cozette supercharger, 61-79bhp, plate clutch, four speed gearbox, spiral bevel axle, semi-elliptic suspension. The Hyper, as it became known, was Van Eugen's classic, good for 85mph in road trim and amongst the first standard production blown British cars. Four wheel servo assisted brakes made it stop as well as it went and it had numerous competition successes including victory in the 1928 TT. Delaney picked the name Hyper, but some touring models like the V and the W shared its sloping radiator style.

LECOY

Northolt Road, Harrow, Middlesex

In 1921-22 Lambert Engineering of St Hilda's Works offered this friction transmission cyclecar with Blackburne 8hp twin-cylinder engine for £185 (a JAP engine is also referred to). Final drive was by chain and there was coil front and cantilever rear suspension. With wire wheels (detachable types were an optional extra) it weighed 5½cwt. Finished in buff brown, it had a primitive, spindly appearance resembling the pre-war breed of cyclecar and had a small luggage well exposed above the back axle.

Front and rear views of the 1921-22 Lecoy.

The 1½-litre Lea Francis Hyper.

LEWIS

Abbey Wood Works, London SE2

Abbey Industries was responsible for this 10hp car in 1923-24. An air-cooled MAG 1092cc twin or a Coventry Climax sidevalve four could be specified at £195 and £225 respectively for a two-seater. The cars had quarter-elliptic suspension, Opperman three speed gearboxes, single plate clutches and spiral bevel axles. The standard body finish was polished aluminium. Chassis numbers commenced at 201 in 1923 and 601 in 1924 but it is most unlikely that so many were built, especially as the marque died in April 1924. See also Abbey.

Lewis 10hp, 1923.

LEYLAND

King Street, Leyland, Lancashire

Described as "The Lion of Olympia" when displayed at the 1920 Motor Show, this splendid machine was the work of J G Parry Thomas and Reid Railton, who were normally involved with Leyland's commercial vehicles. However, like Henry Spurrier, the boss of Leyland, they admired fast and powerful cars and decided to create the best. At the opposite extreme Leyland was also to adopt the utilitarian Trojan, with which Parry Thomas would have no truck. The Leyland Eight was in its day Britain's most powerful and expensive car, but it lacked the carriage trade traditions and high class associations so essential for its sales success.

EIGHT. 1920-23 (prod: approx 18). Chassis £2500 1920, £1875 1922. S8 OHC 7 then 7.3 litres, single plate clutch, four speed gearbox, helical then spiral bevel axle. Semi-elliptic front, quarter-elliptic with torsion bar rear suspension. 110bhp was delivered, or 145bhp with twin carburettors, and this 90mph car bristled with novelties including coil ignition, hemi head, and automatic chassis lubrication activated by shocks to the suspension. Leaf springs closed each pair of valves, the gearbox was cushioned on leather, and there were vacuum servo brakes and a suction controlled ignition cut-out. A suction governor on the cooling fan put it out of

1920 Leyland Eight tourer.

operation at light throttle openings. The starter motor was in-unit with the gearbox (and was activated by the gear lever) and there was a radiator thermostat. The Maharajah of Patiala bought two and Michael Collins was shot and killed in one during the Irish Troubles. Late in 1921 Parry Thomas developed the racing versions and in 1922 left to concentrate on his successful Brookland career, also breaking the World Land Speed record in 1924 at 129.73mph in his Leyland-Thomas. He died in his Liberty aero engined "Babs" record attempt of 1927 and in that year one further Leyland Eight was built up from spares by Thomson and Taylor. See also Marlborough and Arab.

LINCOLN

Lancaster Gardens, Ealing, London W

A 1920 three wheel cyclecar with a 1000cc two-stroke Blackburne engine and chain drive. There was of course no connection between it and the luxury American marque of that name which joined Ford in 1922.

1920 Lincoln three wheeler.

LINGTON

Bedford and London Road, Twickenham, Middlesex

Another ephemeral cyclecar, this time shaft driven and powered by a vee-twin 10hp engine that could be kick-started from the driver's seat.

Lington cyclecar, 1920.

LITTLE GREG

King Street, Wigan, Lancashire

It appears that H H Timberlake Ltd were agents for the French Grégoire car and added another French make to their range in 1923-24. This was built by Hinstin and called the Little Greg in England, where the Northern Greg Syndicate was listed as concessionaires in 1923. The Little Greg had an 1100cc 20bhp CIME engine, but in addition Timberlake was an agent for Dorman and bought considerable quantities of Dorman engines. It is conceivable that some of these were used in Anglicised versions, though the majority were supplied to the makers of Westwood cars and Pagefield lorries.

L M, LITTLE MIDLAND

Southgate Works, Preston, Lancashire

A light car of this make first appeared in 1905 in Clitheroe. A different design then came to some prominence as one of the first cyclecars in the teens. Revived in 1919 in Duke Street, Blackburn and then under the auspices of the Little Midland Light Car Co. (1920) Ltd in Preston, it survived until 1922.

Little Midland 8hp, 1920.

8-10HP. 1919-22 (prod: chassis numbers commenced at 700 in 1921 and 890 in 1922). V2 980cc JAP water-cooled 9hp RAC, cone clutch, three speed gearbox, chain drive, quarter-elliptic suspension. A substantial half-ton machine with two seats plus dickey for 250 guineas, reduced in August 1921 to £200. It had Michelin disc wheels, was finished in grey, and a 45-55mpg fuel consumption was typical. The sole concessionaire, John White, operated from The Albany, Liverpool.

LITTLE SCOTSMAN

See Scotsman

LOCKWOOD

Eastbourne, Sussex

Made by a garage, the Lockwood was billed in 1921-22 as the smallest car in the world and was actually suitable only for publicity stunts or mechanically minded children.

LONDON-PULLMAN

Adelaide Road, London NW3

This was described as a British assembled American car and came from the Arcade Motor Co. Ltd. It had the same four-cylinder 3-litre Golden, Belknap and Schwartz engine as late examples of the Pullman cars from York, Pennsylvania which went out of production in 1917, and it seems probably that Arcade was using up old spares or else had brought the remnants of Pullman. In any event the car was listed from 1922 to 1925 and had largely American accessories (and presumably components) but with British coachwork and the option of Michelin detachable disc wheels. Tourers cost from £395 and landaulettes £695.

LOTHIAN

London SW9

One of the numerous hopefuls that probably never got beyond the prototype, or even only the literature stage in 1920. 11.9 and 10hp models with four-cylinder engines were planned by the would-be makers, W J M Auto Engineers Ltd. Lothian was also the name of commercial chassis made in 1913-24 by bus operator Scottish Motor Traction Co. Ltd of Edinburgh.

LOYD-LORD

High Road, Chiswick, London W4

A O Lord had designed the engine for the Albert car before starting a car firm in 1922 with a partner called Blythe. In December a new partner named Loyd joined Lord. Loyd (see Carden) became noted for his Carden Loyd tracked military vehicles (which, under the auspices of Vickers from 1928, had Meadows engines and gearboxes). Initially assembled cars, Loyd-Lords soon incorporated Lord's own two-stroke engines. When the project foundered Lord's Lord-Six Motors of West Kensington came up with the LFS engine for Vulcan

and Lea Francis, and he became Vulcan's chief car engineer.

Loyd-Lord 14/30, 1923.

12/20, 14/30, 14/40. 1922-24 (prod: 38). Chassis (in red and grey) from £375. S4 OHV 1795cc and 2120cc Meadows, cone clutch, four speed Meadows gearbox, right hand change, Timken spiral bevel axle, semi-elliptic suspension. An assembled car using similar engines to Phoenix, Hampton, Seabrook, Westwood, Autocrat, Wigan-Barlow, Airedale, Meteorite, Bayliss Thomas, Vulcan and others. The first engines and gearboxes arrived from Meadows in April 1922 but Lord's heart lay with his two-stroke ideas and from 1924 only the 14/30 was left (in fact the same car as 1923's 14/40).

11, 18/60. 1924 (prod: n/a). Chassis £160, £500. S2 TS 1082cc air-cooled, S4 TS 2009cc air-cooled, plate clutch, Meadows three and four speed gearboxes, Timken spiral bevel axle, four wheel brakes on 18/60. Both engines had separately cast cylinders and finned heads and were blown with rotary superchargers. All these eccentricities were far too much for the sensible buying public. The badges of all models were overlapping Ls in the manner of Rolls-Royce with Loyd above and Lord below in bold capitals.

LSD

Linthwaite, Huddersfield and Nunbrook, Mirfield, Yorkshire

Longbottom (designer) and Sykes and Dyson (backers) made this three-wheeler. Soon the partners were just Sykes and Sugden, and at its height the enterprise employed 50, some of whom were also involved in making household gaslight fittings. In 1923 the firm became LSD Motor Co. Ltd at Mirfield. When this venture expired in 1924 Ivor Blakey acquired the remnants and built about 30 cars. Parts to build several more still exist in Norfolk.

The LSD 8hp.

8HP. 1920-25 (prod: approx 640). Grey two-seater from £245. V2 MAG or JAP (986cc), cone clutch, two speed gearbox, chain drive. Horizontal coil spring independent front, quarter-elliptic rear suspension. Curious for both its suspension and the provision of a reverse gear on a three-wheeler. Weighing over 7cwt, this was no skimpy cyclecar but a robust runabout for rugged Yorkshire conditions.

MAGNETIC

See Crown Magnetic

MAIFLOWER

See Ford

MARENDAZ

Brixton Road, London SW9

Captain D M K Marendaz had been involved with T G John and de Freville in the original Alvis before making gearboxes for the Emscote and creating the Marseal. The Marendaz Special was conceived and built on the first floor of the premises of the London Cab Co. in Brixton, with much help from Mrs

Marendaz. Most of the income for their ambitious racing and record breaking programme came from the sale of exotic secondhand cars – The London Cab premises were also shared by the concessionaires for Bugatti and the American Graham-Paige. In 1932 Marendaz moved to the same site as GWK in Maidenhead, and made about 60 six-cylinder cars before going out of business in 1936 despite considerable competition success, notably in the hands of the Moss family (see Crouch). Capt. Marendaz then concentrated on aircraft and later in South Africa on small diesel engines.

1½ LITRE. 1926-30 (prod: approx 25). Chassis approx £400, sports £650 1928, £495 1930. S4 SV 1496cc 11/55hp British Anzani (also 9/90 with Anzani linered down to 1087cc), plate clutch, three or four speed gearbox, spiral bevel axle. Semi-elliptic front, cantilever rear suspension. After the first few cars a Bentley-style radiator was adopted. The brakes were unusual in that the pedal worked on the front drums and the handbrake on the rear. Shock absorbers on all four wheels were also a rarity at the time. A supercharged version was called the 11/120, and theoretically available was a straight-eight 1½-litre 14/55 (14/125 when supercharged) with Anzani crankshaft but other parts

A Marendaz sports.

made specially for Marendaz in Birmingham. A 1093cc OHV version took the world Class G 24 hour record in February 1928. The normal 11/55 could do 75mph.

MARLBOROUGH

Dering Street, off New Bond Street, London W1

This Anglo-French make started life in 1906 and from 1909 was under the control in Britain of T B André (of shock absorber fame). French MAB chassis components and proprietary engines were used, assembly taking place in Notting Hill Gate. Two thousand cars are said to have been made in total, ending with the 2-litre six-cylinder OHV Coventry Climax engined Grand Sports model of 1926, which sold at £525 and would do 75mph. These were assembled in J G Parry Thomas' (see Leyland) shed at Brooklands, where some Marlborough-Thomas racing cars were also made. The initial address of the Marlborough-Thomas was given as Thomas Inventions Development Co. Ltd, Spring Gardens, Whitehall SW1, where the car was envisaged as the Thomas-Special.

Other 1920s Marlboroughs had French Fivet, Ballot and CIME engines, or British Anzani sidevalve 1½-litre units. The Roadspeed version of the Anzani engined car was guaranteed to do 60mph and was capable of 70mph (with a following wind!).

André also appears to have had links with the makers of Blackburne engines, Salmons coachwork, Martinyde motor cycles, and Bleriot Whippet and Eric Longden cars. It was the importer of the American Grant.

A 1921 Marlborough 10-20 Roadspeed model, costing £525 (a De Luxe was also available for £50 more).

MARLBOROUGH-THOMAS SPORTS. 1923-24 (prod: a handful). S4 OHC (both DOHC and SOHC quoted) 1493cc, four speed gearbox (some with additional epicyclic reduction ratio), spiral bevel axle, quarter-elliptic or torsion bar suspension, four wheel brakes. The sports was listed as a production model, at £575 for the chassis in 1923 (when the usual 9.5

Streamlined Marlborough-Thomas 12.1hp Sports.

Marlborough cost only £160) and had four André shock absorbers as standard. Two of the Sports fared badly in the 1923 Brooklands 200 mile race but with their low-slung chassis at least they looked very stylish. The engine had originally been conceived as a Leyland 2-litre taxi engine and had leaf spring valve gear similar to that of the Leyland Eight.

MARSEEL & MARSEAL

Atlantic Works, Stoke, Coventry

Captain Marendaz, apprenticed at Siddeley-Deasy, was involved with the the original Alvis and made gearboxes for the Emscote, a light car made by Marlowe and Seelhaft. The latter teamed up with Marendaz to make the Marseel (Marseal after Seelhaft, also ex-Siddeley, withdrew in 1923). Marendaz used competition to promote the marque, which gained many trials awards (over 250 were claimed by the Captain) and even raced at Brooklands. Most cars were bodied by Lawson or Hancock and Warman, the latter well known in connection with Riley. Capt. Marendaz's next venture into car manufacture after a spell on the Stock Exchange was with the Marendaz Special.

A 1920 Marseal tourer.

VARIOUS 9-12HP. 1919-25 (prod: approx 1200 total). S4 SV Coventry Simplex/Climax (also briefly an OHV S6 14/48 in 1924), cone clutch, mid-mounted three speed gearbox, bevel or worm axle.

1923 Marseal four-seater with all weather side curtains.

Semi-elliptic front, cantilever rear suspension. Early production figures indicate an output of 2-300 cars per year and a brief flirtation with an oil-cooled four in 1922. A blue and white racing version used by the flamboyant Marendaz was nicknamed Blancmange.

MARSHALL

Gainsborough, Lincolnshire

There is no known connection between the 1919-20 car and the famous steam and oil engined heavy vehicle manufacturer of the same name in Gainsborough. P F E Marshall is said to have used Coventry Simplex sidevalve engines in the very small number of cars he built.

MASCOTTE

Kensal Road, London W10

Very similar in appearance to the Meteorite (and indeed the Albert, Eric Campbell and others with radiators of Rolls-Royce shape), the Mascotte was an assembled car which lasted only 1919-21 and employed Belgian designed but English built Peters engines, plus 12 from Dorman (11 in 1919 and one as a replacement or attempted revival in 1924).

The 11.9hp Mascotte two-seater tourer.

10, 11.9. 1919-20 (prod: chassis nos. from 109 in 1920 and 240 in 1921). Chassis £415, two- or four-seater £475, S4 SV Peters 1645cc, 1820cc, cone clutch, three speed gearbox, bevel axle. Semi-elliptic front, cantilever rear suspension. There was nothing to distinguish this from many other assembled cars of the time, and it was too expensive and had few mod. cons. (no self-starter, for example).

MASS

Milverton Street, Kensington, London W

This was a French car built specifically for the London importer Masser-Horniman. From 1912 cars destined to remain in France were called Pierrons. Neither brand was offered after 1923.

MATCHLESS

Plumstead Road, London SE

H Collier and Sons, makers of the famous Matchless motor cycles, added three wheel cyclecars in 1913. Their postwar car production did not start until late 1922 and was technically far more interesting. In 1931 Matchless offered special sports bodied versions of the Austin 7 with its own style of radiator shell.

1924 Matchless Model K.

MODEL K. 1922-24 (prod: started at K1 for 1923 and K500 for 1924 though one source suggests only 50 were built). HO2 OHV air-cooled 1.35 litres 10hp, single plate clutch, in-unit three speed centre change gearbox, worm drive, independent front suspension by double transverse springs. This very advanced car was first tried in the 1922 Exeter Trial and entered production in April 1923. It had four wheel brakes, unitary chassis/body con-

struction and independent front suspension. It commenced at £225 but fell to £185 and was quickly discontinued.

MAUDSLAY

Parkside, Coventry

This near neighbour of Armstrong-Siddeley built cars from 1902 and was founded by a member of the same family as started Standard. From the earliest days it favoured overhead camshafts, even on the commercial vehicles that became its staple product. No cars were made from 1914 to 1923, but then came a startling twin cam sportscar intended to help the firm recover from a slump in demand, from 263 heavy chassis in 1920 to only 35 in 1921. As it was, low-level safety coaches of similar technical specification to the sportscar revived the firm's fortunes and the cars were quietly forgotten.

Maudslay 15/80 Six chassis.

15-80 SIX. 1923 (prod: possibly only two). Chassis £825. S6 DOHC 1991cc, plate clutch, in-unit four speed gearbox, spiral bevel axle, semi-elliptic suspension with shock absorbers, four wheel brakes. J A Kemp (later of Albion) and J R Hamilton designed the 15-80 under the supervision of engineering director Alexander Craig (also a director of Rover), and *The Autocar* thought it was the most exciting arrival since the Fergus (see OD) of 1915. The crankshaft ran in seven roller races and the hemispherical cylinder head had inclined valves operated by an oscillating Y working eccentrics on the camshafts via roller races. One car was destroyed by fire at the coachbuilders and another got to the 1923 Motor Show as a chassis. Parts for others were made but probably never assembled.

MAXWELL
See Chrysler

MB

St George's Road Works, Bolton, Lancashire

In 1920 Merrall Brown Motors succeeded a garage firm called Premier Motors which in the previous year had launched a vee-twin 10hp Precision engined car with rear wheels very close-set to avoid the need for a differential. About 17 were made before the MB emerged as the more conventional four-wheeler described below.

The MB 10/12hp.

10/12HP. 1919-21 (prod: 7 in 1919 then n/a). Chassis £300, complete £375. S4 SV 1498cc Coventry Simplex, cone clutch, two speed and reverse gearbox, chain drive, quarter-elliptic suspension. About the only claim to fame of the short-lived MB was a bronze medal in the Scottish Six Days' Trial and the claimed lowest price for a four-cylinder light car. Two gears and chain drive were of course primitive compared with many other rivals and the car came with an MB badge surrounded by the Latin tag *Facile Princeps Sui Generis* (though it had no connection with the Princeps car!).

McCURD

Hayes, Middlesex

W A McCurd was a well known London motor trader who built lorries from 1912 in Cricklewood and moved production out to Hayes after the Great War (during which his premises were taken over by the Government for tank experimental work). In 1923 cars were introduced and these and commercials lasted until 1927 – even longer in some buyers' guides.

1923 12hp McCurd.

12/20. 1923-27 (prod: chassis numbers were 1000 per year but output was far less). Chassis £425 falling to £375. S4 SV 1645cc, plate clutch, amid-

Chassis of the prototype 12hp McCurd.

ships mounted four speed gearbox, spiral bevel axle, semi-elliptic suspension. Relatively primitive and with no front wheel brakes (though McCurd coaches had them in 1926 under the slogan "Thought out first, not found out afterwards"). A nice touch was a watch in the centre of the steering wheel which, when pressed, sounded the horn. Various body styles were available in the standard colours of grey and wine, with leather upholstery.

McKENZIE

Charles Henry Street, Birmingham

A maker of sidecars, car bodies, invalid chairs and woodwork, Thomas McKenzie introduced in 1913 a light car that may have had a home-built 1162cc engine, but after the war engines were bought in from Alpha and then Coventry Simplex. The quality of manufacture was high and the cars were regular trials contenders. Thomas McKenzie's grandson, writing in *The Automobile* in 1989, stated that the number produced was impossible to ascertain though chassis number allocations show 50 or less cars per year from 1919 to 1922, and then a jump from chassis number 501 to 799 in 1922.

9 TO 11HP. 1919-26 (prod: approx 300). Chassis £360 1919, £255 1924. Initially S4 SV Alpha 11hp then S4 SV Coventry Simplex/Climax 10.5hp 1498cc from 1921. 9hp 1074cc version of latter added 1924. Cone clutch, in-unit three speed Meadows gearbox from late 1922, spiral bevel axle (worm in 1919-20), quarter-elliptic suspension. Above average small cars which played on their Scottish sounding name for thrift and toughness and had a stag's head as trademark. The 9hp would do

1924 McKenzie 11hp two-seater.

50mph and 44mpg and a contemporary test spoke of light steering. Some stylish saloons and coupés were offered.

MENDIP

Southmead, Bristol

Originating at a little foundry and blacksmithy high in the Mendips (which still exists as a pheasant farm), this firm introduced cars in 1914. W H Bateman Hope acquired the business that year and transferred production to Southmead. Virtually everything was made in-house. The proprietor died in 1921 but works manager G R Thatcher continued assembly at Atworth, Melksham, Wiltshire into 1922, whilst Baines Manufacturing of Westbury on Trym, Bristol offered spares following its takeover of the Mendip Motor and Engineering Works. The rest of the business continued as general and then aircraft engineers and ultimately joined the Dowty Group.

1250cc Mendip 11hp, 1920.

10 to 12HP. 1914-22 (prod: 300-400). S4 SV 1100 to 1330cc (16bhp) from 1920, cone clutch, three speed gearbox, worm axle, semi-elliptic suspension. Designed by W L Adams, also responsible for the Day-Leeds, these cars had Belgian chassis. The early engines were made by Mendip and had ingenious one-piece castings incorporating manifolds and ancillaries. Later cars had Alpha engines. An interesting example of a purely local rural make.

MENLEY

Etruria Road, Basford, Stoke on Trent, Staffordshire

This 1920 cyclecar had an 8hp air-cooled Blackburne engine with three speed gearbox and chain/belt transmission. An employee named Titley who had worked for Sheffield-Simplex and Austin before joining the Menley Motor Co. told the author that 16 were built and that motor cycle racer Archie Cox managed 60mph in one and lived to tell the tale. The frame was of ash with tubular metal cross-members and the complete price £250.

Menley cyclecar, 1920.

MERCURY

Gould Road, Twickenham, Middlesex

A new maker in 1914 with a 12/14hp car and a light commercial chassis, revived after the war with different bore and stroke. The maker was initially Medina Engineering of the above address but in April 1920 became Mercury Cars (Productions) Ltd of Mercury Works, May Road, Twickenham, which was in liquidation by 1922. There were several other Mercury cars including a London built car in veteran times. All the others with the name were American, including of course the famous upmarket Ford type of 1938 onwards.

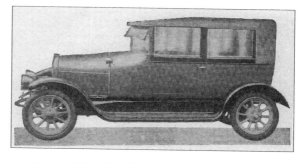

Mercury 10hp with all-weather body by W H Arnold.

9.5 1920, 11.9 and 10.2 1921-22 (prod: chassis numbers 1000-2000 quoted for 1920 but probably

Mercury chassis on test.

never attained). **Chassis £350-£495, complete £450-£600. S4 SV 1230cc, 1945cc, 1300cc, in-unit three speed gearbox, right hand change, bevel axle. Semi-elliptic front, cantilever rear suspension.** The 10.2 Treasury hp model was an enlarged bore version of the 9.5 (both called 10 by Mercury). Most components bore the Medina name so this may have been more than simply an assembled car.

METEORITE

142 Uxbridge Road, Shepherds Bush, London W12

The "light car with high-powered car advantages" was built from 1912 to 1924 and much was made of its very full equipment. In 1924 this included aeroplane mascot, CAV lighting and starting, magnetic inspection lamp, gradient meter, cast aluminium number plates, dimmer switch, petrol can carrier, luggage rack, spring gaiters and folding screen for rear seat passengers, along with other items that together would have cost nearly £100 as accessories. Before the war a 10hp engine of uncertain origin, a six by Aster and JAP vee-twins

had been used, the latter in a cyclecar which was revived briefly in 1919 along with the 10hp. However, production in the 1920s centred on an 11hp Coventry Simplex engined model and a short-lived 14/30 six. Coachwork was frequently by the locally based firm Strachan and Brown. Manufacture was "postponed" that October "until times become more normal", but they never did and spares passed to C E Humphreys of Bedford.

11 1920-23, 11.9/12 1924 (prod: approx 400). Chassis £430 falling to £290, standard colour heliotrope. S4 SV 1488cc Coventry Simplex, cone clutch, mid-mounted three speed gearbox with right hand change, torque tube, bevel axle. Semi-elliptic front, cantilever rear suspension. Though well equipped, these models and the mysterious 1753cc six (listed, presumably incorrectly, as both 14/30 and in 1924 14/60) never got to the four wheel brake stage – this probably being the last financial straw that broke the camel's back. A final attempt to halt the slide in 1924 with the 45mph 11.9 as a Twelve two-seater for £375 failed. After about 1921 the Rolls-Royce shaped radiator had a curved inner surround to the upper part of the radiator core.

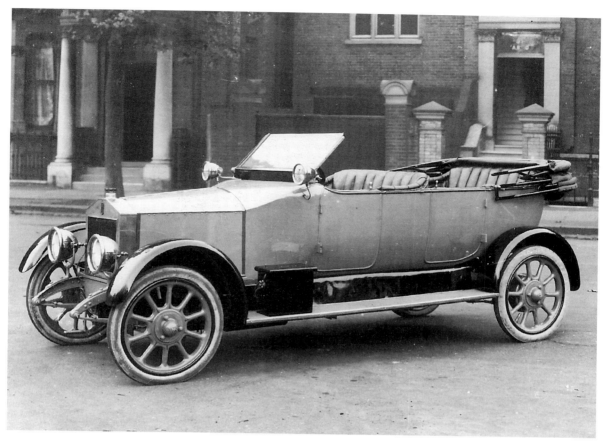

1922 Meteorite 11hp.

METRO-TYLER

Bannister Road, Kilburn Lane, London W10

This cyclecar was the product of a motor cycle firm which grew from the 1912-founded Metro Manufacturing and Engineering Co. of Birmingham. Tyler Apparatus Ltd acquired the company in 1919 and transferred it to London. The motor cycles had 269cc singles and the cyclecars of 1922-23 two-cylinder versions of the same engine, though a 758cc Blackburne was in use in 1923 and perhaps earlier.

5/6HP. 1922-23 (prod: chassis numbers 100-150 in 1922, 200 up in 1923). £125-155 complete. Two-cylinder TS 540cc or Blackburne two-cylinder SV 758cc, plate clutch, Sturmey-Archer three speed and reverse gearbox, belt and on later models chain drive, no differential, quarter-elliptic suspension. A cheap and basic cyclecar with an eight foot wheelbase, blue paintwork and Rexine upholstery. It weighed 6cwt, and the separate foot and hand brakes worked on opposite rear wheels.

Metro-Tyler 5/6hp.

MG

Oxford, then Edmund Road, Cowley from Sept 1927; Pavlova Works, Abingdon from Sept 1929

The MG evolved from The Morris Garages' sideline of supplying special bodies on the Morris chassis. In June 1924 the manager, Cecil Kimber, produced the 14/28 MG Super Sports. At this stage MG was not a make of car but a Morris Oxford fitted with a Morris Garages – MG – Super Sports body. All 14/28 MGs were registered as Morris Oxfords and carried a Morris Motors chassis plate. However, the body had coachbuilder's plates on the thresholds

1927 "Flatnose" MG 14/28.

1925 "Bullnose" MG 14/28.

1927 MG 14/40 two-door Salonette.

below the doors stamped *The Morris Garages* and bearing the famous octagon trade mark.

MG became an individual make of car, separate from Morris, from the start of production at a newly built factory at Edmund Road, Cowley in September 1927. The 14/40 MkIV Sports is the first production model of MG. Thereafter, MGs developed increasingly distinctive models, including one of the first cheap and universal sports cars and some exciting sixes, both of which types had ohc engines.

14/28 SUPER SPORTS 1924-26, 14/28 (flat radiator) 1927, and 14/40 1928-29 (prod: approx 1300 of which around 400 were Bullnose types). 1927 Mk

IV chassis £280, four-seater sports £350, Salonette £475. S4 SV 1802cc, wet plate cork clutch, three speed in-unit gearbox, spiral bevel axle, semi-elliptic suspension (three-quarter elliptic at rear until 1927). In 1923 Cecil Kimber drove a Morris Oxford with Morris Garages special chummy body in the London-Exeter Trial and gained a gold medal. One of the 1925 Bullnose types is shown together with a two years newer Salonette bodied model incorporating the Flatnose radiator which was adopted for 1927, the year in which MG won its first race. Four wheel brakes were servo assisted until 1928, and the sidevalve cars ended with the move to Abingdon. The enamelled octagon appeared on the radiator for 1928. A maximum of 60mph and pleas-

MG M-type Midget, 1928.

ant manners were features though the slogan "The car which cannot skid" was perhaps a trifle over-optimistic!

A MkI MG 18/80, 1930.

18/80. 1928-33 (prod: approx 740). Chassis £420 1929, complete up to £555. S6 OHC 2468cc, single plate clutch, in-unit three speed gearbox (four speed on 1929 MkII) with central change, torque tube (open propshaft on 1929 MkII), spiral bevel axle, semi-elliptic suspension. The Morris Light Six shown at Olympia in 1927 had the new JA OHC six-cylinder engine designed by Woollard and Pendrell squeezed into an elongated Morris Oxford frame. The result was a sparkling performer with roadhold-

One of the five sports/racing 18/80s made in 1930, known as the 18/100.

ing that courted disaster. W R Morris was furious with Cowley and gave The Morris Garages permission to design their own frame for the JA running gear. The result was the MG Six, which was unveiled at the 1928 London Motor Show. Early cars had bolt-on wheels but the Rudge Whitworth type was soon adopted, and all cars had the archetypal MG radiator. The MkII had improved brakes, twin carburettors (like most MkIs) and a new chassis with wider track, though the MkI continued alongside it until early 1931 as a cheaper option, accounting for 500 sales. Five MkIII sports/racing versions were made in 1930. These were capable of 100mph whilst the normal 18/80 was good for 80mph.

M TYPE MIDGET. 1929-32 (prod: 3235). 1929 chassis £150, two-seater £175. S4 OHC 847cc, plate clutch, in-unit three speed gearbox, spiral bevel axle, semi-elliptic suspension. The MG that brought sports cars within reach of young enthusiasts. Based closely on the Morris Minor, it was sometimes known as the 8/33 and first appeared at the 1928 London Motor Show, early production in 1929 taking place at Cowley. The engine provided 60mph and 38mpg and its output was increased from 20 to 27bhp in 1930 for even more noisy fun. Midgets were used in club racing in 1929 and official teams ran at Le Mans and the Double-Twelve in 1930, the year in which a four speed gearbox became a desirable option.

MILTON

Sunbury Mews, Belford Road, Edinburgh

From 1920 Milton offered 9hp and 10.5hp models with friction transmission, chain drive and engines by Alpha and Decolange. Suspension was by transverse leaf at the front and quarter-elliptics at the rear. At a chassis price of £315, or £385 for a four-seater, the cars stood little chance, and their maker, the Belford Motor Co., was in liquidation by 1922, after between 12 and 20 had been built.

A 1920 Milton.

MOLLER

Charing Cross, London WC2

Despite its very British sounding 11.9hp specification and locally produced bodywork, the chassis was actually built in Lewistown, Pennsylvania specifically with right hand drive. The car was listed 1920-22 but at 400 guineas for a chassis very few can have been sold. Perrens and McCracken were the British concessionaires.

This seems to have been the best picture of the Moller 11.9hp that the British concessionaires could offer in 1920.

MONARCH

Castle Bromwich, Birmingham

Though listed 1925-28 there is little evidence of any sales of the Monarch, and there is no known connection between it and the pre-Great War Birmingham built Monarch cyclecar. Though the later Monarch claimed to have the Monarch Motor Company of Monarch Works' own four-cylinder overhead-valve 2121cc engine, the prototype was probably powered by a 14hp Meadows. The specification included an in-unit four speed gearbox, cone clutch and Salisbury spiral bevel axle. Four wheel brakes were fitted and the chassis cost £360, or £525 with a Mulliner saloon body. Monarch supplied components to the Bond car.

MORGAN

Pickersleigh Road, Malvern Link, Worcestershire

Between 1919 and 1923 Morgan moved most of its factory into new Malvern Link premises, still in use today, where capacity was theoretically 40-50 cars per week from about 160 employees (4500 cars had been made 1919-22). Founder H F S Morgan lost two fingers in a lathe at this unpropitious moment, but still took an active part in the trialling and racing for which his marque was famous. The original 1909/10 features of sliding pillar independent front suspension, two speed chain transmission without

A Morgan in competition on a typical 1920s back road.

reverse, and vee-twin engine, were retained. The touring types became hard to sell after the Austin Seven arrived but by dint of reduced prices and a fanatical following from ex-motor cycle owners the firm could still sell around 1000 three wheelers a year, falling to 659 in 1934 and 29 in 1939. Darmont and Sandford made versions in France, where in 1929 Gwenda Stewart did 115mph in a Morgan. In 1924 the JCC had banned them from racing against four-wheelers after a well publicised accident, and in 1925 a Blackburne engined Morgan was the fastest unsupercharged 1100cc car in the world at 104.68mph for a flying kilometre.

1924 Morgan standard model.

Aero model Morgan, 1924.

THREE WHEELER. 1919-30 (prod: approx 18,000 1910-30 of which perhaps 15,000 made after the war). From £128 1923, £110 1924, £86 1928. Various SV and OHV air- or water-cooled engines, 976-1098cc. Cone clutch with two speed chain transmission (three speed for 1932 season and plate clutch in 1932. Two speeder available into 1933.) Coil spring independent front, quarter-elliptic rear suspension. Best known of all the three-wheelers, and available in a bewildering assortment of two- and four-seat family and sporting guises.

The Grand Prix was current 1913 until 1926, when it was replaced by the more streamlined Aero (Aero first seen in 1919 and available in 1921). The Standard, De Luxe and Family ran through the decade. The Super Sports Aero from 1927 was responsible for much of Morgan's competition success. Light three wheelers like the Morgan paid only £4 road tax. All manner of engines were used, notably MAG, Blackburne, JAP, Precision, and in the later 1930s Matchless and Ford. The accelerator was a lever on the steering wheel and the rear wheel was detachable from 1921. Three wheel brakes and geared steering became available later in the decade.

MORRIS

Cowley, Oxford

William Morris turned the British motor industry on its head. From humble roots in an Oxford garage he launched the immortal "Bullnose" in 1912. By shrewd manipulation of component suppliers and price he achieved an amazing mass-production formula that saw the acquisition of component firms like Hotchkiss engines, Wrigley gearboxes, SU carburettors, and body firm Hollick and Pratt. He overtook Ford's sales in Britain in 1924 and was inadvertently responsible for the demise of dozens of the makers of handbuilt family cars listed in this book. During "our" decade Morris spawned both MG and Morris-Commercial as well as acquiring Wolseley and Leon Bollée in France. Morris, with Citroën, was amongst the European pioneers of pressed steel bodywork, his pressing plant in 1927 covering eleven acres and employing 1000 men. Sales of 3077 cars in 1921 rose to 32,939 in 1924, 54,151 in 1925 and 63,000 in 1929. 1927 was the first year in which over 10,000 Morris cars were exported.

COWLEY. 1919-20 (prod: 282). Two-seater 1919 £295. S4 SV 1495cc 11.9hp Continental, dry plate clutch, in-unit Detroit three speed gearbox with centre change, torque tube, spiral bevel axle. Semi-elliptic front, three quarter elliptic rear suspension. The early Morris Oxford had engines by White and Poppe but, to create the cheaper Cowley, William Morris bought components in America. The Type U Continental Red Seal engine cost £18 instead of £50 for the White and Poppe, the gearbox a mere £8 10s, and axles and steering gear £16 5s. Supplies were severely disrupted by enemy action and could not be renewed after the war, so only the last 281 of the 1400 such Cowleys were made in 1919, with a final one in 1920. The Continental engined Cowley was William Morris' masterpiece and its sound design was a key factor in his subsequent success. Although it would have been hard for a leading "Buy British" campaigner to admit it, Morris must often have thought that the Cowley's American running gear, and subsequently the rights to the designs for him to copy for his postwar cars, were the best investment of his career.

A Morris Cowley with coupé-cabriolet special body.

1924 Morris Cowley 11.9hp occasional four.

COWLEY 11.9. 1919-26 (prod: approx 150,000 with Oxford incl. commercials). Two-seater 1920 £465, 1925 £162. S4 SV copy of Continental, cork insert clutch in oil, in-unit three speed centre change gearbox, torque tube, spiral bevel axle. Semi-elliptic front, three quarter elliptic rear suspension, with Gabriel Snubber available from 1923 and standard in 1925. White and Poppe was bought by Dennis in 1919 and 11.9hp engines were no longer available from Continental, so Morris went to a new engine supplier, the Coventry branch of the French armaments and car firm Hotchkiss. It agreed to make slightly modified versions of the Continental engine and gearbox for Morris, which acquired Hotchkiss in 1923. To shift accumulating cars Morris sales manager Hugh Wordsworth Grey dropped the price in February 1921 and saw sales boom. Further reductions coupled with sound specifications and first class materials quickly made this Britain's most popular car.

OXFORD. 1919-26 (prod: see Cowley). Two-seater 1919 £360, 1925 £240. Same engine as Cowley until 13.9hp 1802cc version offered from beginning of 1923 and standardised September 1924, cork insert clutch in oil, in-unit three speed gearbox, torque tube, spiral bevel axle, suspension as Cowley. The Oxford started out as a posh version of the Cowley, with such additional fittings as a Lucas dynamotor, five lamp lighting set and leather upholstery. In 1923 it was offered with a larger 13.9hp engine as an extra. The 13.9 engine was standard for 1924 and cooled by a larger radiator – Bullnoses ran on the warm side. In 1925, the 13.9 Oxford completed the process of growing up into a distinct model from the Cowley with an increase in wheelbase from 8' 6" to 9' and four wheel brakes with 12 inch drums as standard. The excellent Barker headlamp dippers were standard for 1926. A notably comfortable and quiet car, it was capable of 50mph and 28mpg. A Super Sports version was offered by MG.

The Morris Oxford "Silent Six" at the 1920 motor show.

1926 Morris Oxford four-seater tourer.

F-TYPE OXFORD SILENT SIX. 1920-26 (prod: approx 50). Chassis 1923 £375, 1924 £325. S6 SV 2320cc 17.9hp Hotchkiss, cork insert clutch in oil, in-unit three speed gearbox with centre change, torque tube, spiral bevel axle, semi-elliptic suspension. Starting as an OHV prototype in 1920, the Silent Six was a rare failure for Morris. It shared as many parts as possible with the 11.9 engine, which resulted in hopeless crankshaft dimensions, and the six soon gained a reputation for crankshaft breakage. Virtually all were made before mid-1924, and the unused parts for about 500 cars were allegedly used in the foundations of the Osberton Radiator factory in Oxford. Though the chassis was nine inches longer than the fours the extra space was taken up by the engine, leaving no more room for passengers in what was supposed to be an up-market 60mph car. The unique survivor is at BMIHT Gaydon.

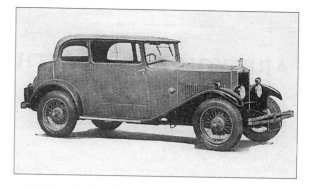

1929 Morris Six with Gordon England Club Coupé body.

SIX (JA SERIES). 1927-29 (prod: approx 3,500). Chassis 1928 £285, saloon £375. S6 OHC 2468cc 17.7hp, cork insert clutch in oil, in-unit three speed gearbox, torque tube, spiral bevel axle, semi-elliptic suspension. Eleven cars were built utilising the Frank Woollard designed engine that also appealed to MG for its 18/80. The narrow Morris chassis handled badly and a wider Oxford Six was ready in 1928. In mid-1929 the car was revised as the Isis, though a cheaper sidevalve Oxford Six was offered alongside this.

A late 1920s Morris Oxford gets a wash.

COWLEY and OXFORD. 1926-30 (prod: 185,000 including commercials). Chassis 1929 from £122 10s, saloon £240. S4 SV 1548cc, 1802cc, similar to earlier cars in 11.9 and 13.9 sizes, cork insert clutch in oil, in-unit three speed gearbox with centre change, torque tube, spiral bevel axle, semi-elliptic suspension. The Bullnose became a Flatnose in late 1926, and these were updated versions of the old faithfuls, now often with the all-steel bodies built under Budd licence that William Morris had studied in America in late 1925. Four wheel brakes were now the rule except on the simplified Cowley of 1927. In 1928 an 11.9 version of the Oxford was briefly offered to counter increased petrol prices but was found to be no more economical than the 13.9. Versions of the Cowley with more modern styling carried on to 1935. Overland offered a car with Oxford running gear in 1925-26.

A 1929 Morris Minor.

MINOR. 1928-32 (prod: 39,083 including commercials). Chassis £100, tourer £125, saloon £135. S4 OHC 847cc 20bhp, single plate clutch, in-unit three speed gearbox, spiral bevel axle, semi elliptic suspension. The success of the Austin Seven caused Miles Thomas of Morris to consider a rival. The acquisition of Wolseley brought production space for the new baby along with the six-cylinder engine of the Hornet , then at its development stage. Two thirds of this engine powered the Morris, launched in August 1928, and also the MG Midget. For 1931 the Minor was joined and soon overtaken by a sidevalve version (of which a two-seater model could be bought for £100), and hydraulics replaced the cable brakes for the following season.

The Morris Isis saloon, 1929.

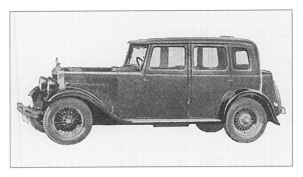

The 15hp Morris Oxford Six fabric saloon.

ISIS. 1929-31 (prod: 3939). Saloon 1930 £385, chassis £250. S6 OHC 2468cc 17.7hp, cork insert clutch in oil, in-unit three speed gearbox, torque tube, spiral bevel axle, semi-elliptic suspension. All-day cruising at 50mph, with 28mpg, and a 65mph maximum, were features of this remarkably American-looking car, which shared Budd body dies with Dodge and Ruxton. This was the first Morris to have Lockheed hydraulic brakes when introduced in July 1929, and it had the new features of chrome plating, thermostatic radiator shutters and safety glass. 2730 were built in 1929-30.

OXFORD SIX (LA SERIES). 1929-33 (prod: 32,282). 1929 tourer £275, fabric saloon £285. S6 SV 1938cc 15hp, cork insert clutch in oil, in-unit three speed gearbox, torque tube, spiral bevel axle, semi-elliptic suspension. No less than 15,545 were sold in the

first year and the same engine also went into the Cowley chassis to create the Major for 1931. Good for 60mph, this Oxford shared many of its modern features with the more expensive Isis.

MORRIS-COMMERCIAL

Soho and Adderley Park, Birmingham

In 1923 the Wrigley gearbox and axle works was acquired by Morris, and in 1924 production of a range of commercial vehicles using 13.9hp engines commenced. Some of these with larger engines became the basis for special purpose cars such as cross-country six wheelers and the rugged Empire Oxford. Morris-Commercial began to expand into the Wolseley works after its acquisition by Morris in 1927.

An early Morris (-Commercial) six wheeler with a half-track conversion by Roadless of Hounslow.

SIX WHEELER. 1925-31 (prod: about 20). S4 SV 2513cc 15.9hp (see Empire Oxford), from 1930 S6 SV 4256cc, four speed gearbox, drive to both rear axles, semi-elliptic suspension, hydraulic brakes. The late types often looked like elongated Isis with additional rear axles, but an early model is shown with Roadless of Hounslow half-track conversion to make a forerunner of the Land-Rover.

Morris (-Commercial) Empire Oxford staff car.

Morris (-Commercial) Empire Oxford Taxi.

EMPIRE OXFORD. 1926-29 (prod: 1742). Chassis 1927 £245, 1929 £210. S4 SV 2513cc 15.9hp, dry plate clutch, in-unit four speed gearbox, torque tube, overhead worm axle, semi-elliptic suspension, four wheel brakes. This was a tough, no-frills vehicle designed by Morris-Commercial to take sales away from the American vehicles so popular in the colonies. By Morris standards the 16/40, as it was sometimes called, was not a commercial success and many of the vehicles produced were dismantled when found to be too expensive to be saleable. Customers wanted more powerful sixes and Morris soon responded. Many components were used up in the 840 type G International taxis, and engines were common to some other Morris-Commercials. Lots of Empire Oxfords were sold to the RAF in 1928 and some if not all of the car versions were assembled at Cowley.

MORRISS-LONDON

Piccadilly, London

F E Morriss had these cars built exclusively for him by the Century Motor Co. of Elkhart, Indiana. What else Century did is uncertain, though it may have been a subsidiary of Crow-Elkhart in the same town, which built its own cars, the prototype Morriss-London and early production Morriss-Londons as well as components for them. The London-Pullman was a similar type of car. After a while Autocars of Woodstock Street, London, and Queensbridge Motor Co. of Belfast sold the cars, and then in 1922 Saunders Garage and Motor Car Co. of The Parade, London, bought what was left at London Docks – 69 in packing cases. They often called the cars Saunders, and like their predecessors claimed that at any rate some were British assembled. A slight increase in bore size at this stage is believed to have been because water had penetrated the engines in storage and they had to be rebored! Saunders became H A Saunders, the Austin distributors, and those with experience of the Morriss-London recall its totally inadequate external contracting rear brakes.

Morriss-London 18hp, 1922.

18. 1919-25 (prod: 69). Two-seater 1922 £375, 1925 £195. S4 SV 2872cc Supreme. Borg and Beck clutch, three speed Peru gearbox, spiral bevel axle. Semi-elliptic front, cantilever rear suspension. Supreme engines, made in Warren, Ohio, were used by a few obscure American firms plus one model of the better known Auburn (from the same state as Century). Whatever the truth about British assembly, all cars seem to have had British bodywork, a Gwynne all-weather type being shown. Morriss-London's badge showed the dome of St Paul's and the firm's slogan was "A capital car at a price that defies competition".

NAPIER

Acton Vale, London W3

An engineering firm which made cars in 1900, after nearly 100 years of diverse experience, and in

1919 Napier 40/50.

1904 offered the world's first commercially successful six-cylinder model. S F Edge (see AC and Cubitt) was closely involved in the firm's early years of racing and record breaking. During the Great War, Napier made about 2000 vehicles and a great many aero engines, including the immortal Lion which was later to power a number of land speed record cars. In 1919 a one model policy based on a 40/50 designed by A J Rowledge (designer of the Lion, who departed to Rolls-Royce in 1921) failed to produce adequate sales and car production was axed in 1924. Napier nearly returned to vehicle manufacture in the 1930s, when it developed the Mechanical Horse, which was adopted by Scammell, and it narrowly missed acquiring Bentley when outbid by Rolls-Royce.

40/50. 1919-24 (prod: 187). Chassis 1919 £2100, 1924 £1500. S6 OHC 6150cc 38.4hp RAC 82bhp, dry plate clutch, separate four speed gearbox with right hand change, torque tube, spiral bevel axle. Semi-elliptic front, cantilever rear suspension. The first car with SU carburettors, incorporating the Napier-developed metal dashpots. Many chassis were bodied by the Cunard Motor and Carriage Co., which Napier bought for the purpose. Production of 500 was intended but despite reduced prices sales were slow – though better than those of the Leyland Eight and British Ensign. Top speed was about 60mph and final cars had four wheel brakes.

NEC

Hythe Road, Willesden Junction, London NW10

G F Mort designed the two-stroke engine that was a feature of the cars made by the New Engine Company from 1905. The engines of all lived beneath the front seat, and with forward control there was room for capacious bodywork. They were ideal as town cars, though one ran from London to Edinburgh non-stop in 1910. The cars offered up to 1921 may well have been pre-war stock and still had oil and acetylene lamps when photographed, though CAV electrics were shown in contemporary specifications. NEC carried on in the motor field, making car components.

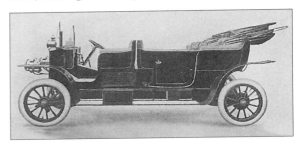

The NEC 30hp had a 4.6-litre flat-four two-stroke engine.

40 and 30HP. 1919-21 (prod: few, possibly of pre-war origin). Chassis from £1000. HO4 TS 5776cc and 4654cc, cone clutch, four speed gearbox, worm axle, quarter-elliptic suspension. Various body styles had been built before the war but D-fronted landaulets were the standard offering afterwards. Overall appearance had changed very little from 1905 and wooden artillery wheels remained non-detachable to the end.

NEW BRITISH

Overend Road, Cradley Heath, Staffordshire

Cradley Heath was famous for chains, and the Colonial Works of Charles Willetts Junr Ltd was a lifting tackle manufacturer with around 250 employees. From 1921 the company made friction driven light cars in batches of six in its under-utilised winch department, but when sales diminished it wisely abandoned the project.

Air-cooled New British 10hp, c1920.

10HP. 1921-23 (prod: chassis numbers to end of 1922 1-125). Two-seater 1922 £215, 1923 £170. V2 SV air- or water-cooled Blackburne, friction transmission, chain final drive, no differential, quarter-elliptic suspension. Supplied only as a two-seater in a standard colour of blue, the car was initially sold by New British Motors of Corporation Street, Birmingham. There was 6 volt lighting and handle starting. In the final year only the water-cooled type was made. An original 12hp prototype was retained by the works for many years.

NEW CARDEN
See Carden

NEWEY

Bristol Street, Birmingham

An Aster engined Ten first seen in 1913 was revived after the war and joined by a Chapuis-Dornier engined 12/15hp listed until 1922. An American engined car, the GNL, had also been offered in the later stages of the war by the ailing Gordon Newey, who had commenced his vehicle selling and assembly career in Colwyn Bay, North Wales. He abandoned car manufacture due to ill-health and to the appointment of a Receiver to his business Gordon Newey Ltd in 1921.

The Newey 12/15 "sporting model".

12/15. 1920-22 (prod: n/a). Chassis £595 later £500. S4 1795cc Chapuis-Dornier, cone clutch, three speed gearbox, bevel axle, semi-elliptic suspension. A typical over-priced assembled car though, curiously, its 10/12hp stablemate had a better specification with four forward gears and cost less (£425 as a chassis).

NEW HUDSON

Icknield Street, Birmingham

This bicycle and motor cycle firm made the first of several diminutive four wheelers in 1910 but offered only three wheelers after the war. Motor cycle production ended in 1933 but the name was revived by BSA after the Second World War.

New Hudson 10hp Runabout.

10HP. 1920-24 (prod: n/a). Two-seater 1920 £250, 1923 £195. V2 1250cc to 1922 then MAG V2 IOE 1093cc, dry plate clutch, three speed and reverse gearbox, chain drive. Quarter-elliptic front, semi-elliptic rear suspension (cantilever to 1922). Neat in royal blue, this little car was 10ft 4in long and weighed a little under 8cwt. New Hudson bikes took various speed records at the time with Bert Le Vack, who was also involved with the Swiss MAG factory.

NEW ORLEANS
See Owen

NEW PICK
See Pick

NEWTON

William Street, Salford, Manchester

Newton and Bennett had made the NB car in an Italian factory owned by the company, and had employed R O Harper (see Harper Runabout) as their manager for several years. In 1914 the Italian Government insisted on the name changing to

Newton and in 1916 the factory was sold to Diatto. What the origins of the 1923-25 Newton were is hard to ascertain, though Newton and Bennett were Ceirano concessionaires at this stage and N B Newton ran a design office in Italy and entered a Newton at Brooklands. The Newton does not match the specification of any Ceirano, though the 1923 Diatto Ten shared the same bore with a shorter stroke.

The Newton Ten, 1924.

Newton Ten engine and gearbox.

TEN and TEN SPORTS. 1923-25 (prod: n/a). Chassis £395. S4 DOHC 1086cc 40bhp, cone clutch, in-unit four speed gearbox with centre change, spiral bevel axle, semi-elliptic suspension. Bore and stroke of 60 × 90mm allied to a fixed cylinder head and twin OHC was a very unusual combination. Electric equipment was Bosch and the carburettor a Claudel Hobson. There were four wheel brakes and Rudge-Whitworth wire wheels. Fuel consumption was said to be 45mpg. The sports model had a 7ft 9in instead of 9ft wheelbase.

NOMAD

See Gnome

NORTH-LUCAS

Robin Hood Engineering Works, Putney Vale, London SW15

A truly revolutionary design for 1922 from the pens of Oliver North (ex-Straker-Squire and later with Scammell) and Ralph Lucas (maker of the veteran Lucas Valveless). Built in the home of KLG spark-plugs, the car had aluminium unitary construction, all-independent suspension, and a rear-mounted radial engine. It was so far ahead of its time that neither the public nor potential series producers took up the challenge, and after nearly 100,000 miles in 16 years the prototype was scrapped.

The North-Lucas used a five-cylinder radial engine.

NORTH-LUCAS. 1922 (prod: one). Cost £2500 to make. Radial air-cooled five cylinder (each 300cc SV JAP) mounted horizontally in rear and in-unit above three speed gearbox and worm final drive. Swinging arm dampers with integral coil spring independent suspension. Vanes on the flywheel kept the engine cool and the brakes were inboard mounted at the rear, with universally jointed drive shafts. The boat-shaped riveted aluminium bodywork, by the Chelsea Motor Building Co., had a doped translucent aircraft fabric roof. Tested by *The Motor*, the car was found to have incredibly resilient suspension and to be capable of 60mph.

NORTH STAR

Lee Green, London SE

Like the Edmond and the Swallow this was made by Sir J F Payne-Gallway Brown and Co. Ltd. The

1920 North Star 4hp cyclecar.

NP all-weather four-seater.

North Star and Edmond shared the same manufacturing address, the former being a Blackburne 4hp single cylinder engined cyclecar with Gradua variable belt drive as on Zenith motor cycles. It was available in 1920-21 and cost £159.

NP

Tickford Street, Newport Pagnell, Buckinghamshire

This was the work of coachbuilders Salmons and was made in the factory which has been occupied by Aston-Martin and Lagonda since the mid 1950s. The SLC Co. Ltd (Salmons Light Car Co.) utilised Meadows engines and ceased activity when competition grew too fierce and the cars became unprofitable. NP stood for Newport Pagnell. T B André (see Marlborough) is believed to have had financial links with Salmons.

11.9 and 13.9 (12/16 and 14.22). 1923-25 (prod: 395). Chassis 14/22 1923 £420, 1924 £300. S4 OHV 1796cc and 2120cc Meadows, cone clutch, in-unit four speed Meadows gearbox with right hand change, spiral bevel axle. Semi-elliptic front, cantilever rear suspension. Presumably all cars carried Salmons coachwork, a two-seater on the 14/22 in 1924 costing £375 and other types up to £675. Only 99 engines have been positively identified for SLC in Meadows' sales ledger so output may have been less than the officially quoted figure, or else other makes of engine utilised.

OD

Dunmore, Antrim Road, Belfast, Northern Ireland

Standing for Owner Driver, the 1921 OD was the final version of the Fergus which had appeared in 1915. Because of component shortages Fergus production had been moved to Newark, NJ, USA, to a company with a capital of $200,000. Supply difficulties again halted sales, but the marque existed again briefly, with a six-cylinder car in 1921-22, before becoming an Austin agency. Meanwhile the principal garage, motor agent and bodybuilder in Belfast, J B Ferguson (whose brother Harry Ferguson invented the eponymous tractor in the 1930s) attempted to revive Irish interest in his Fergus project. The name, however, had to be changed as Ferguson was a Rolls-Royce agent and the car was intended to sell in that league. To distance it from the chauffeured Rolls-Royce image, Owner Drivers were to be catered for. The slump of 1921 caused the backers to depart and OD Cars Ltd became an engineering firm and garage. After the Second World War its successors became the principal suppliers of electric hares for greyhound racing.

OD. 1921 (prod: one). Chassis £650. S6 OHC 25.7hp 80bhp, single disc clutch, three speed gearbox, cantilever suspension. Designed by J A McKee of Fergusons, who manufactured most of the parts, the Fergus and OD had a very rigid girder chassis (boxed channel section on the OD) with cantilever

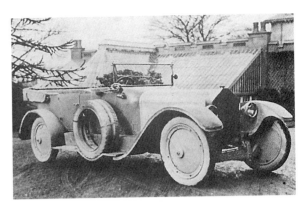

The 1921 OD had an 80bhp straight-six engine.

springs at each corner. There was automatic lubrication of every moving part, electric starting, and the first use of rubber engine mounts. Front wheel brakes were offered on the postwar American version, which had coil ignition, and both types bristled with other advanced features.

OMEGA

Swan Lane, Coventry, Warwickshire

W J Green Ltd of Omega Works made Omega motor cycles from 1920, Green having been works manager of the Premier motor cycle factory, which became Coventry Premier. Singer acquired Coventry Premier and ended production of its three wheeler, though presumably some of this vehicle's features remained familiar to Green when he introduced his own version. This was a year ahead of the rival Coventry-Victor, which no doubt became one of the causes of the Omega's speedy demise. Omega motor cycles also ended in 1927, some having had proprietary engines and some the firm's own.

Omega 8hp three-wheeler, 1925.

8HP. 1925-27 (prod: n/a). Two-seater £95, four-seater £115. V2 SV 980cc JAP, shaft drive, Moss spiral bevel gears driving high and low chain sprockets on either side of rear wheel, quarter-elliptic suspension. A neat little three wheeler with a

dummy radiator when air-cooled – water-cooling was a £10 extra. De Luxe versions had polished aluminium bodies, the standard finish being royal blue. An exhaust valve lifter on a hand grip gave the driver something to hang onto when hand cranking the engine. Front wheel brakes cost £3 extra and *The Light Car and Cyclecar* journalist Harold Hastings, who owned an Omega from new, said that he never encountered another. He dreaded having to mend a rear wheel puncture but on the plus side enjoyed a 60mph top speed.

ORLEANS

See Owen

ORPINGTON

High Street, Orpington, Kent

Smith and Milroy allegedly used the Model T Ford as the basis of their car, though there is little evidence of this in the size of the car or the choice of engine and gearbox. Axle, brakes and steering may have been Model T on the prototype, though in contemporary specifications the spiral bevel axle is specifically described as the firm's own and there is no transverse suspension.

The Orpington 10/12.

10/12. 1920-24 (prod: possibly 200-300). Chassis £395 falling to £200. S4 SV 1505cc Coventry Simplex, cone clutch, three speed Moss gearbox with right hand change, spiral bevel axle. Semi-elliptic front, quarter-elliptic rear suspension. Another uninspiring assembled car that was doomed when Morris began to cut prices. It was marketed as "The Business Man's Light Car".

OVERLAND

Heaton Chapel, Stockport, Manchester

William Letts of Crossley was a friend of the American J N Willys and in December 1919 a major assembly operation for Willys-Overland cars got under way at a former aircraft factory a few miles from the British Ford T factory. Partially completed chassis arrived from Canada and were assembled at Heaton Chapel, jig-built British bodies being fitted on three quarters of them by late 1922. In time only components arrived from Canada and America, and true manufacture took place, incorporating British accessories under the supervision of American foremen. Along with the other Willys models it seems that production peaked in 1927-28, at around 250 cars and 100 commercials per week, though J N Willys had spoken of anticipating 7000 sales in 1920 and 12,500 per annum thereafter.

By August 1928 8000 commercials had been produced, some body press work was taking place and the workforce stood at about 1000. The McKenna duties ensured that a higher proportion of parts were British sourced, and indeed from 1925 there had been an all-British model with Morris Oxford engine, (the others were said to be 70% British and 30% Canadian at this stage). Overland Commercials were known as Manchesters in the late 1920s, and the last profitable year for the group was 1929. Full-scale assembly ended in 1931 and Overland-Crossley (by then making AJS cars as well) collapsed in 1933.

1925 Overland 13.9hp.

13.9. 1925-26 (prod: n/a). Chassis £195, complete £270. S4 SV 1802cc Morris, cork insert clutch in oil, in-unit three speed gearbox, torque tube, spiral bevel axle, quarter-elliptic suspension. Various 18hp Overlands had been assembled from North American parts since 1920 but a combination of import duty and higher road tax (£19 instead of £14) made the Morris-based model expedient. It did not sell as well as expected, probably because the larger models had chassis prices starting at £145. An unusual Overland feature was that chassis came to a point at front and rear because no outer attachment point was needed for the splayed quarter elliptic springs. Four wheel brakes were soon offered.

The Overland Whippet.

WHIPPET. 1926-30 (prod: possibly 25,000). Complete 1927 £198-285, 1930 £210. S4 SV 2387cc 15.6hp, dry plate clutch, in-unit three speed gearbox, spiral bevel axle, semi-elliptic suspension. This one gave Willys-Overland a small enough engine of its own for British tax purposes. Unlike earlier cars it had underslung semi-elliptic springs and four wheel brakes. It was good for 55mph and an optimistic sounding 35mpg. The Whippet became a brand in its own right, and following American 21.6hp sixes in 1925 there were also 2400cc six-cylinder versions from 1927, of which one in 1930 became the Willys-Overland Palatine Six. British output was said to be running at 50 cars per day in 1929, when the four was known as the Superior Whippet and could accelerate 0-40mph in under 20 seconds.

OWEN

Orleans Car Co., Comeragh Road, London W14

A mystery which greater minds than the author's (including the late Michael Sedgwick) have been unable to fathom. E H Owen listed a plethora of models between 1899 and 1935. His premises appear to have been a private house, with no provision for the showroom claimed to have been at 6 Comeragh Road. Press reports in 1921 spoke of a Birmingham factory said to have been making engines, gearboxes, axles and so forth for 20 years.

The Owen of 1920 was a long stroke 20hp four with such abundant torque that only one forward gear was deemed necessary. Its sister, the Owen Dynamic, was a 40hp petrol-electric, and in addition came a range of Orleans 10, 15 and 20hp models (the latter being listed through the decade).

In 1921 the Owen itself became a 7.6-litre V8 costing more than a Silver Ghost or Napier. The only magazine photograph of its betrays an uncanny resemblance to the American Kenworthy, and this car was listed to 1928, and then to 1935 by Stone and Cox, which mysteriously asserted that spares in the later 1930s were avail-

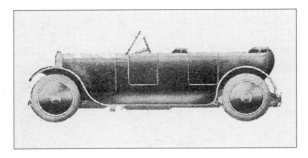

The 20hp New Orleans listed by Owen in 1920 at £695 with 3-litre engine and "infinitely variable" (Entz?) transmission.

able from T A Jenner of Richmond Road, Twickenham.

It has been suggested that E H Owen was a car enthusiast who hoodwinked the motoring press with his "dream cars", but this is hardly consistent with the availability of spares. Lots of chassis code letter and numbers were quoted but the only consecutive ones suggest that 70 10hp and 130 15hp models were made in 1922, plus 200 V8 types between 1922 and 1929, at which point the chassis cost £1775.

The early mention of petrol-electric transmission makes one wonder if there was some connection with the American Owen Magnetic car, which inspired the Magnetic and one model of British Ensign. Likewise, Orleans perhaps implies some association with the New Orleans made before the First World War in the town that saw the end of the Owen mystery, Twickenham.

PALLADIUM

Felsham Road, Putney, London SW

Like McCurd, this grew from a successful motor sales business. John Ross McMahon in 1912 began to assemble cars from French components. Heavy trucks and aero engines were made during the Great War, and then in 1919 came an interesting but short-lived cyclecar. Larger cars with Dorman engines followed in 1922 alongside the commercials, but the firm was in trouble by 1925. It moved to Premier Place off Putney High Street, and there offered British Anzani 1½-litre engined New Victory and Empire models without success. Bodybuilder E C Gordon England is said to have been behind this revival and he used the premises for a time for his own business before moving out to Wembley. Also at Premier Place was the maker of Surrey cars, some of whose models seem to have been the same as Palladiums.

10HP. 1919-20 (prod: few). Two-seater 265 guineas. HO2 1.3 litre air-cooled, friction disc variable transmission, chain drive, differential-less

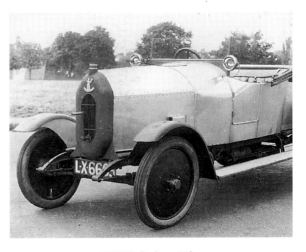

1919 Palladium 10hp.

axle, semi-elliptic suspension. A neat little car with forced-draft fan cooling from an air intake in the dummy radiator. The makers claimed a 45mph top speed and up to 40mpg. Truck sales boomed briefly, so this model was only pursued half-heartedly.

12hp Palladium on the 1922 Scottish Light Car Trial.

12. 1922-25 (prod: 280). Chassis from 298 guineas. S4 SV 1496cc Dorman, plate clutch, in-unit four speed gearbox (three on Speed Model), spiral bevel axle, semi-elliptic suspension. By now truck sales had collapsed and Palladium made a more determined effort to get back into the car field. The Touring and Victory 1½-litre models had attractive looks, and front wheel brakes were available as early as 1923. 60mph and 35mpg were claimed for the Victory sports tourer. A Meadows 1800cc model was listed but possibly only one was built. As noted above, an attempt to revive the marque in 1925 came to nothing. The 1922 Scottish Trial model shown was said to be well sprung and have surplus power, with no inclination to boil and a "great future". Victory trials cars sometimes had four white overalled occupants to emphasise four seats, four gears and four wheel brakes.

PALM, PALMERSTON

Palmerston Road, Boscombe, Hampshire

The Palmerston Engineering Works of Messrs Goddard Lawrence and Fish (latterly Palmcars Ltd) made the Coventry Victor 5-7hp engined Palmerston light car in 1920-21 and the 9hp Palm in 1922-23. The cars had three speed gearboxes, shaft drive to a bevel axle, and semi-elliptic suspension. Olympic Aeros and Autos of Boscombe had the unenviable task of trying to sell a two-seater with outdated polished brass radiator, acetylene lamps and fittings, for £275 in 1921 and £250 in 1923.

The Coventry Victor 5-7hp engined Palmerston light car.

PARNACOTT, PARNACAR

Penge Lane, Penge, Surrey

A E Parnacott built a prototype car in 1913 with a 3½hp FN motor cycle engine, returning to the fray in 1920 with a 1½-litre water-cooled flat twin (in-line vertical twin also mentioned) which also seems to have got no further than the prototype stage. It was intended to be sold for £300 and had shaft drive and the unusual feature of all-round independent suspension. There was a multi-plate clutch and foot lever starting.

The Parnacott 12/20.

PAYDELL

The Hyde, Hendon, London NW9

Paydell Engineering's 2120cc OHV car was only made in 1924. It had a Meadows in-unit four speed gearbox, which probably gives a clue to the identity of the engine maker. The spiral bevel axle was by Wrigley and there was a cone clutch, torque tube and cantilever rear suspension (semi-elliptic at the front). Hobdell, Way and Co. of Church Street, London E1 were also listed as makers, but were more likely the sales outlet. At a chassis price of £450, sales of this 13.9hp assembled car cannot have been helped by the availability of a complete 13.9hp Morris from £300, and Paydell was dead by September 1924.

PAYZE

Cookham, Berkshire

RAF Captain A Payze started the Payze Light Car Company in 1920 in the sleepy Thamesside village not far from the homes of HE and GWK cars. His car was technically conventional, with a Coventry Simplex 1498cc 10.5hp engine, cone clutch, three speed gearbox, spiral bevel axle and semi-elliptic front, three-quarter elliptic rear suspension. Where it differed from others was in having a three-seater arrangement under the hood, with access to the single back seat through a gap between the front seats. The radiator was of Rolls-Royce shape but this did not help to sell the over-priced £450 car, which lasted no longer than 1921.

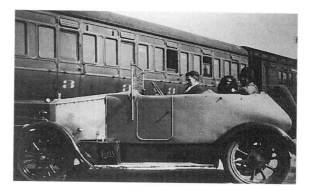

1921 Payze 10hp.

PERFEX

Holdenhurst Road, Bournemouth, Dorset

Like the Morriss-London and London-Pullman this was the British version of an American make. It had a London headquarters in Holborn and the directors were two members of the family that became famous for its Arnott supercharger, fitted to such cars as the 1930s Atalanta. The original Perfex, from Los Angeles, was made up to 1914, and its English revival used the same unusual proprietary engine, a Golden, Belknap and Schwartz, as also found in the London-Pullman.

The 22.5hp Perfex.

22.5. 1920-21 (prod: few). Chassis £515, saloon £975. S4 SV 3062cc, cone clutch, three speed gearbox, bevel axle. Semi-elliptic front, cantilever rear suspension. The car had Autolite electrics, coil ignition and nickel plating; it was also over-priced and expensive to tax even for the brief postwar boom. Surviving artwork of an intended advertisement reports that a limited number of £850 coupés could be supplied for early delivery. Despite the London address of directors S H and A T Arnott, the London agents were quoted as the Atom Motor Co. of St James's Street.

PHOENIX

Letchworth, Hertfordshire

An old established London motor firm which moved out to the rural delights of Letchworth Garden City in 1911. During the Great War it was approached by Monsieur Citroën of Minerva to make an 18hp model for him whilst his own factory was under German occupation. This came to nothing, though it gave Phoenix the idea for a car of this size, which appeared in 1921 based on the Arrol-Johnston Victory. It was not a success and very few were built (possibly only one, though parts for hundreds were allegedly ordered and in some cases used up in the Ascot later to be made in the Phoenix factory). More successful was a revival of the pre-war 11.9, but an interesting unitary construction 8hp car from chief engineer Albert Bowyer-Lowe was not pursued and he left to make the Foster.

A 1922 Phoenix 11.9hp with front mounted radiator on a trial.

1920 Phoenix 11.9hp with scuttle mounted radiator.

11.9. 1919-22 (prod: about 400). Chassis 1919 £340, 1921 £420. S4 SV 1496cc, metal cone clutch in oil, three speed gearbox, worm axle, semi-elliptic suspension. One of the last British cars to be built with a scuttle-mounted radiator – useful for keeping the car's occupants warm and the engine accessible – it was designed by Bowyer-Lowe in 1912 and made at the rate of seven per week by the 150-strong workforce until war intervened. Most parts were made in-house and construction was massive and heavy, but the car was at least strong and reliable. A conventional front-mounted radiator was adopted for the last year and both types are shown.

The Phoenix 12/25.

12/25. 1922-25 (prod: 168). Chassis £310, tourer £395. S4 OHV 1795cc Meadows, cone clutch, in-unit four speed Meadows gearbox with right hand change, Timken spiral bevel axle, semi-elliptic suspension. When announcing this modern model *The Motor* commented: "Memory harks back to days of strange cars and stranger motor cycles", and went on to imply that until then the Phoenix had been left behind. The car was supplied as a tourer, with very thorough weather equipment incorporating glass windows that folded down and also opened with the doors. The firm went into liquidation in 1924 but limped on for a while, latterly making nine Meadows engined six-cylinder 18/45 cars in 1924-25. One last four-cylinder model was made in 1926, and then the flame went out at Phoenix.

PICK

Great North Road, Stamford, Lincolnshire

A country garage and engineering firm that made cars from 1898 in small numbers – the peak before the Great War seems to have been 50 in a year. In 1922 a final attempt to sell Pick cars resulted in a 3.6-litre model rated at 22.5hp. It had some similarity, including a 95mm bore, with the Golden, Belknap and Schwartz engines found in the London-Pullman and Perfex, though 95mm

was also the bore of the pre-war New Pick car, which is believed to have had a home-produced engine (engine makers and iron founders Blackstone and Co. Ltd existed at Stamford and could have been involved). In 1925 Jack Pick turned his back on the motor trade and became a vegetable grower and greengrocer. Presumably he used a Pick 30hp tractor – a product offered 1919-24.

1924 Pick 22.5hp saloon.

22/45 and 22.5hp. 1923-25 (prod: few). £265-£450 complete. S4 SV 3.6 litres, cone clutch, separate three speed gearbox with right hand change, worm axle, semi-elliptic suspension. As noted above this car could have had American origins, a theory supported by the low price. The "Scorching" sports model (literally, one imagines, judging by its exposed exhaust pipe) was capable of 60mph (40mph at 1000rpm) and 30mpg. A bizarre 1924 advertisement is shown.

PICKNELL

Penrith Road, Basingstoke, Hampshire

In 1919 *The Model Engineer* magazine published a detailed account for home handymen on how to

The Picknell car with Douglas Picknell at the wheel.

construct a cyclecar. The starting point was plans based on the D. Ultra car made in Clapham 1914-16 by Harold E Dew (also responsible for the contemporary Dewcar and Victor). No doubt these home made cars appeared under several different names, one being the Picknell made by Douglas Picknell in his bedroom between 1919 and 1922. It used a Fafnir 7.7hp vee-twin with friction transmission and chain drive, and gave good service for seven years.

PLYMOUTH
See Chrysler

PONTIAC
See Chevrolet

POMEROY
Named after Laurence Pomeroy of Daimler Double Six fame, this was in fact a short-lived American car from the period when he was promoting the use of aluminium to the motor industry in the USA in the early 1920s.

PRINCEPS
A friction drive light car of uncertain origin in 1920 with Coventry Simplex four-cylinder sidevalve engine. G R Doyle's *World's Automobiles 1931* listed an earlier car with this name made in Nottingham.

The four-cylinder Princeps, 1920.

PRINCESS
Streatham Hill, London SW2

As the telegraphic address Jayemshoka confirmed, the Streatham Engineering Co. Ltd made shock absorbers. In 1923 only it offered an 1100cc vee-twin air-cooled cyclecar with coil ignition, multi-

plate clutch, three speed gearbox, worm axle and quarter-elliptic suspension for £225. Despite a reduction to £175 and an invitation to compare it with any car up to £400 few were sold.

The 9/20hp Princess 3/4-seater.

PROGRESS
See Seal

PULLINGER
Peckham, London SE and Putney, London SW

Whether Pullinger Engineering, with its registered office at 52 Holborn Viaduct EC1 and two works as above, was connected with T C Pullinger, originally of Sunbeam and then Arrol-Johnston, is unclear. In 1919 the "Speedy Two-Seater" was listed at 110 guineas, and was a streamlined two-seater capable of 60mpg fuel consumption. It had an 8hp air-cooled vee-twin, cone clutch, two speed and reverse gearbox, belt final drive and quarter elliptic suspension. Though advertised it did not make it into most sales guides. See also Speedy.

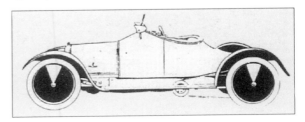

The Pullinger "Speedy Two-Seater".

PULLMAN

See London-Pullman

PUTOL

London Road, Sheffield

This 1922 car from the Tolputt Co. appears to have progressed no further than the prototype stage.

RALEIGH

Lenton, Nottingham

Though well known for its three wheelers in the 1930s this famous bicycle firm got no further in our period than a flat-twin engined four wheel prototype in 1922, following a few experimental cyclecars in the Great War period.

R & B (REABA)

Kings Road, Tyseley, Birmingham

After working for Grahame-White and Enfield-Allday, A C "Gus" Bertelli joined Woolf Barnato (see Bentley) and made three Bertelli sleeve-valve racing cars based on Enfield-Allday chassis at Barnato's Lingfield mansion. The cars were never fully developed as millionaire Barnato returned to America on the election of the 1923 Labour Government and Bertelli joined ex-Armstrong Siddeley designer W S Renwick. Renwick and Bertelli built one example of the 1781cc OHC R & B, or Reaba, better known as Buzz Box, but were then snapped up, along with their new design, by the new backers of Aston Martin, becoming directors of that firm in 1926. Bodywork was by Gus Bertelli's brother Enrico, who did similar work for Aston Martin.

The R & B, or Reaba, was better known as Buzz Box.

REEVES RADIAL

See Enfield-Allday

RENAULT

Westfields Road, Acton, London W3

This French firm had sold vehicles in London since around 1900 and formed a British company in December 1904. It became an important supplier of taxis, notably to the London Cab trade. From Seagrave Road, West Brompton it supplied and serviced Renault vehicles and aero engines in the Great War, and most vehicles thereafter were bodied locally. In 1926, taking a leaf from Citroën's book at Slough, Renault acquired a former aircraft factory for expansion. New premises were added alongside it at Acton where limited assembly took place in order to reduce the effects of the increased McKenna import duties levied from July 1925. From 1927 to 1932 British wheels, lamps, upholstery and other items were used and the cars were painted in the Acton factory. Further British assembly took place there from 1934 to 1939 and again from 1949 to 1960. Acton is still the HQ of Renault in Britain.

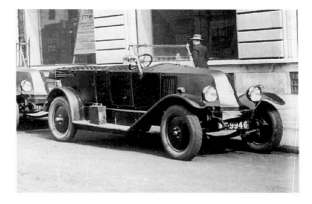

A typical mid-1920s Renault.

Early types (no British production figures available). All sidevalve, three speed gearboxes, spiral bevel axles and semi-elliptic front and transverse rear suspension. Four wheel brakes had been standardised on the 13.9 as early as 1923 and soon spread to the rest. In 1926 these included 8.3, 13.9, 17.9, 26.9 and 45hp types. The 8.3 cost £219 as a tourer in 1926 and gave 50mph and 45mpg. The smaller models (the 8.3 was called 6CV in France) had round badges instead of the angular badges of the cars above 15CV from 1926.

VIVASIX. 1928-32 (prod: n/a) Price falling from £330 for chassis to £269 for complete tourer. S6 SV 3189cc 21hp (16CV French), three speed gearbox in-unit with spiral bevel rear axle. Semi-elliptic front suspension, cantilever and transverse at rear. With the opening of the Acton factory all cars were tested on a rolling road for pre-delivery adjust-

A 21hp Renault Vivasix outside the Acton factory.

ments. 1927 saw the arrival of the Monasix, a 1474cc 12.5hp six, and shown outside the Acton factory is its bigger 21hp sister, bearing its British Vivasix Renault Ltd badge and the last traces of the sloping nose (the scuttle radiator lasted on some models to the end of the decade). 21 to 45hp models also had an oil cooler.

RESTELLI

Lawrence Pountney Hill, London EC

This was an Italian car made 1920-23 in Milan, but in 1923 it was claimed that manufacture was being undertaken by Restelli Patents Ltd at the above London address. Whether some degree of assembly of Italian parts took place cannot be ascertained. Of principal interest in a British context is that Antonio Lago used a Restelli in trials here. Lago was of course later involved with Sunbeam-Talbot-Darracq and ultimately acquired the latter firm's French factory.

10.8. 1923 (prod: n/a). Complete £450. S4 OHC or DOHC 1500cc 12/15hp, dry plate clutch, four speed gearbox, spiral bevel axle, semi elliptic suspension. This unusual sports car was of chassisless construction, with engine, gearbox and axle in-unit and attached to sprung trunnions. A F Lago of High Holborn was concessionaire and enthusiastic test driver. Some parts, such as Sankey detachable wheels, were British, though electrics were by Bosch.

RHODE

Blythswood Road, Tyseley, Birmingham/ Webb Lane, Hall Green, Birmingham

F W Mead and T W Deakin were motor cycle component suppliers who were particularly successful with their Canoelet sidecars. Occasional light car experiments were tried and in 1921 they launched the Rhode, named in honour of Cecil Rhodes, founder of Rhodesia. This was unusual in having an overhead camshaft engine (made by Rhode) and for being a family car of deliberately sporting type. The rather crude rocker gear was lubricated by a splash arrangement in the absence of an oil pump. 5-600 cars per year were made in the peak early years and, though chassis numbers ultimately reached 5000, more like half that number were probably produced. These early Rhodes were lively and noisy, and more refined pushrod OHV models joined them in 1926, by which time the firm was in financial difficulties. It was bought in 1928-29 by H B Denley, the firm's old test driver, whose business was later to acquire the remnants of Star. Mead then made trailervans before joining Morris-Commercial, and his son later offered coachwork on a number of early post-Second World War cars.

The 1925 Rhode 11/30 "Sportsman's" with curiously angled windscreen.

becoming the 10.8 again in 1926 when pushrod OHV was adopted. Frames of most if not all had the channel section facing outwards, as on the 1925 "Sportsman's" shown.

Rhode 9.5hp.

9.5. 1921-24 (prod: approx 1000). Tourer 1921 £275, 1924 £189. S4 OHC 1087cc, plate clutch, three speed centre-change Wrigley gearbox, spiral bevel axle (initially without differential), quarter-elliptic suspension. Often sold as the original "Occasional four" because there was a small compartment for passenger or luggage under the hood instead of exposed in the "dickey". There was also space for a horizontal spare wheel under the seat. This body style became the Norwood in 1923, when the Rhode was said to be capable of 45-50mph and 35-45mpg. A weight of only 12cwt gave it a lively performance.

10.8, 11/30, 10/30. 1924-30 (prod: approx 1500). Chassis £200, £173 from 1927. S4 OHC (OHV on later 10.8) 1232cc, plate clutch, in-unit four speed gearbox, torque tube, spiral bevel axle. Quarter-elliptic suspension, later semi-elliptic front. Initially the 10.8 was simply a larger-engined version of the 9.5 but in 1925 came the 11/30 with Rhode's own gearbox (Wrigley had been bought by Morris in 1923), revised suspension and powerful four wheel brakes. The cheapest version was called the 11,

Rhode Hawk fabric saloon, 1928.

An artist's impression of the Rhode Hawk saloon.

HAWK. 1928-35 (prod: possibly 50). Fabric saloon 1928 £285, 1930 £335. S4 OHC 1232cc, plate clutch, in-unit four speed gearbox, torque tube, spiral bevel axle. Semi-elliptic front, quarter-elliptic rear suspension. The Hawk was the final version of the 10.8, wearing the latest style of fabric saloon body complete with trendy pram irons and porthole windows in the rear quarters. The engine returned to OHC, developing 37bhp, and there was a longer chassis and revised suspension. When production moved to Hall Green in 1929 there appears to have been no engine-making facility, and six 1½-litre Meadows engines were acquired. Though listed to 1935, it seems unlikely that any Hawks were built after 1930.

RICHARDSON

Finbat Works, Aizlewood Road, Sheffield, Yorkshire

Brothers Charles and Ebenezer Richardson were pioneers of children's scooters and amongst the first toy makers to produce model aircraft. Booming business led Finbat Toys to open a new factory at the above address in 1914. After war work, and making toy guns, the brothers launched the Richardson car in 1919. Over 100 men were employed, but the moulders' strike damaged sales and bankruptcy followed in 1922. Charles became a property magnate but Ebenezer sold ice cream before becoming a lathe operator.

The Richardson cyclecar.

8 or 10HP. 1919-22 (prod: approx 600). From £200 complete. V2 air-cooled 1090cc Precision or 980cc JAP, shaft drive to cork lined friction disc, thence chain (initially belt) to back axle without differential, semi-elliptic suspension. Typical cyclecar which gained slightly more conventional looks when a nickel plated vertical dummy radiator was adopted in 1921.

RILEY

Foleshill, Coventry

Yet another Coventry firm with roots in textile machinery and bicycles. Riley's first powered vehicle came in 1899 and the company became a very important supplier of detachable wire wheels (around 200 firms used them in the teens). Members of the Riley family ran different Riley companies, the Riley Engine Co. being responsible for the 17/30 and for making early examples of the famous Nine for Riley (Coventry) Ltd. This car was considered by LTC Rolt to be the most important landmark in automobile history during the 1920s, and it turned Riley into a front runner. Later in the 1930s Riley joined the burgeoning Morris empire.

Riley 17/30 on wedding duty.

17/30. 1913-22 (prod: approx 6 postwar). S4 SV 2951cc 18.2hp RAC, cone clutch, four speed gearbox (three speed pre-1914), worm axle. Semi-elliptic front, ¾-elliptic rear suspension. "As old as the industry, as modern as the hour" was a famous Riley slogan first used in 1920, though this car was archaic, having been designed by Harry Rush for the Riley Engine Co. of Castle Works, Aldbourne Road, Coventry, before the war. It lost its circular radiator in postwar guise. It was Riley's first in-line four-cylinder car and its largest. The car was listed to 1926 but production ended in 1921-22. Naturally there were Riley detachable wire wheels from the Riley Cycle Co., which had become Riley (Coventry) Ltd. in 1912, plus the pioneering Riley "silent third" gearbox. This had constant mesh top and third with helically cut gears in third – a feature of subsequent Rileys.

10.8, ELEVEN, 11/40. 1919-24 (prod: 3300). Chassis £395 falling to £300. S4 inclined SV 1498cc 35bhp, cone clutch in oil (dry plate from 1925), four speed gearbox with central change (right hand optional), spiral bevel axle, semi-elliptic suspension. This made one of the earliest uses of self-lubricating bushes and had only six grease nipples. Unlike previous cars designed by the Riley family, the Eleven was created by Harry Rush, the Works Manager also involved in the 17/30, and was attractive and beautifully made. The engine had a detachable head from the outset and there were four wheel brakes from 1925. Several sporting variants were offered including the well-known Redwing.

Four-seater Riley 11hp.

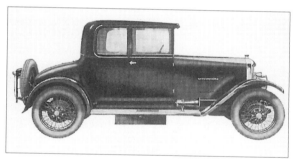

Riley Twelve Wentworth coupé.

The Riley Nine Monaco saloon.

11.9, TWELVE. 1925-28 (prod: 2300). Chassis £300. S4 SV 1645cc 42bhp, cone clutch in oil (soon dry plate), four speed gearbox with optional right hand change, spiral bevel axle, semi-elliptic suspension. Confusingly, for 1925 this enlarged engine was still called 11/40 but now had a bigger chassis and front wheel brakes. Various factory body styles were offered, often made by Midland Motor Body (another Riley family owned firm). In 1927 these included the Chatsworth steel saloon, the Wentworth coupé and the Lulworth fabric saloon, the latter reminiscent of the Nine Monaco. The Lulworth was actually made by a local trade coachbuilder named Hancock and Warman Ltd. To combat the OHV Nine, later cars had higher compression Ricardo "swirl" heads.

NINE. 1926-37 (prod: to October 1930 approx 6000). 1928 Monaco saloon from £298, tourer £280. S4 OHV 1087cc, single plate clutch, in-unit four speed gearbox, torque tube, spiral bevel axle, semi-elliptic suspension. "The Wonder Car" was designed by Stanley and Percy Riley in 1925, C H Leek being General Manager in charge of getting the immortal Nine into production. He later moved to Lea Francis, whose 1930s engine was closely based on the Riley. The PR (Percy Riley) cylinder head bristled with novelties including hemispherical combustion chambers, its inclined valves worked by short pushrods from high-mounted camshafts on either side. 60mph and up to 40mpg were a remarkable combination in a cheap 1100cc car and bring back happy memories of the author's first vintage car.

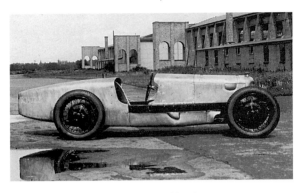

Riley 9hp Brooklands.

BROOKLANDS. 1927-31 (prod: about 100). Complete 1928 £395, 1930 £420. S4 OHV 1087cc twin carburettor approx 50bhp, plate clutch, in-unit four speed gearbox with centre change (right hand on prototypes), torque tube, spiral bevel axle, semi-elliptic suspension. J G Parry Thomas (see Leyland) developed sports-racing versions of the Nine, and Reid Railton (see Arab) carried on the work after Thomas' tragic death in March 1927. These highly competitive cars were offered for sale in 1927 and were assembled at first by Thomson and Taylor at Brooklands. The first of many racing victories was in 1927 in the hands of Railton, who averaged 91.37mph at Brooklands.

Riley Six, c1928.

SIX. 1928-37 (prod: approx 500 to October 1932). Complete 1929 £455. S6 OHV 1633cc 50bhp, plate clutch, four speed gearbox, torque tube, spiral bevel axle, semi-elliptic suspension. This was effectively a Nine with two additional cylinders. The Nine had a two-bearing crank and the Six had a third in the middle which was water-cooled and, if not separately drained, could wreck the block after frost. It was launched as the 14/50 Six, often with Stelvio Weymann type coachwork, though also as a tourer or Deauville coachbuilt saloon by Hancock and Warman. 62mph and 20mpg were achievable, and there was the usual "Silent Third" gearbox with optional freewheel device.

RLC

Priory Road, Hornsey, London N8

Priory Road was the London address of Argyll, which had been bought by its manager A H Lindsay. He was the L of the RLC, a car also known as the Rubury-Lindsay. The R was Capt J M Rubury, former chief designer at Sheffield-Simplex and before that with Argyll, where he had worked on Rubury four wheel brakes.

10.8. 1920-21 (prod: possibly only one). Chassis £250, two-seater £315. Three-cylinder radial OHV 1230cc air-cooled, serrated aluminium cone clutch, three speed gearbox, bevel axle, semi-cantilever suspension. What semi-cantilever was unless semi-elliptic was not explained. There is some suggestion that the 1920 London Show car was built and that the whole design was then sold to France, where it became the basis of the Lafitte (a car in which A G Grice of GWK later had some involvement).

RMC

See Seabrook

ROB ROY

Shettleston, Glasgow

Hugh Kennedy had made Kennedy and Ailsa cars in veteran times, had worked with T C Pullinger (see Arrol-Johnston) and had run the first Scottish Ford agency in 1909. After the war he ran the Koh-i-noor Works (named after the famous diamond) at Shettleston, making engines for Kingsbury. His 8/10hp flat-twin Rob Roy (a character from the pen of Sir Walter Scott) was based on the Kingsbury and used the same engine, whilst the 10/12 employed Coventry Climax and the 12/20 an engine by Dorman. All were sold in competition with the Kingsbury by United Transport of Vauxhall Bridge Road, London.

The flat-twin engined Rob Roy 8/10, 1922.

8/10, 10/12, 12/20. 1922-26 (prod: 240 numbers allocated first year – possibly 500 in total). 8/10

see Kingsbury, 10 and 12 S4 SV 1248cc and 1491cc, all cone clutch, in-unit three speed gearbox, torque tube, Wrigley bevel axle, quarter-elliptic suspension. The four-seater tourer versions of each model in 1924 cost respectively £210, £230 and £295. From 1925 the company was run by liquidator W Duncan. The firm's telegraphic address of Minervanyt is puzzling, because there is no obvious connection with the Minerva Knight engined Belgian luxury cars that were popular in Britain at the time. However, it may be a legacy from Kennedy's garage interests.

10/22hp Roger two-seater, 1924.

ROGER

St George's Parade, Wolverhampton

Thomas Rogers and Co. Ltd introduced a friction driven Eleven in 1920 but in 1923 added a model with conventional gearbox. The cars were sold in London through the Ogle Motor Co. of Ogle Street, W1, and chassis numbers had reached only 109 in 1923. Chassis and many of the mechanical components came from Turner.

10/22, ELEVEN. 1920-24 (prod: under 200). Two-seater 1922 £245, 1924 £185. S4 SV 1370cc Coventry Climax, friction transmission to Meadows chain drive axle (optional Meadows three speed gearbox and Meadows bevel axle from 1923). **Semi-elliptic front, quarter-elliptic rear suspension.** Leather upholstery, royal blue paintwork and disc wheels were about the only distinguishing features of this assembled car, which didn't stand a chance against the falling prices of Clyno up the road. A self-starter was £13 optional extra and the car had exposed pinion and quadrant steering.

ROLLS-ROYCE

Nightingale Road, Derby

Quickly dubbed by the press "The Best Car in the World", the 40/50 was Henry Royce's masterpiece. His entrepreneurial partner, the Hon.

Rolls-Royce 40/50 Silver Ghost, a late example with front wheel brakes.

Charles Rolls, died in a flying accident in 1910 and Royce with Claude Johnson guided the company through the 1920s, adding a smaller car to suit the new breed of owner driver. An output of around 10,000 cars in the decade must have been the envy of many a rival. Aero engines and chassis for staff and armoured cars were specialities in the Great War. Many of the latter were rebodied after the War, the 40/50 being virtually impossible to wear out. All pre-1940s Rolls-Royce cars have bodywork by specialist coachbuilders and some very fine styles were adopted in the 1920s as well as some magnificently appointed formal bodies.

40/50 SILVER GHOST. 1906-25 (prod: 6173, plus 1703 in USA). S6 SV 7428cc 48.6hp Treasury rating, cone clutch, separate four speed gearbox with right hand change, torque tube, spiral bevel axle. Semi-elliptic front, cantilever rear suspension. Progressively modernised over its long life, the Silver Ghost (as the model became known after the 1907 demonstrator of that name) gained electric lighting and starting in 1919, a starting carburettor and twin ignition in 1921, and four wheel brakes in 1924. Virtually everything was made by Rolls-Royce, though the brake servo had actually been invented by Hispano-Suiza. The car offered unbelievable levels of silence, refinement and comfort, and at Brooklands in 1911 one was even timed at 101.8mph with streamlined single-seat bodywork! (See picture on previous page.)

Rolls-Royce Twenty with Mann Egerton saloon body.

TWENTY. 1922-29 (prod: 2940). Chassis £1100 and £1185 in last two years. S6 OHV 3127cc, plate clutch, in-unit three speed gearbox with central change, from 1925 four speed right hand change, torque tube, spiral bevel axle, semi-elliptic suspension. A big seller compared with other handbuilt cars, especially when its high price is considered, the Twenty was intended for owner drivers, though many were chauffeur driven. Lots of amendments were made during the decade, not least the axeing of the "new-fangled" centre gearchange. Four wheel

servo brakes were adopted in 1924, and horizontal radiator shutters, initially enamelled and then nickelled, gave way to vertical shutters to give a closer family resemblance to the New Phantom. Here were all the attributes of the big cars in a model that was still bigger and better than most.

1928 Rolls-Royce 40/50 New Phantom with "saloon limousine" body by Barker.

40/50 NEW PHANTOM. 1925-29 (prod: 2212, plus 1241 in USA). Chassis £1850. S6 OHV 7668cc 43.3hp Treasury rating, plate clutch, in-unit four speed gearbox with right hand change, torque tube, spiral bevel axle. Semi-elliptic front, cantilever rear suspension. This model had a bi-bloc engine unlike the Twenty's monobloc but with similar pushrod OHV, and it incurred less tax than the Silver Ghost despite an increase in capacity. There were four wheel brakes with the usual R-R mechanical servo, and friction shock absorbers to begin with, but, as on the other models, the hydraulic type was soon adopted. The American cars were unknown here, but unlike the Springfield Ghost they differed in many ways, not least in having a centre change and left hand drive. The American factory ceased production in 1931, making the New Phantom long after it had been discontinued in Britain.

40/50 PHANTOM II, 1929-35 (prod: 1767). Chassis £1850. S6 OHV 7668cc 43.3hp, plate clutch, in-unit four speed gearbox with right hand change, hypoid bevel axle, semi-elliptic suspension. The New Phantom had incorporated a new engine looking for a new chassis, which it got with the PII. The engine had the same aluminium cylinder head as used from 1928 on its predecessor (conveniently known as the PI after the PII arrived). This was a powerful car (R-R did not disclose bhp) capable of 90mph. 21 inch wheels shrank to 20 inches in 1930 as part of a modernisation process that saw partial synchromesh in 1932 and more than fifty other modifications.

20/25. 1929-36 (prod: 3827). Chassis £1185. S6 OHV 3699cc 25.3hp Treasury rating, plate clutch,

1930 Rolls-Royce Phantom II.

Rolls-Royce 20/25.

in-unit four speed gearbox, spiral bevel axle, semi-elliptic suspension. As sales of the big Phantom slowed in the Depression so the "Baby Rolls" blossomed. Owners now did more of their own driving and appreciated the 20/25's enlarged engine, which offered remarkable flexibility and silence with a top speed of about 75mph. As with all Rolls-Royces of the period, the coachwork fitted can be almost an insult to the beautiful engineering, and some dire styles were perpetrated on this chassis.

ROVER

West Orchard, Coventry and Tyseley, Birmingham

Safety bicycle pioneers (they discarded two wheelers in 1925) and important producers of cars from 1904, Rover spent the Great War making motor cycles, staff cars to Sunbeam design, Maudslay lorries and ammunition. They adopted a former munitions factory at Tyseley to make the new Eight but continued manufacture at Coventry with revived pre-war designs by Owen Clegg. Rover's total output averaged about 5000 cars per year from a workforce of 3500, but the firm frequently made losses. A director at this time was Alexander Craig – see Maudslay. Two steps in the right direction were the appointment of S B Wilks from Hillman in 1929 and the offer of two-year guarantees. Wilks reorganised the firm to create one of the most important makers of competitively priced, above-average cars for professionals and their families. He became managing director in 1933 and was joined by his brother Maurice, though a departure to the new Rootes Group was publicity manager Dudley Noble, who since 1923 had been responsible for several publicity stunts by Rover cars, culminating in the celebrated 750-mile dash to beat the Blue Train.

14hp Rover 4/5-seater, 1924.

TWELVE, 14. 1919-23, 1924 (prod: approx 13,000 in total, perhaps 8000 postwar). Chassis 1919 £600, 1923 £415. S4 SV 2297cc, plate clutch, three speed gearbox, (four available on 14), worm axle, semi-elliptic suspension. This solid and reliable car first appeared in 1912 and almost 2000 had been made in 1914. It was designed by Owen Clegg from Wolseley, who left afterwards to prepare rather similar models for Darracq. The monobloc engine gained a detachable head and electric starting in 1919. The 14 was virtually the same car making better use of the 13.9hp Treasury rating and actually developed 40bhp. 50mph and 25mpg were available on both models.

The Rover Eight.

EIGHT. 1919-25 (prod: 17,700). Two-seater 1919 £230, 1925 £139. HO2 SV 998cc (from late 1923 1135cc) air-cooled, disc clutch, three speed gearbox, worm axle, quarter-elliptic suspension. A much loved little buzzbox whose detachable cylinder heads glowed through scoops in the bonnet sides, the Eight was designed by Jack Sangster, who left to make a similar car for Ariel in 1922 and was later Chairman of BSA. 45mph and 45mpg were possible from the 13bhp (later 18bhp) on tap. Clare's Motor spares broke up over 300 to provide cheap

secondhand parts to keep Eights on the road in later life. In a Midlands ballot 26,000 placed Rover ahead of 40 other makes of car in 1922.

1927 Rover 9/20 saloon.

9/20. 1924-27 (prod: 13,000). Complete from £175. S4 OHV 1075cc, plate clutch, in-unit three speed gearbox with centre change, worm axle, quarter-elliptic suspension (semi-elliptic front on Super from late 1925). A 1926 RAC Trial to discover how far a 9/20 could travel on £5 worth fuel and oil discovered that 2007 miles was the answer, at a public road average of 19.9mph and 40.9mpg. This car was a more sophisticated successor to the Eight with a water-cooled four-cylinder engine. A Super version from late 1925 had a wider chassis with revised suspension and four wheel brakes. Roughly the last 1000 cars had a similar engine to the 10/25, and a pointed-tail sports model was available at the same time for £220.

A 1925 Rover 14/45 coachbuilt saloon, priced at £760.

14/45, 16/50. 1925-27, 1927-28 (prod: approx 4000). Chassis £455 falling to £385. S4 OHV, 2136cc, 2425cc, plate clutch (in oil on 16/50), in-unit four speed gearbox, torque tube, spiral bevel axle, semi-elliptic suspension. Alexander Craig, a director of both Maudslay and Rover, persuaded his friend Peter Poppe (of the former White and Poppe engine and carburettor firm) to design these technically interesting cars, in which the high-camshaft

1929 Rover Light Six Sportsman's saloon.

engine, clutch, gearbox and steering gear were all in-unit. They had hemispherical combustion chambers with inclined valves, and a 100mph 90bhp racing version called Odin was built for test purposes. A 14/45 won a Dewar Trophy on an RAC test that included 50 consecutive ascents of the Bwlch-y-Groes Pass. Many 14/45s were fitted with 16/50 engines but retained their old engine numbers. It is believed that 2778 of the former type and 1364 of the latter were built.

The 2 litre came with all manner of body styles, often with Weymann type coachwork. A shallower ribbon radiator with less pronounced Viking shield came in August 1929 on the Light Six version, followed by a slightly more dished design with centre strip for 1931. This was also seen on the Meteor, available with 2023cc or 2565cc engine of which about 1700 were made into 1933. A Light Six beat the Blue Train across France in January 1930.

Rover Six Weymann saloon, 1927.

Rover 10/25 owned by VSCC secretary David Franklin.

SIX. 1927-32 (prod: approx 7000 to end 1930 and roughly 1000 after). Weymann saloon 1927 £425, Light Six Sportsman's saloon 1929 £325. S6 OHV 2023cc 15.72hp Treasury rating, cork insert in oil clutch, three speed gearbox, torque tube, spiral bevel axle, semi-elliptic suspension, shock absorbers standard, coil ignition (magneto extra). At the 1923 London Show a 21hp 3½-litre Six was unveiled but only three prototypes were built. The 2-litre Six was a more accomplished design by Peter Poppe which, unlike his four, had pushrod OHV.

10/25. 1927-33 (prod: approx 15,000). Chassis £185, £150 in 1930. S4 OHV 1185cc, cork insert plate clutch, three speed gearbox, torque tube, worm axle. Semi-elliptic front, quarter-elliptic rear suspension. Marketed as the Nippy Ten and tracing its origins from the Eight, the 10/25 was closely related to late examples of the 9/20 and was often seen with Weymann bodywork. The Riviera version for £250 with Weymann body had a fully opening roof, and the same money bought the fancifully named Paris saloon. Coil ignition replaced magneto during 1929.

ROYAL RUBY

Manchester

Royal Ruby built high quality motor cycles from 1909 to 1933. It offered four wheel cyclecars in 1913-14 and then, briefly in 1927, a three wheeler with a single-cylinder JAP 5hp engine.

1927 Royal Ruby three wheeler.

RTC

Chapel Street, London NW1 and St Peter's Road, Croydon, Surrey

The René Tondeur Co. of Croydon, with works at Marylebone (occupied by Vici Engineering), offered a cyclecar in 1922-23 powered by an 824cc Blackburne vee-twin air-cooled sidevalve engine. It had twin belt drive with the brakes working on the belt pulley, hopefully the one on the dead axle! The ratio was allegedly made automatically variable by a governor enlarging and reducing the diameter of the pulleys, a bit like the system used on the pre-war Clyno motor cycle and the Rudge Multi motor cycle and pre-war cyclecar.

The 9hp two-seater RTC, finished in maroon, grey and blue, cost £160 and had cantilever springs at both ends.

RUBURY-LINDSAY

See RLC

RUGBY

Despite its English-sounding name this was an export version of the American Star, a product of the Durant empire. Called a Star in America and in countries where Star of Wolverhampton had not registered its name, it was a direct competitor to the Model T Ford and very cheap.

RUSTON-HORNSBY

Boultham, Lincoln

This massive agricultural and industrial steam engineering group was created in 1918 from the Ruston Proctor and Richard Hornsby firms, which had employed 13,000 during the Great War. They had built 35,000 carts, 440 crawler tractors, 2750 air-

Ruston-Hornsby 16/20 tourer.

craft and 3200 engines. Something was urgently needed to keep the factories occupied in peacetime, and diversification included furniture, bodywork and the American-inspired Ruston-Hornsby car. Despite mass production the car was too big, heavy and expensive for British tastes, and production did not exceed 35 per week. However its rugged qualities were appreciated in the far-flung corners of the Empire. Sales in Britain were undertaken by C B Wardman (see Lea Francis, to which Ruston Hornsby engineer H E Tatlow had departed as works manager) who was managing director of Vulcan and also involved with the sales of Bean, Swift, ABC, etc., in the British Motor Trading Corp.

16/20, FIFTEEN. 1920-24 (prod: 1050). Tourer 1919 £600, 1923 £475. S4 SV 2614cc Dorman, cone clutch, three speed gearbox with centre change attached to helical rear axle. Semi-elliptic front, ¾-elliptic rear suspension. Built in a former aircraft factory, these models had Dorman detachable cylinder head engines. 18mpg and a 50mph top speed were quoted. For some strange reason, but presumably after a good lunch, *Motor Trader* in 1923 testified: "The car which represents value for money never surpassed in any country or time". Sadly the public did not agree and Ruston-Hornsby stopped accepting orders in August 1924.

Ruston-Hornsby Sixteen.

SIXTEEN, TWENTY. 1919-24 (prod: possibly 500). Tourer 1920 £650-750, 1923 £525-575. S4 SV 2614cc 40bhp, 3308cc 50bhp, cone clutch, in-unit three speed gearbox with centre change, helical bevel axle, semi-elliptic suspension. Ruston-Hornsbys had a Lincoln Imp radiator mascot and the above models, with the firm's own fixed cylinder head engines, were described as De Luxe, whilst the Dorman types were Standard. The engine, gearbox and steering gear were assembled together and the firm built its own bodywork. The company was particularly proud of its hood and weather equipment, whilst other good features were wiring in conduits, and full pressure lubrication with unusually comprehensive filtering.

RYNER-WILSON

Western Road, Merton Abbey, Wimbledon, Surrey

This was such an unusually well conceived car that one wonders if the Wilson concerned was not Walter Wilson, the co-inventor of the Great War tank and exponent of pre-selective gears and the Wilson gearbox. The intention was to make an ideal car for the owner-driver to maintain himself. For example, the clutch could be adjusted from outside and water temperature could be controlled by a lever in the cockpit operating a tap. The engine was flexibly mounted. Twin Vici carburettors were used, possibly from the makers of the RTC car. Mr Ryner was an American car enthusiast and many of the good features of his OHV Buick found their way into the Ryner-Wilson.

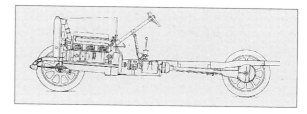

The 15hp Ryner-Wilson chassis.

15. 1919-21 (prod: about 12). Chassis £700. S6 OHV 2290cc, cone clutch, four speed gearbox, torque tube, bevel axle. Semi elliptic front, double cantilever rear suspension. A small six as early as this was most unusual. The valves were operated by pushrods from camshafts on either side of the block, and dry-sump lubrication was provided. The cars were so expensive and production so brief that poor Mr Ryner never managed to own one himself. His son reports that the factory still existed in the grounds of a paintmaker in 1990.

SALMSON

Kingston Bypass, Raynes Park, Surrey

This French firm made British GN cars under licence from 1919. F W Berwick (see Sizaire-Berwick and Windsor) helped establish British Salmson at Raynes Park in 1929, but until launching its own car in 1934 the firm's only British products in our period were aero engines. The French cars were earlier sold from premises adjoining Gwynne.

SANTLER

Malvern Link, Worcestershire

Sporadic car maker from as early as 1898, Santler occupied premises near to Morgan. After the Great

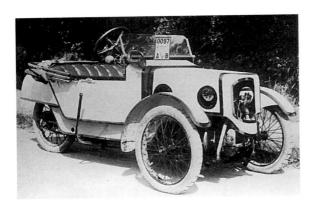

The rather "Morganesque" Santler Rushabout. This is the prototype of 1920-21.

A Scotsman at the top of Rest and Be Thankful in 1929.

War it made motor ploughs and about a dozen Rushabout three wheelers looking suspiciously like Morgan's Runabout. The Rushabout's price commenced at £165 and ended at £85. Water- or air-cooled MAG 10hp engines were utilised and like Morgan, though by a different system, the cars had independent front suspension. Four Dorman 1.5- and 2.6-litre engines were also used though whether for cars or agricultural purposes is not recorded. Santler died in 1940 in New Zealand, where he had gone to install railway signalling equipment after the cars were discontinued in 1924-25. The 1920-21 prototype is shown by courtesy of F W Ring-Santler.

SAUNDERS

See Morriss-London

SCOTSMAN

St Vincent Street and Wigton Street, Glasgow, and Gorgie, Edinburgh

In its first incarnation in 1922-23 the Scotsman Motor Car Co. Ltd made cars with thistle-shaped surrounds to their radiator cores and had financial backing from music hall artist Sir Harry Lauder, who was certainly on the Board in 1922. Scotsman Motors Ltd of Edinburgh in 1929-30 probably had no connection with the former and used licence-built French SARA air-cooled engines until water-cooled Meadows were substituted in the Little Scotsman.

SCOTSMAN. 1922-23 (prod: approx 12). 13hp Flying Scotsman chassis 1922 £475, 1923 £380. 1.5- and 2.35-litre listed, probably cone clutch, three speed Meadows gearbox, semi-elliptic suspension. Designed by pioneer Scottish motorist J Hall Nicol, this would appear to have been an assembled car, and presumably a long-lived and workmanlike one,

as our photo shows one at the top of Rest and be Thankful in 1929. The 2.35-litre engine in the Flying Scotsman model had OHC and the unusual bore and stroke measurement of 72.5 × 140mm, and was allegedly by Sage (who perhaps built engines for the 10/20hp models too).

Scotsman 17hp Sports with a "Krolite" four-seater body.

The Little Scotsman.

17HP and LITTLE SCOTSMAN. 1929-30 (prod: 30-40). Saloons from £550 and £450. S6 OHV 1.8-litre and S4 OHV 1.5-litre, plate clutch, four speed gearbox (centre change on six, right hand on four), spiral bevel axle, semi-elliptic suspension. The six had an air-cooled engine and was the French SARA (Soc. des Autos à Refroidissement par Air). It was allegedly produced under licence by Scotsman, though all ancillaries seem to have been French, which suggests that only the bodywork may have been made in Scotland. The four had a Meadows engine and in contemporary road tests was said to be the result of exhaustive testing of two prototypes in Scotland and Wales (and presumably England in between). 60mph and 32mpg were possible and quality was said to be above average, SARA collapsed in 1930 and Scotsman quickly followed.

SCOTT SOCIABLE

Clayton Road, Lidget Green, Bradford, Yorkshire

Designed by A A Scott of Scott motor cycle fame for military purposes (but not bought by the army) this strange vehicle became the Sociable made by the separately constituted Scott Autocar Co. Ltd. Scott had early engineering involvement with Jowett, whose factory he originally shared. So convinced was he that his cross between a motor cycle and a car would be a commercial success that he established a new factory separate from that of Scott Engineering, but he died in 1923 and production lasted little longer in the face of mass-produced cheap cars.

The Scott Sociable, unclothed and clothed.

5/6. 1921-25 (prod: approx 200, chassis nos. commenced at 80 in 1922). Complete 1921 £273, 1924 £135. S2 TS 580cc, cone clutch, in-unit three speed (no reverse) gearbox, torque tube, spiral bevel drive to offside rear wheel, helical suspension. Water-cooling, a steering wheel and rack and pinion steering were about the only things to justify the "car" label. The price plummeted as real cars became affordable; presumably real bikers thought Sociables cissy and stuck to their combinations.

SCOUT

Bemerton Road, Salisbury, Wiltshire

Product of the watch and clockmaking Burden family as early as 1904, Scout was a typical regional manufacturer. Most parts, including engines, were made in-house and at the firm's peak shortly before the Great War the 150 employees were turning out 100 vehicles per year. One of the few outside suppliers, the S R O Ball Bearing Co., forced bankruptcy over an unpaid bill in June 1921, and Whatley and Co. of Avonside, Pewsey bought the spares and probably assembled a few more cars into 1923.

Scout was also well known for local delivery vehicles. Its factory is now a Telecom depot.

The 15.9hp Scout chassis.

15.9. 1919-23 (prod: few). Chassis £750, complete £950. S4 SV 2610cc, cone clutch with cork insert, four speed gearbox with right hand change, bevel axle. Semi-elliptic front, ¾-elliptic rear suspension. This, and a briefly offered 10/12, were hang-overs from pre-war days, and were the firm's only monoblocs. The cars were well made and included Scout's own bodywork, but inevitably prices were too high to compete. Interesting features included an electric self-starter and Rudge-Whitworth detachable wire wheels. The brakes were on the transmission and the rear wheels, as was typical at the time.

SEABROOK

Gt Eastern St, London EC and Kings Road,
Chelsea, London SW3

A long established firm of motor factors, whose
early success was attributed to bicycle bells,
Seabrook imported the American Regal Underslung car from 1911 and last displayed these,
renamed Seabrook-RMC, at the 1919 London
Show. An all-British car had been under development since 1917 and it duly appeared, selling
slowly until the Seabrook Brothers retired in early
1926. The firm was then run by Frank Burgess in
Chelsea, who bought only three further Meadows
engines, though the marque was listed into 1928.

1925 Seabrook 12/24 saloon.

brakes were available and the cheapest tourer could
be bought for £250, which makes one wonder why
the car sold so slowly – 1924 was the peak year.

SEAL

Percy Street, Hulme, Manchester

Rather like the Scott Sociable, which it beat into
production by some seven years, though with its
motor cycle origins less disguised. It had tiller
steering to start with but gained a conventional
wheel in 1914. The postwar three wheelers all had
980cc JAP engines and three forward gears. Shaft
drive was briefly offered, though most made until
the end in 1924 had chain drive. After that, versions simply for trade purposes were made, the
design finally becoming a more conventional tri-
angular three wheeler with single front wheel in
1932. From 1930 the products were known as
Progress and they lasted to 1934.

Seabrook 10hp.

**10. 1920-22 (prod: 41). Chassis £385, complete
£475. S4 OHV 1795cc, cone clutch, four speed
gearbox with right hand change, bevel axle. Semi-
elliptic front, cantilever rear suspension.** An
attractive and relatively sporty offering. Some
sources claim that the car originally had Seabrook's
own engine (sometimes quoted at 1.5 litres) but its
description otherwise matches that of the 41 Dormans it is known to have used. These had aluminium water jackets and developed 22.5bhp at
2000rpm, using twin high camshafts like the later
Riley, though without its hemi head. The magneto
was mounted on the head and access for sump oil
was through a cap on the steering box, which also
lubricated the steering worm.

**9/19, 10/20, 12. 1923-28 (prod: approx 160). Chas-
sis 1924 £209, 1928 £230. S4 OHV 1497cc (9.8) others 1496cc, cone clutch, three speed in-unit Meadows gearbox with right hand change, torque tube,
spiral bevel axle. Semi-elliptic front, cantilever
rear suspension.** All had Meadows engines, the 12
being marketed as the 12/24, 12/27 and finally 12/40
(offered alongside the 12/24). By then four wheel

The 1921 Seal.

**SEAL. 1919-24 (prod: n/a). V2 (fore and aft in frame)
980cc, three speed gearbox, chain drive (shaft and
bevel in 1920).** This curiosity came in two-, three-
and even four-seater versions and the Family model
had hood and sidescreens, though the area alongside the engine had to be kept open for running
adjustments! The makers were Haynes and Bradshaw
until 1920 and then Seal Motors Ltd. Two or three
Seals survive so a fair number must have been made.

SEATON-PETTER

Nautilus Works, Yeovil, Somerset

Petters were reknowned for fire grates, cream separators and engines, a few of the latter being used in cars in late Victorian times. The Petter family later created Westland Aircraft, and in the mid 1920s decided that their mass production experience made a £100 car feasible. Percival Petter helped to design the car and set up the Petter Car Co. to make it. Douglas Seaton, a motor dealer who helped him design it, had been apprenticed at Petters and established the British Dominions Car Co. Ltd to market it, this title being chosen as the car was seen as simple, robust and ideal for the colonies. What went wrong is hard to guess, though two-cylinder two-strokes, even when water-cooled, were not what the upwardly mobile motorist was looking for anywhere on earth, even at a rock bottom price (initially £150 though down to £110 for a complete half-ton van). Petter's next roadgoing two-strokes went into Shefflex (Sheffield Simplex) lorry chassis in the 1930s, but again enjoyed only very limited success, despite being early examples of diesels.

The Seaton-Petter 10-18, 1926.

10-18. 1926-27 (prod: about 70). S2 TS 1319cc, plate clutch, in-unit three speed gearbox with central change, spiral bevel axle, ¾-elliptic suspension (suitable for off-road use). One of the first British cars with artificial cellulose paintwork, and a bit like a Camionette Normande in that the rear seats could be removed to make a goods vehicle. There was coil ignition and crankcase compression to force the next charge into the cylinders. Two wheel and transmission brakes were rather primitive. In 1927 Douglas Seaton tried a 1.5-litre Meadows, but to no avail.

SHEFFIELD SIMPLEX

Tinsley, Sheffield, Yorkshire. Canbury Park Road, Kingston, Surrey

Maker of very expensive six-cylinder cars in the teens, Sheffield Simplex was backed by coal magnate Earl Fitzwilliam (involved with Invicta in the 1930s), who lived in Wentworth Woodhouse, Britain's largest private home. After the war Cecil Kimber (see MG) worked for the firm, with Percy Richardson (originally with Daimler) as MD, and the company attacked both ends of the market with the Neracar motor cycle and a 50hp car, as well as some Commer based trucks.

At Kingston Capt. J M Rubury (see RLC) designed the 50, which unlike the tri-bloc pre-war 30 had separately cast cylinders. Compressed paper gears designed to give silent operation were rapidly abandoned when it was discovered that grease from the bearings destroyed them. Earl Fitzwilliam allegedly lost £250,000 on Sheffield Simplex, only 1500 Neracars per year and a handful of cars finding customers.

30. 1919-20 (prod: few). Chassis 1914 £895. S6 SV 4.8 litres, multi-plate clutch, mid-mounted four

The Sheffield Simplex 50hp two-seater.

The 30hp Sheffield Simplex saloon.

Service car version of the Sheret Family Model.

speed gearbox, worm axle. Semi-elliptic front, cantilever rear suspension. Sheffield Simplex had made a series of Renault-inspired cars before the war with gearboxes in their back axles (an earlier 45hp model was so flexible that no gears were needed, though an emergency low was available in the back axle). The Renault types were replaced by the 30 in 1913, and this was revived after the war and displayed at the 1919 Olympia Motor Show. Presumably a few were sold before the 50 arrived a year later.

50. 1921-24, listed to '26 (prod: few). Chassis £2250. S6 SV 7777cc 48.4hp Treasury rating, multiple-plate clutch, mid-mounted four speed gearbox, helical bevel axle. Semi-elliptic front, cantilever rear suspension. The 50 was new at the 1920 Show and had an engine allegedly based on the Ricardo tank unit made by Peter Brotherhood during the war. It had coil and magneto ignition, engine governor, self-starter and optional front wheel brakes in 1921. Thirty orders were apparently taken, but whether so many cars were ultimately sold seems unlikely, especially when a Silver Ghost could be acquired for substantially less money.

SHERET

Hythe Road, Willesden, London NW2

As noted under Carden, Arnott and Harrison Ltd acquired Capt. Carden's design and made the New Carden at Willesden. Alongside it in 1924-25 came the somewhat less basic Sheret.

FAMILY MODEL. 1924-25 (prod: n/a). 2+2-seater £130 reduced to £115. Two-cylinder TS 707cc, plate clutch, three speed chains and dogs, chain final drive, quarter-elliptic suspension (semi-elliptic at rear on service car shown). Fairly conventional looking but with too many eccentricities under the skin for the average motorist, who was by now used to four water-cooled cylinders.

The New Carden as made by Sheret.

SHORT-ASHBY
See Ashby

SILENT RECORD

Tatbury, Burton on Trent, Staffordshire

The Record Engineering Co. Ltd probably never progressed beyond the prototype stage in 1922 and no specification details appear to have been published.

SILENT UNIT
See Unit

SILVER HAWK

Glengarrif, Cobham, Surrey

These sports cars were made in the same domestic garage as spawned the prototype Invicta. Noel Campbell Macklin had conceived the Eric-Campbell, and the Silver Hawk was a more overtly sporting type made when Vulcan Iron and Metal Works adopted the former. Three were tried in the 1920 Voiturettes Race at Le Mans with only modest success, which did not help sales prospects.

The Coventry Simplex engined Silver Hawk of 1920.

A Silver Hawk two-seater, 1921.

SILVER HAWK. 1920-21 (prod: approx 12). S4 SV 1498cc Coventry Simplex, cone clutch, three or four speed gearbox, spiral bevel axle. Semi-elliptic front, cantilever rear suspension. Each car had to be able to reach 70mph within 500 yards of starting at Brooklands. The engine internals were lightened by a team of three or four including H L Bing, who had been works manager at Iris and who went on to join BAC. The marque became a well-known race and sprint contender, notably at Brooklands, and one car was equipped with a Sage engine. The external exhaust pipe was a distinguishing feature, even on the wasp-tail touring model.

SIMPLIC

Jessamy Road, Weybridge, Surrey

This grew from a garage and motor cycle repair business that had introduced the Autotrix cyclecar in 1911. Finance came from George Wadden, a local hairdresser who reformed the business in 1914 in Cobham with a partner named West to build the Simplic. Initially with 5/6hp or 8hp JAP engines and belt drive, it was redesigned at the end of the war (West had left and Wadden returned to Weybridge) and now had an 8/10hp vee-twin JAP unit and twin speed chain drive in a

wooden chassis with quarter elliptic suspension. 75mpg and a list price of £185 in 1920 must have seemed attractive, but few were built before the end of production in 1923.

1920 Simplic.

SINGER

Canterbury Street, Coventry. Coventry Road, Small Heath, Birmingham

Another of the Coventry bicycle pioneers who were early on the motoring scene, Singer's Ten of 1912 was one of the first good "big cars in miniature". This and developments of it provided the company's staple background through the 1920s, during which it became the third biggest British owned car firm and, unlike many of its rivals, maintained profitability. Managing Director W E Bullock, who had been with the firm since 1909, was credited with much of the success and he recruited designers S C Poole from Clyno in 1920 and then H C M Stephens from Sunbeam. Singer expanded rapidly, acquiring Coventry Premier, Calcott, Coventry Repetition, Sparkbrook Manufacturing and then, in 1926-27, the enormous BSA/Daimler armaments premises in Birmingham.

Singer made most of its own parts including castings, bodywork and even chassis, and at the end of our period had 8000 employees and 44 acres of factories, with a capacity of 20,000 vehicles p.a. (though only 8000 were made in 1930, down from a claimed 11,000 in 1927).

Calcott had been acquired as servicing premises, and for the same purpose the former Aster factory in Middlesex was in use from 1929.

10. 1919-24 (prod: possibly 6000, see below). S4 SV (OHV from 1923) 1096cc, cone clutch, three speed gearbox (in back axle to 1922 then amidships, then from 1923 in-unit with engine), bevel axle, semi-elliptic suspension (quarter-elliptic from 1922). The Rootes Brothers' sales network helped make this a great success from its launch in 1912

Singer 10hp, c1919, with unusual protection for the dickey seat.

(Rootes eventually acquired Singer in 1956). 40-50 per week were being made in mid-1920, though chassis numbers confirm only 750 in 1922. 50mph and 40mpg were possible. A basic version was sold for £210 in 1923 as a Coventry Premier following the takeover of that factory. One of the earliest Weymann saloons was available in 1923. A single-seater racing 10 was tried in 1921 but most fame attaches to an earlier variety developed by Lionel Martin before he introduced Aston-Martin.

15hp Singer six-cylinder 4/5-seater.

15. 1922-25 (prod: approx 150). Two-seater 1923 520 guineas, 1924 £450. S6 SV 1992cc, cone clutch then plate, three speed gearbox, spiral bevel axle. Semi-elliptic front, cantilever rear suspension. A prototype of one of the earliest small sixes was running in 1920. 60mph and 25mpg were mentioned, and twin carburettors and front wheel brakes were

available in 1924. Very complete weather protection for rear seat passengers was afforded by sidescreens that could be converted to a vee-screen.

The Singer 10/26, 1921.

10/26. 1925-27 (prod: approx 15,500). Complete car from £220. S4 OHV 1308cc 26bhp, plate clutch, in-unit three speed gearbox, spiral bevel axle, quarter elliptic suspension (semi-elliptic in 1927). A modernised version of the 10, with four wheel brakes from 1926, this one put Singer into the top five sales league. 150 per week were made early in 1925, with around a third of them saloons – smoke blue or grey were standard colours. 50mph and 30mpg were obtainable, though not necessarily at the same time!

Singer Six saloon, advertised at £350.

14/34, SIX, SUPER SIX. 1926-27, 1927-28, 1929-31 (prod: approx 5000). Saloon 1926 £375, 1930 £340. S6 OHV 1776cc/1920cc, single plate clutch, in-unit three speed gearbox, spiral bevel axle. Semi-elliptic front, quarter elliptic rear suspension. Another of Singer's pushrod OHVs, claimed to provide 60mph and 26-28mpg. Features in 1929 included safety glass, pedal operated centralised lubrication, chromium plating and Newton shock absorbers, all for £300 in tourer form and £350 as a saloon (the latter shown, though the same picture was also used by Singer to advertise its Senior!).

The Singer Light Six, 1929.

LIGHT SIX. 1929-31 (prod: approx 2000). Saloon £275. S6 SV 1792cc, plate clutch, in-unit four speed gearbox (three speed when announced Oct 1929), spiral bevel axle, semi-elliptic suspension. Real leather, walnut cappings and wire wheels were plus points, but the sidevalve engine was a backward step, even if it did provide a car of remarkable flexibility (and gutlessness, 10-30mph in top taking 16 seconds!). 55mph was the maximum speed and top gear could cope with everything above 4mph.

A 1930 Singer Junior driver receives a road fund licence reminder.

Singer Senior saloon, 1928.

SENIOR. 1927-30 (prod: approx 7000). Chassis 1929 £180, saloon £260. S4 OHV 1571cc 12hp 32bhp, plate clutch, in-unit three speed gearbox with right hand change, spiral bevel axle, semi-elliptic suspension. This started as a development of the 10/26 and gained a 4-inch wider track (8 inches on the Colonial version) and a larger engine in the autumn of 1927. Very similar bodywork was used on the Senior and the Six. The Senior was made alongside the Junior at the newly acquired Birmingham factory. The artist's impression from late 1928 accompanied an advertisement referring to two-tone cellulose paintwork, chrome plate, Triplex screen, Dewandre servo and leather covered pneumatic upholstery. The car could be "Bought on Deferred Terms without the need for Guarantors".

A Singer Junior ploughs a lonely furrow on the 1927 Monte Carlo Rally.

JUNIOR. 1927-32 (prod: approx 40,000). Tourer 1927 £148-10s, 1930 £135. Initial specification S4 OHC 848cc 16.5bhp, cone clutch, three speed gearbox, spiral bevel axle, quarter-elliptic suspension. As launched in September 1926, the Junior's early specification included only two wheel brakes, and top speed was 48mph. For 1928 came semi-elliptic front suspension, four wheel brakes and a plate clutch. 1929 saw semi-elliptics all round, aluminium pistons, hydraulic shock absorbers, and a 56mph top

speed allied to a 42mpg touring consumption. In 1930 coil ignition, wire wheels, chrome and Triplex glass arrived, and four gears were adopted in 1931.

In 1929 a Junior stormed Porlock Hill one hundred times, and other publicity stunts included a six days and nights marathon at Montlhéry. It is curious that the Morris Minor and the slightly more up-market Singer Junior should have come out with pint-pot overhead cam engines: coincidence or industrial espionage?

SIZAIRE-BERWICK

Cumberland Avenue, Park Royal, London NW10

F W Berwick was a motoring enthusiast and dealer who, with financial backing from jam manufacturer Alexander Keiller, organised the Sizaire brothers, ex-partners in the French car firm Sizaire et Naudin, to produce a luxury car to English taste. It resembled a Rolls-Royce when production started in France in 1913, and 139 had been sold (many in Britain) when war intervened.

Berwick built up a factory at Park Royal which at its height covered 16 acres and employed 5800 making De Havilland aircraft and French designed aero engines. The cars were built there from 1919 with Maurice Sizaire on hand (he had been taught English by S-B employee Jack Warner, later Dixon of Dock Green on TV). Park, Ward and Webb all worked at Park Royal before going into coachbuilding on their own account, Webb with Freestone.

Keiller's nominee at Park Royal had worked for a road roller manufacturer and soon fell out with Maurice Sizaire over "lightweight" construction. He also ordered parts for 1000 cars when sales never exceeded 5 per week.

After Austin took a controlling interest in 1922 Sizaire returned to France to make Sizaire Frères cars, Berwick later becoming involved with the Windsor car and with British Salmson. Sizaire-Berwick made an assortment of cars in France until 1928, latterly with OHV engines and finally a Lycoming straight eight.

25/50. 1919-23 (prod: possibly 200 in UK). Four-seat tourer 1923 £1250. S4 SV 4536cc 22.4hp Treasury rating, plate clutch, four speed gearbox with right hand change, spiral bevel axle, semi-elliptic suspension (rear underslung). Though there were technical advantages at the time in making smooth in-line four-cylinder engines, they were not fashionable. Motoring magazines claimed that the average motorist could not tell the difference, but the majority paying a high price wanted a six. The cachet provided by the Rolls-Royce-like radiator shape was lost when Rolls-Royce insisted that the radiator be

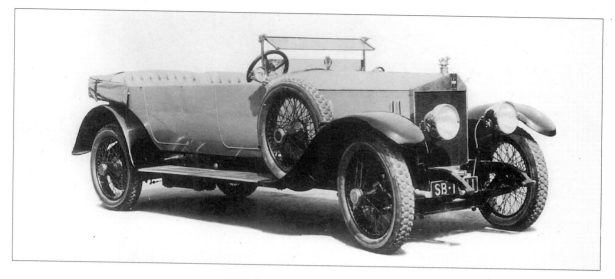

1920 Sizaire-Berwick 25/50 tourer.

altered. The cars were high-quality machines with the firm's own coachwork. High gearing gave long-legged performance with marine engine-like revs, according to onetime owner Bunty Scott-Moncrieff.

The 23/46hp Sizaire-Berwick Limousine Landaulette.

13/26 Sizaire-Berwick saloon sporting artillery wheels.

13/26, 23/46, 26/52, 15. 1922-25 (prod: n/a). S4 SV 1660cc (13/26), 3610cc (23/46), 1997cc (15), S6 SV 3250cc (26/52), in-unit four speed gearbox (three speed 26/52), spiral bevel axle, semi-elliptic suspension. The first two were based on the Austin 12

and 20, with special radiators and bonnets, and bespoke coachwork on the larger car. They lasted to 1925, when only the somewhat mysterious 15 was available. The six-cylinder car is believed to have been based on an early prototype for the Austin 20 Six. All must have been inspired by the marketing strategy of making a cheap car expensive by adding lots of luxury features, as tried so successfully by the Vanden Plas Austins of the 1950s-70s. Unfortunately for Sizaire-Berwick and Austin, this plan did not work in the 1920s.

SKEOCH

Burnside Works, Dalbeattie, Kirkcudbright

Made in 1921 by J B Skeoch, formerly of commercial vehicle manufacturer Belhaven, this £165 light car had a single-cylinder Precision 348cc engine, Burman two speed gearbox and chain drive. Between eight and ten were made before the factory was destroyed by fire.

1921 Skeoch light car.

SNOW

Morland Road, Croydon, Surrey

Yet another early 1920s car that probably never made it into production, it was credited in 1922 to a firm or individuals called Baseby and Sadler.

SPEEDY

Peckham, London SE, and Putney, London SW

This was the continuation of Pullinger and was the same car. An output of 5000 was envisaged in the first year but, as the project fizzled out in 1921, presumably very few were sold.

STACK

Mayo Road, East Croydon, Surrey

G F Stack's cyclecar lasted a little longer than most but fared no better than its rivals. Complicated chassis numbering indicates that six were made in 1921 followed by 41 in 1922 and five in 1923. What happened after that is not clear, except that the final model for 1925 had grown up into a four-cylinder 1526cc monobloc sidevalve with in-unit three speed gearbox, torque tube and spiral bevel axle. Suspension was by transverse leaf at the front and quarter-elliptic springs at the rear. Though competitively priced at £160 for a four-seater, it did not survive the year.

1921 Stack 6hp two-seater.

6, 8, 10HP. 1921-24 (prod: about 60). Complete £289 falling to £137. Two-cylinder SV water-cooled, friction transmission, chain drive. Transverse leaf front, quarter-elliptic rear suspension. These cyclecars were finished in grey and with their water cooling and plated radiators looked more like real cars than some. They had an ingenious device to apply more pressure to the disc when revs on gradients made it likely to slip. For a description of the conventional car which replaced them for 1925 see above.

STAFFORD

Cannon Street, London EC4

Like Ruston-Hornsby and so many others, this was an attempt to mass-produce a large, conventional car from proprietary components, and it was no more successful. As it picked Dorman's slogan, "The heart of the car is the engine", for its own 1920 advertisements, it is reasonable to assume that Dorman, which after all was based in Stafford, had put money into Stafford Associated Engineering Co. Ltd.

In 1919 Dorman had in its fleet two Morris Cowleys with 4MV engines, which may have been prototypes of the Stafford. Where the car was made is unclear, though Battersea has been suggested.

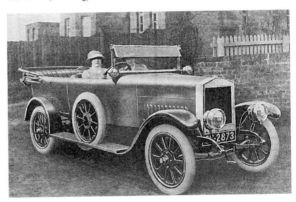

The 1920 Stafford 12.

12, 16/20. 1919-21, 1921 (prod: n/a). 12 complete 1919-20 £495, 1921 £595. S4 OHV 1790cc, 2613cc Dorman, cone clutch and three speed gearbox on 12, plate clutch and four speed gearbox on 16/20, bevel axle. Semi-elliptic front, cantilever rear suspension. "You cannot beat the best" was Stafford's claimed reason for buying Dorman engine, Zenith carburettor, Watford magneto, P&H and Smith electrics, Sankey wheels, Ubas steel gears, Ferodo linings and Vislok locknuts (curiously the Vislok firm bought four MV Dorman engines in January 1923, though there is no sign of Stafford Associated Engineering in Dorman's archives – unless its records were kept separate).

The 22.5bhp 12, with a chassis weight of only 13cwt, must have been a reasonable performer.

STANDARD

Canley, Coventry

Standard was founded by R W Maudslay, a member of the same family as had started the Maudslay Motor Co. Like Singer it made a very successful "big car in miniature" before the war which was still modern in the 1920s. By then it had the benefit of a large "green field" wartime aircraft factory at Canley, where 2630 were on the payroll in 1919 and where 200 cars per month were made by 1921 and 10,000 per year in 1924 (which made it Britain's third largest car manufacturer, a position also claimed by Singer at another stage in the decade). The factory had been expanded to 10 acres by 1926. Chief engineer (and chairman) John Budge retired after creating the OHV models that made Standard so successful. He was succeeded by A J Wilde (ex-Hotchkiss) who designed a very successful sidevalve 9 that made up for the disappointing sales of Standard's six-cylinder types.

The resourceful John Black became managing director in 1929 from Hillman, where like his colleague S B Wilks (Hillman then Rover) he had married a Hillman daughter. He forged links with Swallow coachwork that would bring lasting benefits, and increased Standard's output to 50,000 per year by the end of the 1930s.

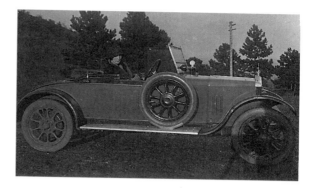

Standard 11hp two-seater.

8, these all had the factory model code SLO (O for OHV) and had the usual open radiator sides.

From 1922, like other models, they also had the Roman IX Legion Standard radiator mascot. Standard's slogan at the time was "Count them on the road", and sales were certainly booming. Body styles bore place names like Knowle, Piccadilly, Pall Mall, Warwick and Kineton.

The 9.5hp Standard tourer.

9.5 1919-20 and 8 (11) 1922-26 (prod: 1750 and 1500). Complete £550 and £295. S4 SV (9.5), OHV (8) 1100cc later 1300cc, disc clutch, three speed gearbox with right hand change, worm axle, semi-elliptic (9.5) quarter-elliptic (8) suspension. The 9.5 was revived in 1919 as the S, much as it had been before the war, and was joined that year by a 1340cc SLS version that would ultimately gain overhead valves and became Standard's main seller. The low-built 8 (actually 11hp rating) originally shared the 9.5's engine dimensions, but with OHV and coil ignition, and grew from the V1 and V2 to the V3 of 1924-25 with the same engine but now called Eleven.

A 1920 road test found a 42mph top speed, good weather equipment and economical and reliable running over 2000 miles.

11.6, 11, 11/14. 1920-21, 1922-23, 1924 (prod: approx 12,000). S4 OHV 1600cc 11.6hp, plate clutch, four speed gearbox, worm axle, semi-elliptic suspension. Not to be confused with the 11 alias

Standard 14/28hp "Stratford" tourer.

14, 14/28, 14/32. 1925-26, 1926-28, 1928 (prod: approx 15,000). S4 OHV 1945cc 13.9hp Treasury rating, plate clutch, four speed gearbox, worm axle, semi-elliptic suspension. These 14s were the final versions of the excellent SLO series. The October 1926 14/28 shown has the new enclosed radiator sides and also the front wheel brakes that had been available, initially as an extra, since 1924. A 14/28 on test was found to have a top speed of 55mph and to average 24mpg. Brakes and ride (augmented by Hartford shock absorbers) came in for favourable comment.

18/36, 18/42. 1926-28, 1928-29 (prod: n/a). Chassis 1927 £285, Stratford tourer £345, Sherborne saloon £395. S6 OHV 2230cc, multi-plate clutch, three (later four) speed gearbox, worm axle, semi-elliptic suspension. Initially offered in fawn, blue or crimson and with Dewandre servo brakes, these six-cylinder models gained a reputation for unreliability

1927 Standard 18/42.

The six-cylinder Standard 18/36.

1929 Standard Envoy 15hp.

and in spring 1929 agents Jack Olding and Archie Simmons bought the unsold stock and offered saloons at £155 off the £440 list price. The 18/36 seems to have had vertical bonnet louvres whilst the 18/42 mostly or always had the pattern shown (later used on the Nine).

15, 16. 1928-30, 1929-30 (prod: n/a). Chassis 1929 £245, Exmouth saloon £325-375. S6 SV 1930cc, 2054cc late 1929, plate clutch, four speed gearbox with central change, underslung worm axle (spiral bevel with bigger engine), semi-elliptic suspension. Standard stayed true to tradition with its

shouldered radiator and worm axle, but gone were magneto ignition and the distinctive overhead valves. However, many buyers were no doubt more concerned with the Stanlite sliding roof supplied as original equipment, a feature which had been pioneered by the company on the 1927 14/28 and 18/36. A larger engine was offered with the longer wheelbase and the larger bodied 16hp saloon announced in August 1929, which became the Ensign. In mid-1930 a 2552cc 20hp Envoy semi-Weymann model became available, sporting a new ribbon radiator without Standard's traditional domed header tank.

1929 Standard Nine Teignmouth saloon.

NINE and BIG NINE. 1927-30 (prod: approx 10,000). Selby tourer 1928 £190, Fulham saloon £199. S4 SV 1155cc, 1287cc (Big Nine), plate clutch, three speed gearbox with centre change, underslung worm axle, semi-elliptic suspension. The Nine is said to have been developed in just six months, after which two prototypes were driven virtually non-stop round the Cotswolds for a month. Launched in September 1927, the car was allegedly based on a French Mathis design. A top speed of 45mph with four aboard and 38-40mpg were attainable (a halfpenny per mile for petrol and oil!) and, like the Austin Seven, the chassis soon came in for attention from the more sporting coachbuilders like Gordon England (who made a £300 75mph supercharged two-seater), Jensen, Avon and Swallow. (On the way to creating SS, William Lyons designed a new radiator without the shoulders in 1930 which was adopted by Standard.) An enlarged version was available from 1929 which was called the Big Nine from August 1930.

STANHOPE

Dixon Lane Road, Lower Wortley, Leeds, Yorkshire

This strange car resembled the Autogear which was also made in Leeds. The Stanhope family were jewellers and Harry Stanhope, having invented a front wheel drive arrangement, had a prototype three wheeler running in 1915. Production started in 1920 but backer Rowland Winn withdrew and was replaced by pork butcher Walter Bramham, after whom the cars were renamed Bramham in 1922-23. In 1924-25 they were Stanhopes again and included some front wheel drive four wheelers. Harry Stanhope died in the 1925 flu epidemic and the cars expired with him. Like Autogear, Stanhope quoted a Dublin address, in this case concessionaire W E S Gilmour of Eden Quay.

The Stanhope tested by The Light Car & Cyclecar in June 1920, and below, one of the final four wheelers, by courtesy of Terry Stanhope, grandson of its creator.

3 WHEELER. 1920-25 (prod: chassis no. 009 at start of 1924 though survivor from 1922 is no. 128). Two-cylinder JAP 8hp, later Blackburne 10hp, friction drive though latterly three speed Moss gearbox, belt or chain drive (shaft also tried) to fixed front axle on which single front wheel steered. Quarter elliptic front, cantilever rear suspension. Front wheel drive gave this unusual car an advantage in local hillclimbs, and the chain drive four wheeler, with separate chains to each front stub axle on which the wheels pivoted, caused considerable interest, using various types of engine.

The so-called automatic friction drive was actually a spring loaded pulley, the stepped sides of which pressed against the belt and gave different ratios – slack being taken up by a wooden idler pulley.

STAR

Frederick Street then Bushbury, Wolverhampton

A near neighbour of Sunbeam and the maker of similarly high grade and expensive vehicles, Star had been making cars since 1898 and had various sister makes, of which only Briton falls into our period.

Star built approximately 8550 vehicles 1919-32

Star 11.9hp on a trial.

including a few hundred commercials, with most parts except Thompson of Bilston frames (see TB) made in-house, including bodywork.

Guy bought the firm from the founding Lisle family in 1927 and among the new board members were Sidney Guy of Guy Motors and Jack Bean of Bean Cars. Cramped premises were exchanged for a new factory at Bushbury, near Clyno, but sadly the cars were not making any money and in 1932 Star was sold to H B Denley, who had also bought the remains of his former employers, Rhode. Stars were listed by him until 1935.

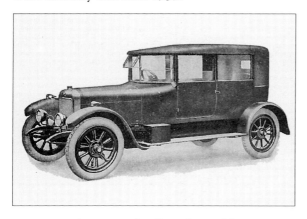

The Star 15.9hp all weather model.

15.9, 20.1. 1919-24, 1919-23 (prod: approx 800 and 100). Chassis 1921 £750-£825. S4 SV 3012cc, 3815cc, plate clutch (initially cone), four speed gearbox with right hand change, bevel axle. Semi-elliptic front, ¾-elliptic rear suspension. These were revivals of successful pre-war models, though with flat instead of bullnose radiators and full electrics. It is believed that production had more or less ended by 1922 but sales continued to the dates above. Both models used virtually the same bi-bloc 150mm stroke engines but with 90mm instead of 80mm bore in the larger.

11.9. 1921-23 (prod: approx 2000). Chassis 1923 £350, tourer £465. S4 SV 1795cc, plate clutch, three speed gearbox with central change, spiral bevel axle, semi-elliptic suspension. Star had made one of the modern breed of monobloc Tens since 1912 so it was not surprising for the firm to return to this expanding market. An attractive D-back saloon on a low-powered chassis was an unusual offering in 1923, one of the features being a passenger seat that folded upwards to give access to the rear through the single nearside door. This saloon cost £725 complete with leather or Bedford cord interior.

SIX 18 and 20. 1923-27, 1924-27 (prod: approx 200 and 50). Chassis 1922 and 1925 £550. S6 SV 2916cc,

The six-cylinder Star 20hp.

OHV 3265cc, plate clutch, in-unit four speed gearbox with central change, spiral bevel axle, semi-elliptic suspension. An early family six that was too expensive to sell well. Four wheel brakes were optional in 1924 and standard in 1925. The original type was the PL 18/40, which gave way to the PL2 20/50. Curiously Star called this a 20/60 in 1926 advertisements although the real 20/60, the OHV PL3, was not ready until 1928. The same advertisement had H Massac Buist of the *Morning Post* claiming "fault finding impossible", which could be taken two ways! 10-30mph in 5 seconds and a top speed of 70mph represented a fine performance by any standard.

Star 14/30 with Joe Lisle of the founding family in the passenger seat.

14/30, 14/40. 1924-26, 1926-27 (prod: approx 1000). Chassis 1925 £360, 1927 £400. S4 SV 2176cc (14/30), OHV 2120cc (14/40), plate clutch, in-unit four speed gearbox with central change, spiral bevel axle, semi-elliptic suspension. This was a completely different car from the 11.9, which had grown into a 12 and continued alongside the 14. Lanchester patent four wheel brakes were an option from 1924. Its flexibility and 55-60mph performance were favourably commented upon and Star made a feature of its use of steel rather than malleable castings. "The antithesis of the mass-produced vehicle – costs least in upkeep", the company claimed.

The 12/40hp Star 4-seater.

12/25, 12/40. 1923-26, 1925-28 (prod: approx 2000). Chassis 1925 £330, £385 with OHV. S4 SV (12/25) OHV (12/40) 1945cc, twin plate clutch, in-unit four speed gearbox with side or central change, spiral bevel axle, semi-elliptic suspension. Here were updated versions of the 11.9, with a substantial increase in bhp from 25 to 40 when Star offered its first pushrod OHV engine. Malcolm Campbell was a London agent: he sold several attractive vee-screen coupés, drove some of the larger horsepower models as his personal transport and raced one at Brooklands. Star body styles had stellar names like Scorpio, Mars, Mercury, etc.

1929 18/50hp Star "Jason" sportsman's coupé.

18/50. 1926-32 (prod: approx 1000). 1929 Jason shown £595. S6 OHV 2470cc, single plate clutch, in-unit four speed gearbox with central change, spiral bevel axle, semi-elliptic suspension with Smiths shock absorbers. This LD series developed into the Jason in 1928, the LDI Comet 18/50 in 1930 and the LDI/X Comet 18 in 1931. In 1931-32 there was also a 2100cc LDS Comet 14, of which 216 were made. A unique feature of the seven-bearing engine was centrifugally cast detachable cylinders. 10mph to 40mph in third took 13 seconds, top speed was 65mph, and touring consumption about 18mpg. At the end of our period ribbon radiator shells with dividing bars were adopted.

20/60, 21, 24/70. 1928-32, 1930-32, 1929-32 (prod: approx 150, plus 24 of the 24/70). Chassis 1930

Star 20/60hp "Norma" saloon limousine.

£450, tourer £695. S6 OHV 3180cc (3620cc 24/70), twin dry plate clutch, in-unit four speed gearbox with central or right hand change, spiral bevel axle, semi-elliptic suspension. The 18/50's big sister, which became known as the Comet 20/60 and then Comet or Planet 21. The 24/70, which became the Planet 24/70 and finally Planet 24, used the same engine as the contemporary Star Flyer commercials and was intended to restore the performance lost with heavier bodywork. Capt. Irving of Sunbeam was employed to improve Star performance and some could do 75mph.

STELLITE
See Wolseley

STERLING

Kingsbury, Hendon, London NW

In 1913 there had been a JAP engined cyclecar made in Leeds but whether this 1922-23 light car was related to it is unclear. It was to have been made by Warbrooke Engineering of Sterling Motor Works, Kingsbury, but never entered series production. Could it have been a continuation of the Kingsbury, as was the Rob Roy?

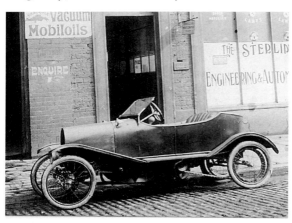

The Sterling pictured outside the company's premises.

STONELEIGH

Parkside, Coventry, Warwickshire

The pre-1914-18 war Stoneleigh had been a joint effort between Siddeley-Deasy and BSA. The version offered from late 1921 was inspired by the Rover 8 and Citroën Cloverleaf, which J D Siddeley had inspected. It was made by Stoneleigh Motors, a division of Armstrong-Siddeley, and had a central driving position with room for a passenger on each side of and slightly behind the driver's seat. Stoneleigh was the name of a Park near Coventry which is now the National Agricultural Centre, and was chosen to avoid demeaning the name of its upmarket parent.

Stoneleigh 9hp with central driving position.

9HP. 1921-24 (prod: probably several 100s). 1923 £185, 1924 £165. V2 OHV 1 litre, forced air-cooling, plate clutch, three speed gearbox (said to be in-unit with back axle on later cars), spiral bevel axle without differential, quarter-elliptic suspension. On offer was 40mph with lots of noise – and an unsatisfactory seating position until a conventional two-seater with offset steering arrived in mid-1924. Nevertheless the vee-twin was quite successful in trials and one even conquered Snowdon. The engine was said to bear close resemblance to both BSA and Hotchkiss units and had coil ignition and hand starting (Smiths self-starter in 1924).

STOREY

Tonbridge, Kent; New Cross SE14; Clapham Park SW12

The Storey family were engineers and toolmakers from Victorian times. The firm was involved with Le Rhône aero engines during the Great War in conjunction with Kingsbury, for whom Storey helped to develop a successful motor scooter. Various prototype cars were built in 1916 and production including bodywork commenced at New Cross in 1919. A 40 acre site at Tonbridge was acquired and was nearly ready for mass-production when the firm was declared bankrupt. Works manager Jack Storey, who had planned a car called the Winchester with E V Varley Grossmith (and supplied parts for his Varley-Woods) revived the Storey at Clapham Park and made about 50 cars up to 1930.

The 20hp Storey saloon.

10-12, 15.9, 20hp, etc. 1919-30 (prod: approx 1000). S4 SV 1327cc, 2815cc, 3817cc, cone clutch, three or four speed gearbox, worm or bevel drive. Semi-elliptic front, cantilever rear suspension. These are the specifications of the cars of the first two years, after which parts were exhausted and occasional other engines, including one each from Meadows and Buick, were utilised. 1921 models had gearboxes in-unit with the back axle and electric starting. Decolange and Chapuis-Dornier accounted for the larger early engines whilst the 10-12 was Storey's own work and was used from late in 1920. An early 20hp saloon costing £1100 is shown. The actress Gladys Cooper helped to publicise the Storey.

STRAKER-SQUIRE

Angel Road, Edmonton, London N18

This firm's forbears made vehicles in Bristol from 1901 and were particularly important in the manufacture of commercial vehicles, which were subsequently made at Twickenham for a few years from 1914. Having been the only firm permitted by Rolls-Royce to make complete aero engines to R-R designs during the Great War, this side of the business separated in 1918 under former chief engineer Roy Fedden's control (see Cosmos).

Straker-Squire then moved to a six acre armaments factory at Edmonton where O D North (ex-Daimler and Wolseley) was chief engineer (see North-Lucas). A new design of commercial vehicle

earned a bad reputation, and Straker-Squire's high-performance and expensive cars sold no better than others of their sort. A brief dalliance with the British Motor Trading Corporation did the firm no good, and although cheaper cars with proprietary engines were introduced it was too late to save the 1000 workforce.

S D Begbie of Aster (the firm's principal commercial vehicle engine supplier – see Arrol-Aster) attempted to sort out the problems, but the business collapsed after years of loss making in 1925, its co-founder Sidney Straker dying four years later. His son Reg went on to sell Rileys.

24/80hp Straker-Squire tourer.

Semi-plan view of the six-cylinder 20/25hp Straker-Squire.

20/25, 24/80. 1919-25 (prod: 67). Chassis 1920 £1350, 1925 £825. S6 OHC 3921cc, plate clutch, four speed gearbox with right hand change, spiral

bevel axle. Semi-elliptic front, cantilever rear suspension. This very desirable "aero of the road" originated in Roy Fedden's fertile imagination and its engine configuration – six separate cylinders, overhead camshaft, aluminium pistons – plainly owed much to Rolls-Royce aero engine experience. 75-80mph was feasible, particularly after hydraulic brakes were fitted to the final examples.

There was electric self-starting from the outset, and Rudge-Whitworth wheels were standard. A racing version with zig-zag striping was campaigned by London motor dealer H Kensington Moir (Straker's nephew).

1922 10hp Straker-Squire chassis.

Straker-Squire 15/20, 1922.

15/20. 1921-23 (prod: approx 40). Chassis 1923 £540. S4 SV 3052cc, plate clutch, spiral bevel axle. Semi-elliptic front, cantilever rear suspension. Although launched in 1919 the OHC Six appears not to have entered production until 1921, and to fill the vacuum the pre-war sidevalve 15/20 had to be revived complete with its fixed cylinder head. In 1913 a tuned version covered half a mile at 98.74mph. One finished fourth in the 1914 TT taking 11 hours 22 minutes to cover 600 miles. Plainly this was a far more interesting car than the specification and appearance suggested.

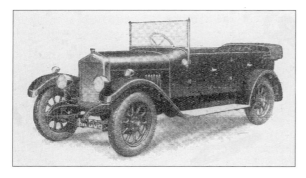

Straker-Squire 11/28hp tourer.

10/12, 10/20, 11/28. 1922-25 (prod: 92). Four-seater 1923 £400, 1925 £350. S4 OHV 1460cc Meadows, cone clutch, four speed in-unit Meadows gearbox with right hand change, spiral bevel axle, semi-elliptic suspension. A fairly typical family car,

though Straker-Squire engineering ensured that it was better than many using the excellent Meadows combination. 55mph and 35mpg were typical. The car became the 10/20 in 1923, with no change of specification but available with various levels of fitments to get the most basic chassis down to £250. The final 11/28 type shown had four wheel hydraulic brakes. The production figure quoted is for Meadows types, though it is possible that there were also a few with Aster engines.

STRINGER

Wincobank Works, Sheffield, Yorkshire

First conceived in 1913 as the Winco by former London General Omnibus designer G Bullock, this was a light car with sporting aspirations. It was called the Stringer Winco after the Great War, then from 1922 the Stringer Smith (shown), finally reverting to Stringer Winco. The car was listed from 1921 to 1932 but it seems unlikely that any were made after the 1920s. Early chassis numbers suggest that two dozen a year were produced, with a possible peak of nearer 100 in 1923.

9hp Stringer Smith two-seater.

9 and 11. 1921-29 (prod: see above). Complete car 1922 £350, 1928 £125. S4 SV 1088cc, 1330cc Alpha,

cone clutch, separate three speed gearbox, torque tube, bevel axle, cantilever suspension. The specification seems to have changed very little over the years and it is difficult to see how a small manufacturer could offer such a cheap car and remain in business. Cone clutch, two wheel brakes, hand starting and magneto ignition were not a recipe for success as late as 1929. In 1923 a 1795cc OHV version with what was claimed to be the firm's own engine was listed. The standard finish for all models was royal blue.

STUDEBAKER

Pound Lane, Willesden, London NW10

Although the above address was given for this American firm's London works, Studebaker does not appear to have gone in for the same degree of local assembly as some of its rivals from North America.

In 1924 the managing director of Studebaker Ltd, Eustace H Watson, stated that his products were Canadian imports. This gave them preferential tariffs and they were very popular in Britain, costing as little as £295 for a complete Light Six at the end of the decade.

After one won its class in the 1929 Brooklands Double Twelve at 71.65mph it was claimed that Studebaker sold more straight eights than any other manufacturer. All steel bodywork was normal from 1923 (including saloons) but traditional English wood-framed coachwork was available.

Two Studebakers in a mid-1920s London Easter parade.

SUFFOLK ROYAL

Woodbridge, Suffolk

The Woodbridge Engineering Co. has some connection with the earlier Ridley Carette and the Lindsay Motor Car Co. (possibly the Lindsay of RLC) and produced the Suffolk Royal. It was listed as a four-seat tourer with self-starter and a Sage 15.6hp engine at £775.

In 1922 H M Taylor of Cheapside, EC2, described the car as being in the experimental stage; only three appear to have been built.

15.6hp Suffolk Royal tourer.

SUMMERS

An 11.8hp car was listed at £295 complete in some 1922 buyer's guides. The engine, with 69 × 100mm bore and stroke (1496cc), sounds like a typical proprietary offering, but confusingly the German Moll with 1595cc engine was sold by ex-racing driver L G Hornsted in England 1922-23 under the Summers name and may have been the same car.

SUNBEAM

Moorfield Works, Wolverhampton, Staffordshire

The "Supreme Sunbeam" bore one of the great names of the British motor (and aero engine) industry, with a long and illustrious history. Things might have turned out differently if it had not teamed up with Talbot and Darracq in the badly managed STD Motors Ltd, which was created in 1920. Vast amounts of money were misspent on a fabulously successful racing and land speed record programme, masterminded by J S Irving, which a firm making only 1000 cars per year (and few of them directed at sporting customers) could ill afford. Virtually everything was made in-house, from castings to bodywork, which necessitated 30 acres of factory floor space and up to 4000 employees. J S Irving was the engineer responsible for the competition cars under legendary Chief Engineer Louis Coatalen. Too many models, including everything from overhead camshaft sports cars to straight-eight limousines, consti-

An early Sunbeam 16hp coupé.

tuted a recipe for disaster – which duly arrived in 1935. The Rootes brothers picked up the name but not many of the pieces.

16, 16/40. 1919-21, 1922-23 (prod: 1049 and 866). Chassis 1919 £790, 1923 £700. S4 SV (16/40 OHV) 3016cc, cone clutch, four speed gearbox, spiral bevel axle, semi-elliptic suspension underslung at rear. This started as a revival of a pre-war model, which had also been produced under licence by Rover during the War. There was a fixed cylinder head until OHV was specified for the 1922 cars. Four wheel brakes with mechanical servo were available in 1923. Bodywork was frequently by Sunbeam.

1924 Sunbeam 24/70.

24, 24/60, 24/70. 1919-21, 1922-23, 1924 (prod: 753, 500, 102). S6 SV 4.5 litres (50bhp until 1922, then 60hp, later 70bhp), cone clutch, four speed gearbox, spiral bevel axle, semi-elliptic suspension underslung at rear. Like the 16, the 24 had the very long stroke of 150mm, giving Edwardian levels of smoothness and flexibility. Also like its smaller sister it gained OHV when it became known as the 24/60. The 24/70 (shown) was broadly similar but with four wheel brakes and a very efficient gearbox driven servo. The 24/60 was described in the press as "The most improved car of 1922".

14hp 1922 Sunbeam with Landaulette body by Bridges of Cirencester.

14, 14/40. 1922-23, 1924-27 (prod: 4356). Tourer 1923 £685, 1926 £625. S4 OHV 1954cc (2121cc after 1922), plate clutch, three speed gearbox with right hand change, torque tube, bevel axle. Semi-elliptic front, cantilever rear suspension. A really up-to-date Sunbeam with coil ignition, automatic advance and retard, an aluminium monobloc engine with both manifolds on the offside, and pump and fan cooling. It started life as a French Darracq with Sunbeam radiator but was soon made here. A reversion to manually controlled magneto was forced by the conservative clientele – iron block too. One contemporary owner did 42,000 miles at a 2 pence per mile total running cost. In 1923-25 a very similar 12/30 was offered, with an engine capacity of 1598cc; only 95 of these were built.

A 1929 Sunbeam 20hp with 'four-under-the-head' coupé body. By this date the radiator had vertical shutters.

20/60hp Sunbeam special 4-door cabriolet, 1924.

20/60, 20 (20.9). 1923-26, 1926-30 (prod: 1060, 2510). S6 OHV 3181cc, 2920cc, plate clutch, in-unit four speed gearbox with right hand change, torque tube, spiral bevel axle. Semi-elliptic front, cantilever rear suspension. The 20/60 was launched at the 1923 London Motor Show and could

be had with artillery or wire wheels. The 20, from late 1926, had a marginally smaller engine – with a cast iron monobloc in place of the 20/60's detachable cast iron block and aluminium crankcase – giving a top speed of 65mph and a touring consumption of 16mpg. The usual Sunbeam standards of comfort, refinement, smooth steering and quality were maintained. A long wheelbase model became available from late 1928 and catered for the carriage trade, Sunbeam's own limo having fore and aft opening doors. A separate set of shoes for the handbrake spread to this and other models in 1929, when the Weymann saloon could achieve 70mph and was "A very fine car of the best class".

16/50, SIXTEEN (16.9). 1924, 1926-30 (prod: 26, 3495). Chassis 1924 £700, 1930 £425. S6 OHV 2540cc, 2035cc, plate clutch, three speed (four speed on 16) gearbox with right hand change, torque tube, spiral bevel axle. Semi-elliptic front, cantilever rear suspension (semi-elliptic 1930).

The 16hp Mann Egerton bodied Sunbeam coupé displayed at Olympia in 1927.

Initially a six-cylinder replacement for the old 16/40, which was handed over to Talbot to become its 18/55 and 20/60. The Sunbeam was then re-designed and lightened for the later 1920s, with the usual Sunbeam feature of engine ancillaries driven by helical gears. It had gear instead of chain timing gear for the first time and could rev to 4400rpm and cruise happily at 4000rpm. The cantilevers on the 16 were directly under an outswept chassis and incorporated running board brackets in their mountings. A 1929 model would do 5-62mph in top with a touring consumption of 18-20mpg.

Sunbeam Super Sport driven by Segrave at Le Mans in 1925.

The six-cylinder three-litre Sunbeam Super Sport engine.

SUPER SPORT. 1925-30 (prod: 305). Tourer 1925 £1125, 1927 £750, 1930 £850. S6 DOHC 2916cc 20.9hp Treasury rating 90-120bhp quoted, single plate clutch, in-unit four speed gearbox with right hand change, torque tube, spiral bevel axle. Semi-elliptic front, cantilever rear suspension. Sunbeam had racing experience of twin cams going back to 1914 and had built seven 3-litre racing cars soon after the war. Nearly all the roadgoing 3 litres were built in 1926, and in 1928 six were offered with 138bhp supercharged engines. There were four wheel brakes (servo available in 1928), fixed hemispherical head, dry sump lubrication, eight-bearing crankshaft, twin Claudel carburettors and, in 1930, dual ignition. A top speed of 90mph was definitely on the cards in what was often known as the "Twin Cam", and owners commended the delightful gear change, though not the poor steering lock and a tendency for the chassis to crack. Hard driving might produce a consumption of 16mpg.

Prince Henry's straight-eight Sunbeam limousine.

30, 35. 1926-29 (prod: 75). Chassis £1175, £1375. S8 OHV 4828cc, 5447cc, multi-plate clutch, in-unit four speed gearbox with right hand change, torque tube. Semi-elliptic front, cantilever rear suspension. Servo brakes stopped these monsters, the larger engine being specified for the biggest limousine. The Duke of Gloucester had a limo in 1926 and a close-coupled Weymann in 1929, so he must have been pleased with this unusual rival to Daimler, Rolls, Lanchester, Armstrong-Siddeley, etc...

Along with the 3 litre (with which it shared dry-sump lubrication) it was the first Sunbeam with a vee radiator (they spread to the rest of the range in the following year). It was also an early example of the commercially ill-fated British straight eight.

25hp Sunbeam Enclosed Drive Weymann Limousine.

"LONG" 25. 1926-32 (prod: 1134). Chassis 1927 £795, 1930 £745. S6 OHV 3619cc, plate clutch, four speed gearbox with right hand change, torque tube, spiral bevel axle. Semi-elliptic front, cantilever rear suspension. A large and stately car with the established Sunbeam attributes of fine steering, braking and handling. The chassis started as a development of the 20/60 and provided over 60mph, even with formal and heavy coachwork. One was official transport for the Governor of Nigeria. A late 1929 Enclosed Drive Weymann Limousine is shown, when the £995 asking price was the "lowest ever offered for enclosed bodywork on this magnificent chassis" – Sunbeam's financial problems were about to escalate.

SURREY

Premier Place, High Street, Putney and
Portsmouth Road, Thames Ditton, Surrey

Charles Alfred West of the West London Scientific
Apparatus Co. Ltd began car assembly in 1921 but
the firm went into liquidation in 1923. It was
reformed as Surrey Service Ltd and continued to
1927, when it had a final fling as Surrey Light Cars
in Putney and finally AC's home town of Thames
Ditton.

Its mid-1920s Putney premises were shared
with the revived Palladium business and some of
the models seem to have been common to both
marques.

The 1922 10hp Surrey.

**10, 10/24, 11. 1921-25 (prod: approx 80). Chassis
1924 £199. S4 SV approx 1500cc Coventry Simplex
or Dorman, cone clutch, in-unit three speed Meadows gearbox with right hand change or friction
drive, Wrigley spiral bevel axle (chain axle with
friction type), quarter-elliptic suspension.** In 1921
the coupé at £310 was claimed to be the cheapest of
its type on the market. The price was allegedly
helped by using Ford T front axle and steering gear.
Only two Dorman engines appear to have been
used (PA types in 1924).

1927 Surrey 10/30 tourer.

**10/22, 10/30, VICTORY. 1925-30 (prod: see below).
Chassis 1926 £185, saloon £275. S4 OHV 1250cc
and 1500cc Meadows, cone clutch, in-unit three
speed Meadows gearbox with right hand change,
spiral bevel axle, quarter-elliptic suspension.**
Remarkably cheap for a limited production car of its
type, which perhaps explains the firm's crises, char-
acterised by changes of name and address. The price
was kept down by having only one door on tourers
and by keeping front wheel brakes as an optional
extra. Only eleven Meadows engines of the above
types have been traced, though also listed were a
12/50 and a sidevalve six-cylinder 18.2hp New Victory Six of uncertain origin. Victory was certainly a
name used by Palladium from the same address,
though few if any of either type can have been built.

SWALLOW

Victoria Street, London SW

Like Carrow, North Star and Edmond, this was an
obscure brand associated with Sir J F Payne-Gallwey, Brown and Co. Ltd. It appeared at the 1921
White City Motor Show overflow at £190 for a plywood bodied two-seater. The 8hp Blackburne
four-cylinder 1122cc engine drove by shaft to a
back axle containing clutch, two speed epicyclic
gearbox and worm drive. A Dorman engine was
available as an option but the Swallow failed to
return next summer (or at any rate it didn't last
beyond 1922!).

There was of course no connection with
William Lyons' Swallow coach-building concern.

SWIFT

Cheylesmore & Quinton, Coventry, Warwickshire

Another of the Coventry bicycle-to-motor pioneers
and one which recalled its origins on many of its
1920s cars with its starting handle resembling a
bike pedal crank.

The company was reformed in 1919 with half
the shares belonging to Bean, but the latter's collapse in 1920 saw Swift regain its independence
under C Sangster who was also involved with Ariel
(though sales continued to be handled for a time
by the ill-fated British Motor Trading Corp.).

Swift made virtually all its own parts and produced cars of high quality. They were all low
horsepower family models, which brought them
into direct confrontation with cheaper mass-produced types. Output was potentially 5000 per
year, but half that was probably the most achieved,
and when efforts to get into the expensive 18hp
and cheap mass-produced 8hp markets failed,
Swift collapsed in April 1931.

The Swift 12hp two/three-seater.

12. 1919-25 (prod: possibly 1500). Chassis 1923 £375, tourer £495. S4 SV 1944cc, cone clutch, separate four speed gearbox with right hand change, bevel axle with torque rod, semi-elliptic suspension. A 15 revived from 1914 was listed in 1919-20 but at the end of 1919 it was joined by the new 12 (first shown in March 1919 with a vee-section radiator when viewed from above). This was designed by W Radford and put into production by Works Manager Robert Burns, a Swift employee since 1897. Swift made its own bodywork in its 150,000 sq ft premises (part of which still stands) and offered most styles including a saloon called the Pytchley for £675.

10. 1919-22 (prod: possibly 1500). Chassis 1922 £320. S4 SV 1122cc, cone clutch, separate three speed gearbox, bevel axle, semi-elliptic suspension. A revival of a pre-war model which had itself grown from a two-cylinder cyclecar, the 10 provided 35-40mph cruising and up to 55mpg. Blue leather upholstery was standard and the normal factory finish was grey. Quality was better than in most such cars of the time, and one example was reported to have covered 10,000 miles in a year with no problems.

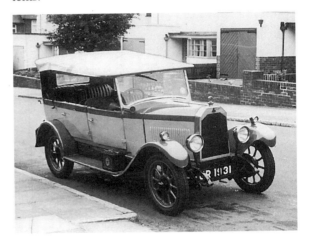

1928 Swift 10 tourer.

10hp Swift on a trial in 1922.

TEN. 1923-31 (prod: possibly 4500). Tourer 1923 £275, 1930 £235. S4 SV 1097cc (1190cc from late 1926), cone then dry plate clutch, three then four speed gearbox, spiral bevel axle, quarter-elliptic suspension (semi-elliptic adopted at front in late 1926 and at rear in 1930). At the end of 1922 the old 10 became the Q type Ten, with Delco-Remy coil ignition and electric starting. 37mpg and a top speed of 55mph were talked of from an engine now giving 21bhp.

The P type, from late 1926, had semi-elliptics at the front to cope better with the front wheel brakes that had previously been optional. It became P2 for 1928, P3 for 1929, etc., and was gradually "improved" within strict limitations of cost. A ribbon radiator similar to that of the Cadet replaced the classic shape in late 1929. Amongst various body styles were Nomad, Fleetwing, Migrant and Paladin saloons for as little as £260 in 1929. About 150 also wore Swallow coachwork.

1931 Swift 8hp Cadet.

The fabric saloon had sliding windows and the four wheel brakes were simplified Bendix-Perrot type.

The 14/40hp Swift tourer.

12/35, 14/40. 1925-26, 1927-30 (prod: n/a). Chassis 1927 £265. S4 SV 1954cc, dry plate clutch, in-unit four speed gearbox with right hand change, spiral bevel axle, semi-elliptic suspension. A replacement for the old 12 and now with four wheel brakes and other mod cons. Swift was now in dire straits, though a reorganisation in 1927 was supposed to have solved the problem. An 18/50 sidevalve four announced at the 1924 Motor Show had not found favour and probably got no further than the prototype stage.

CADET. 1930-31 (prod: about 250). Tourer £149, saloon £165. S4 SV 847cc 23bhp Coventry Climax, dry plate clutch, three speed gearbox with central change, spiral bevel axle, semi-elliptic suspension. Too little too late: Swift could not match the £100 cars and after its collapse spares were handled by R H Collier in Birmingham (who also acquired the remnants of Clyno and others), whilst the engines became the basis of Coventry Climax FSM (SM for Swift Motors) pumps.

TALBOT

Barlby Road, North Kensington, London W10

This distinguished firm started importing Clements in 1903 but soon was making British cars under the crest of its backer, the Earl of Shrewsbury and Talbot, and in 1913 one of its cars was the first to cover 100 miles in an hour. After war years spent producing staff cars and ambulances, as well as parts for other firms including AEC commercials, Talbot joined the British owned but French based Darracq concern and Sunbeam in the Sunbeam Talbot Darracq group, along with components makers and the truck producer W & G du Cros of Acton (where Darracq had a coachworks in The Vale).

Sunbeam designer Louis Coatalen was in overall charge but the Swiss Georges Roesch (born 1891) had joined Talbot in 1916 from French firms and a spell at Daimler. His obsession with lightening moving parts and increasing output by means of higher rpm was to be vindicated by the 10/23 and his famous 14/45. Talbot was starved of funds; in fact it was on the brink of collapse when the 14/45 arrived, yet it would probably have avoided the 1935 Rootes takeover on the strength of its successes if the rest of STD had not been so shaky by then.

French built Darracqs were known as Talbots or Talbot Darracqs in their homeland, but Talbot Darracq, or Darracq, here. British Talbots were sometimes known as Clement Talbots after their maker Clément-Talbot Ltd.

12, 15/20, 16 and 36. 1919-22 (prod: 175). S4 SV 2414cc, 2615cc 36hp, S6 SV 3920cc, cone clutch,

Talbot 12hp, 1919.

four speed gearbox, bevel axle, semi-elliptic suspension (cantilever rear on some). A hotch-potch of models created from pre-war offerings by Georges Roesch. Most barely saw production, the exceptions being the 15 and 16. All had pair cast cylinders, though there was additionally a 1933cc monobloc 14 in 1921 which probably did not venture off the drawing board.

semi-elliptic suspension. A modernised version of a wartime staff car, the 25 was a highly regarded car assembled from old parts in tiny numbers right through the lean years of the mid-1920s when the factory was virtually deserted. An open four-seater weighed nearly two tons and cost £1050 in 1923 – too close for comfort to the sort of car Sunbeam was renowned for.

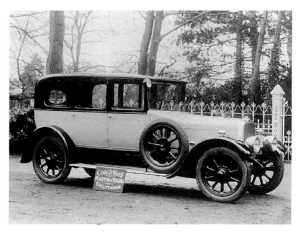

Talbot 25/50 with body by Martin & Young.

25, 25/50. 1919-27 (prod: 1107). Chassis 1920 £850, 1925 £595. S4 SV 4500cc, cone clutch, four speed gearbox with right hand change, bevel axle,

Talbot 10/23.

8/18, 10/23. 1922-26, 1923-25 (prod: 2224, 2850). 8 coupé 1925 £325, 10 coupé £415. S4 OHV 970cc, 1074cc, plate clutch, in-unit three speed gearbox with central change, torque tube, spiral bevel axle, quarter-elliptic suspension. This started off as the same car as the 1-litre Darracq from France sold by Talbot's sister firm down the road at Acton (which also built much of Talbot's coachwork). However, Roesch improved the 8 by increasing engine size and adding a differential to create the 10/23. Both had coil ignition and were sprightly and economical machines capable of 55mph.

The Talbot 12/30, c1925.

12/30. 1923-26 (prod: 860). Chassis 1925 £440, saloon £725. S6 OHV 1612cc, plate clutch, in-unit three speed gearbox with right hand or central change, torque tube, helical bevel axle. Semi-elliptic front, cantilever rear suspension. The 12/30 had the same bore and stroke as the 10/23 and was a very early example of a small six. However, it was very expensive compared with most other Twelves, even if a little smoother and more flexible. It showed what Roesch was capable of and no doubt helped to make the 14/45 a possibility. It is said to have been assembled in the Darracq works at Acton along with the 18/55.

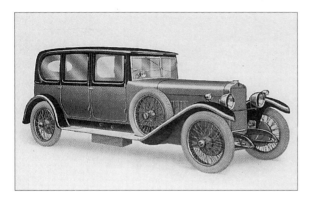

A Grose semi-sports saloon body on an 18/55hp Talbot chassis.

18/55, 20/60. 1924-26, 1926-28 (prod: 292, 99). Chassis 1925 £675, 1927 £685. S6 OHV 2540cc, 2916cc, single plate clutch, in-unit three speed gearbox (four on 20/60) with right hand change, torque tube, spiral bevel axle. Semi-elliptic front, cantilever rear suspension. These were based on the 16/50 Sunbeam, rather than Roesch inspired, and Darracq allegedly had a hand in their assembly. At the time Talbot was also building Sunbeam's twin cam car engines. Roesch had been sent by STD to the Sunbeam and French Darracq factories and did not return to Barlby Road until the autumn of 1925 in a last ditch attempt to make a distinctive Talbot.

The six-cylinder Talbot 14/45.

14/45. 1926-30 (prod: 7018). Chassis 1926 £325, saloon £485. S6 OHV 1665cc, single plate clutch, in-unit four speed gearbox with right hand change, torque tube, spiral bevel axle. Semi-elliptic front, quarter-elliptic rear suspension. The masterpiece that saved Talbot was rushed from the drawing board in six months. Its 65mph top speed and 20mpg consumption were excellent for such a large car. Novel features abounded, from illuminated direction arrows via flywheel fans to light "knitting needle" pushrods and knife-edge rockers, with a "bathtub" head helping to produce 45bhp from a relatively small engine. Marketed as "Britain's safest car" and "the real sportsman's car", it grew into the famous 75, 90, 105 and 110 models. Just 50 examples of the 75 (briefly known as the 18/70) were made at the end of our period in 1930. The motor trade other than Talbot dealers didn't like the cars because they required special service equipment, but their racing successes, against supercharged opposition, ensured a lasting reputation.

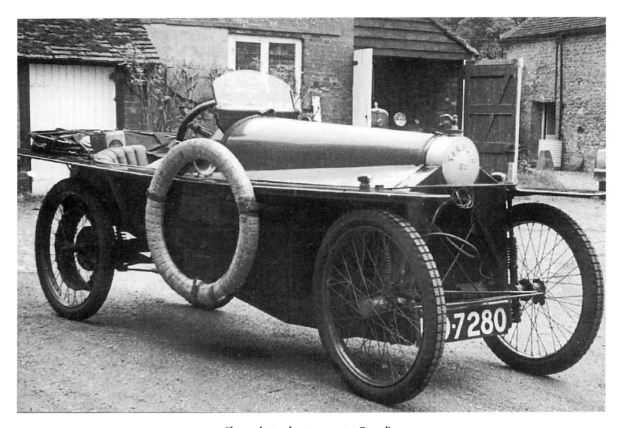

The early tandem two-seater Tamplin.

TAMPLIN

Kingston Road, Staines, then Malden Road, Cheam, Surrey

E A Tamplin of the Railway Garage in Staines was sole agent for the Carden tandem two-seater cyclecar in 1919, and late that year he acquired rights to produce it (by then Capt. Carden's designs had changed – see Carden, Sheret and AV). In late 1923 Tamplin Motors moved to Cheam, where production continued for a couple of years, and even longer to special order.

Later Tamplin reverted to the garage trade, after making more cyclecars than most of its rivals. A figure of 2000 has been quoted but as chassis number 1100 was reached in 1924, and 1185 in 1925, this seems exaggerated.

8/10. 1919-27 (prod: approx 1250). Complete 1920 £185, 1926 £120. V2 SV approx 1 litre JAP or Blackburne air-cooled, multi-disc clutch, chain drive to Sturmey-Archer three speed gearbox (with reverse), belt drive to differentialless back axle (chain drive from 1922). Independent front suspension with coil springs, then quarter-elliptic. Captain Carden had been moving away from front engines, but the Tamplin had a mid-mounted then

1923 side-by-side two-seater Tamplin.

frontal engine position. Usually finished in grey, these were lively cars with fibreboard unitary construction and full-length flat mudguards, sold in touring (JAP) or sports (Blackburne) form. The engine was kickstarted from the driver's seat. Initially a cramped tandem two-seater, the Tamplin became a side-by-side two-seater in 1922.

TANKETTE

Watford, Hertfordshire

A strange little three wheeler of 1919-20 with 2¾hp single-cylinder air-cooled Union engine driving the

1920 Tankette 2¾hp cyclecar chassis.

single back wheel by chain via a Burman two speed gearbox. The track could be narrowed to allow the wheel-steered "sit down" scooter to be stored indoors.

Ronald Trist and Co. Ltd of Watford, and then Tankette Ltd of London N4, were listed as producers.

TAUNTON

York Street, Westminster, London SW1

John Taunton, who had worked for Rolls-Royce, built a few prototypes cars before the Great War and secured massive financial backing. He proposed making 2500 cars in 1914, initially with help from Arrol-Johnston in their factory at Dumfries. Instead he got a cheap short-term lease on the former Hermes car plant in Liège with a view to switching to Britain after three years. War intervened after very few Tauntons had been produced. Attempts to re-launch the firm in Britain after the war were hampered by restrictions on potentially speculative share issues. At any rate one postwar car was built, the 15hp shown being used by Taunton's doctor brother well into the 1930s.

The Taunton 5hp, 1919.

12HP. 1919-20 (prod: few). Two-seater £500, coupé £585. S4 OHV 1800cc, cone clutch, three speed gearbox, bevel axle, quarter-elliptic suspension. Pre-war prototypes had the front axle above the underslung dumb-irons, semi-elliptics and an underslung worm axle. Plainly these features had not persisted but it would be interesting to know whether the pressed crossmember serving as sump and gearbox base was still used.

Shareholders had included Lady Cunard, the Marchioness of Anglesey and two members of the de la Rue family. Whether they or General Kitchener ever got the cars they ordered seems unlikely.

TAYLOR

Bridge Crescent, Scotswood, Newcastle on Tyne

Taylor Motors Ltd. (also written as Taylor's Motors) listed three different types in the 1922-24 period. There was a sidevalve 1498cc Coventry Simplex engined cloverleaf bodied car at £280 with Brown three speed gearbox (whether David Brown or Brown-Lipe was not explained), cone clutch and Brown spiral bevel axle, or two OHV Meadows powered models with otherwise similar specification except for their four speed Meadows gearboxes. Suspension on these 11.9 and 13.9 types was semi-elliptic and they cost £390 and £400 respectively in chassis form.

Only four engines in late 1922 have been traced in the Meadows sales ledgers, so output must have been extremely limited.

TB

Bradley Engineering Works, Bilston, Staffordshire

Thompson Brothers, founded 1810, were best known as tank and boilermakers, but during the war had made mines, shells, aircraft undercarriages, and pressed steel chassis for several motor firms. Complete three wheelers were added in 1920 with horseshoe shaped radiators reminiscent of the Brescia Bugatti.

8/10. 1920-24 (prod: approx 750). Complete 1923 £155-£165. V2 SV 1 litre air- or water-cooled JAP or Precision, plate clutch, two or three speed and reverse gearbox, bevel drive. Quarter-elliptic front, cantilever rear suspension. A neat and well-engineered three wheeler, instead of the usual back street bodge-up. Chassis numbers commenced at 694 in 1923 but probably did not start at 0: hence the production guesstimate above, which compares with the 500 quoted in an employee's reminiscence. A quick-release rear wheel made puncture repair practicable, but the TB could not shake Morgan's

The 10hp TB car.

dominance. Its worst feature was its starting dog on the camshaft rather than the crankshaft, which made it very hard to swing in cold weather due to the gearing-up. 45mph and 45mpg were couted.

THANET

Surrey House Road, Surrey Lane, London SW11

Made by F J Wraight and Co. Ltd in 1920, the Thanet 16/20 had a 2.3-litre monobloc engine, three speed gearbox and worm axle. At £250 complete it should have been a runaway success, though presumably it was uneconomic to make at that figure. Wraight was to have made the bodywork for the Whitehead-Thanet and the two cars may be interchangeable.

THOMAS
See Marlborough

THOR

Palace Street, London SW1

Made by Simpson Taylor Ltd near Buckingham Palace, this was, according to the 1921 publication *Automobiles of the World*, the product of a firm that had made cars since 1906 and had used American engines since 1913. Production in 1921 was said to be three per week.

1919 Thor 15hp coupé.

15. 1919-23 (prod: perhaps 200). Chassis £300, tourer £425. S4 SV 2333cc Le Roi, multi-plate clutch, three speed gearbox with central change, Mepsted Haywood bevel axle. Quarter-elliptic front, cantilever rear suspension. Even the wooden wheels with detachable rims sound American, other definite USA features being American Bosch ignition, Allis Chalmers lighting and starting, Schebler carburettor and, of course, the Le Roi monobloc engine with detachable head.

THURLOW

Kingston Road, Wimbledon, London SW

A Precision 8hp vee-twin powered this three wheeler, which was tested from 1914 and produced in 1921. There was a tubular chassis and a three speed Sturmey Archer gearbox with belt final drive. A decompressor was linked to the mechanical starter operated from the driver's seat. A cone clutch, and suspension by quarter-elliptics at the front and helical coils at the single rear wheel, were other features of the short-lived Thurlow.

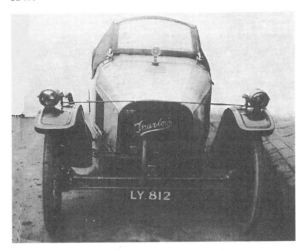

1920 Thurlow 10hp three-wheeler.

TRIDENT

Crayford, Kent

This extraordinary device began as a French prototype and was said in 1919 to be entering production at Vickers' aircraft and general engineering factory in 1920. It seems unlikely that it did, though publicity material for Trident Federated Exporters Ltd shows a tandem two-seater, a parcel car and an extraordinary sedanca.

The detailed view shows the in-line water-cooled twin driving through the steered twin front

The Trident.

wheels to a three speed gearbox that also carried the magneto. There were twin side-mounted radiators and interlinked cantilever springs for front and rear suspension. The price was £160.

TRIUMPH

Priory Street, Coventry, Warwickshire

Two Germans, Siegfried Bettmann and Maurice Schulte, made money from the Coventry bicycle boom and established Triumph motor cycle factories in Nuremberg and Coventry early in the century. The British branch became pre-eminent, and Bettmann became a pillar of the local community, ultimately becoming Mayor of Coventry. He was also Chairman of Standard in 1911, thirty years before the fusion of Standard and Triumph. In

1921 the Dawson factory was purchased to give Triumph an entrée into the car business and the firm became well known for popularising hydraulic brakes in Britain and for making high quality light cars. The bicycle business was disposed of at the end of our period and the motor cycle business in 1936.

Donald Healey was involved with Triumph from the late 1920s (he drove a Super-Seven in 1928 rallies) and joined the experimental department in 1933. The company made increasingly sporty types – amongst the first of which were special bodied 10/20s and, in 1930, supercharged versions of the Super-Seven.

10/20. 1923-25 (prod: approx 2500 with 13 and 15hp). Two-seater 1923 £430, 1925 £325. S4 SV 1393cc 23.4bhp, cone clutch, separate four speed gearbox with right hand change, helical bevel axle, semi-elliptic suspension. General Manager Claude Holbrook organised the ex-Dawson factory to make a design created by the Lea Francis team of Alderson, Lea and Sykes – the latter becoming the Triumph Motor Company's chief engineer. The result was the 10/20, which later in 1923 was the first car in Britain with hydraulic (initially two wheel) brakes. The turbulent-head engine was designed for Triumph by Ricardo and Co. Ltd, and bodywork came from the Regent Carriage Co. of Fulham, London. *The Autocar* commented on superlatively fine workmanship and got 52mph and 40mpg from a sports bodied version. Undoubtedly the Triumph motor cycle reputation helped to establish the 10/20. See picture on next page.

1925 Triumph 13/35 four-door saloon.

13/35, 15/50. 1924-26, 1926-30 (prod: approx 2500 with 10/20). Saloon 1925 £495, 1929 £425 (£375 fabric). S4 SV 1872cc, 2169cc, plate clutch, in-unit three speed gearbox with central change, spiral bevel axle, semi-elliptic suspension. The 13/35 shared with the Horstman the distinction of being the first British car with four wheel hydraulic brakes, at the 1924 London Motor Show. The 1925 saloon

1923 Triumph 10/20 two-seater.

shown cost £495 and was sold with Triumph's familiar globe emblem as well as lots of items, including balloon tyres, that normally were listed as extras. Most other motor cycle makers went for cheap cars but Triumph stuck to quality.

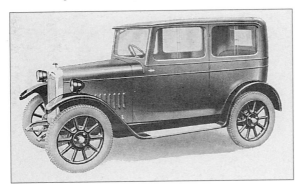

1927 Triumph Super-Seven saloon.

SUPER-SEVEN. 1927-32 (prod: approx 10,500 to end of 1930). Saloon 1928 £182, Gordon England saloon 1929 £190. S4 SV 832cc, plate clutch, in-unit three speed gearbox with central change, torque tube, underslung worm axle. Semi-elliptic front, quarter-elliptic rear suspension. An upmarket Seven designed by Arthur Sykes and Stanley Edge (the latter having played an important role in the birth of the Austin 7). The 40mph cruising gait was marred by a bouncy ride, but there were lots of luxury appointments and other good features, including four wheel hydraulic brakes, an "unburstable" rear axle, and a three-bearing engine. A ribbon radiator was adopted for 1930, when a supercharged 750cc version was briefly offered. Most had Triumph's own bodywork, though Gordon England sold attractive sliding roof saloons. Top speed was 53mph and fuel consumption 35-40mpg. Late in 1930 a six-cylinder version called the Scorpion was unveiled.

TROJAN

Ham, Kingston on Thames, and Purley Way, Croydon

Leslie Hounsfield designed a simple but unusual utility car in 1910 and six were made at Purley Way after the war. They greatly interested Leyland, who moved production to a former aircraft factory at Ham Common. Almost 17,000 were built before rights reverted to Hounsfield at the end of 1927. He recommenced manufacture at Croydon in 1929, whilst Leyland readied Ham for its new Cub commercial range. The first Trojans containing no Leyland parts were made in January 1930. Late in 1929 a conventional looking car arrived, but with

The Trojan Utility Car.

the usual two-stroke engine at the rear. This RE model was still without front wheel brakes and did not see production until well into 1930.

The mid-engined car was also revived, the last being sold in 1937, though van versions continued to 1939 and were replaced by a new range that lasted to 1964.

UTILITY CAR. 1922-26 (prod: 1920s total 16,824 incl. commercials). Tourer 1922 from £230, 1925 £125. S4 TS 1527cc, two speed epicyclic gearbox, chain drive to solid rear axle, cantilever suspension. Apart from the radiator and fuel tank there was little under the bonnet, the engine being under the floor and started by a lever working a ratchet and pawl mechanism next to the "umbrella handle" handbrake to the right of the driver. The cylinders were paired to aid scavenging, with two common combustion chambers. A lever gave the gear positions, with no need for the clutch, though a conventional pedal was also fitted to make drivers of normal cars feel at home. The chassis was a rigid punt shape, and very soft springing made narrow solid tyres acceptable (except when they got into tram rails!). "The simplest car in the world" was cheap to run, Trojan claiming a lower cost than boot leather and socks!

Trojan 10hp.

10. 1926-29 (prod: see Utility). Tourer 1926 £145, saloon 1927 £175. Specification as Utility car but shorter stroke and 1488cc to fit light car taxation class. Crankshaft now balanced and on roller big ends rather than white metal. Brooke Bond Tea had discovered that "even the errand boy was safe with Trojan" and bought hundreds of this type (its total Trojan purchases in the 1920s were 1350, and 5250 by the time production ended in the 1960s). Six wheeler 8-10 seaters were built for grouse moors from 1929. Pneumatic tyres were £5 extra from 1925, and each car came with a 5000 mile guarantee.

TST

An obscure three wheeler of 1922, reminiscent of the Seal in its layout. A Blackburne single-cylinder engine and gearbox drove the rear wheel by chain in conventional motor cycle fashion, but the machine was driven from the sidecar.

TURNER

Lever Street, Wolverhampton, Staffordshire

An engineering firm since 1880, Turner made Belgian Miesse steam cars under licence from 1902 to 1913 and its own designs of petrol engined cars from 1906. It built parts or complete cars for other firms, notably in the 1920s for Varley-Woods and Roger. It employed 160, and had a capital of £50,000 in 1922. Turner cars were listed to 1930, after which components and diesel engines took the lion's share of output. The firm's speciality after the Second World War became truck gearboxes, though it also made farm tractors and other vehicles with its own diesel engines.

1923 Turner 12/20hp saloon, costing £495.

10-14HP. 1920-30 (prod: see below). Chassis 1922 £450, 1929 £250. S4 1131-2203cc, plate clutch (except cone on earliest), three speed gearbox, worm or spiral bevel axle. Semi-elliptic front, cantilever rear suspension (late 1920s semi-elliptic rear on 14/30 and quarter-elliptic on 12/20). Turner began the decade with some light pre-war designs, a 10 alone in 1920, followed by a 13, then a 14 as well as an 11. All probably had Turner's own sidevalve engines, though in 1922 it bought a single Meadows unit followed by forty 1½-litre Dormans in 1922-24. Some of these proprietary engines had OHV. There is no evidence of purchases after 1924 and the 14 was discontinued in 1925, so later output must have been very small.

Turner 10hp 2/3-seater of the Great War period, priced at £220.

UNIT

Holtspur Hill, Wooburn Green, Buckinghamshire

Arthur Grice, the G of GWK cars, had formed a separate company in 1912 named Rotary Units Ltd to make five-cylinder pumping engines. Nothing came of this, but some tin sheds from a Great War hospital at Cliveden were moved to the above address to make the Unit 1 car, sometimes called Silent Unit, following an influx of money from MA Van Roggen (see British Imperia). In 1923 Grice and Van Roggen abandoned Rotary Units and transferred to GWK, having persuaded GWK to buy the remaining Unit cars.

Front engined 1923 Unit.

UNIT No. 1. 1920-23 (prod: about 50). Two-seater 1921 £275. Horizontally opposed rear mounted 1-litre water- or air-cooled engine, friction transmission, chain final drive, quarter-elliptic suspension. The above specification is for the original GWK type cars, but front engines were used from 1921 including four-cylinder Coventry Climax units before the end. LP Lee, later managing director of Coventry Climax, was apprenticed at Rotary Units. A £186 "Service" model with unitary construction was at the 1922 Motor Show. Some cars had conventional three speed gearboxes in place of friction transmission.

Unit No. 1 in 1922.

URECAR

Stedman Road, Southbourne, Bournemouth,
Hampshire

The Urecar Motor Co. offered a 9.8hp Dorman
powered model in 1923 with dog clutches and
chains for its three speed transmission. Only one
Dorman engine appears to have been supplied.

VANDY

Pembridge Villas, Notting Hill Gate, London W11

Major Frank and Lt Percy Vandervell of the CAV
electrical family business sold Italian SPA cars from
Vandy's Ltd at 40 Albemarle Street, London, and
may have assembled American components at the
above address or at a nearby barracks to create
their Vandy. The Vandy (nickname for the Van-
dervells) may however have simply been a variation on the Commonwealth car from America,
with English badge, coachwork and CAV starting
and lighting.

**25. 1920-21 (prod: under 150). Tourer 1920 1000
guineas, 1921 £995. S6 SV 3772cc 55bhp Rutenber,
multi-disc clutch, in-unit four speed gearbox with**

Vandy four-seater tourer, 1921.

**central change, spiral bevel axle, semi-elliptic sus-
pension, detachable wheels and split rims.** Typical
American-type car except that four speeds were by
no means universal at the time. Chassis numbers ran
from 50-200 but not necessarily all were supplied,
though three have been traced by Michael Worthington-Williams to one Welsh dealer. 25mpg was
quoted.

VARLEY WOODS

Shaftesbury Road, Acton, London W3

The High Speed Tool Co. Ltd (also trading as HS
Motors Ltd) introduced an assembled car in 1918

The 1919 Varley Woods 11.9hp.

and in 1919-20 persuaded Turner of Wolverhampton to make it. Some assembly also took place in a disused laundry in Acton using parts obtained from Storey (Jack Storey and E Varley Grossmith had planned a car called the Winchester to be made in the Hampshire city of that name). Grossmith, of the acting and perfumery family, who had already turned his hand to the manufacture of soup and mouth organs, teamed up with J R Woods, an overseas trader, to make the Varley-Woods. (Grossmith sounded too German for the postwar era).

Turner, which was owed money, petitioned for winding up in October 1920 and the final cars were sold during 1921. Woods was subsequently killed by a lion in Africa.

11.9, 14.3. 1918-21 (prod: 160 11.9). Chassis £575. S4 OHV 1795cc Dorman, S4 SV 2200cc Tylor, cone clutch, four speed gearbox, torque tube, worm axle. Semi-elliptic front, cantilever rear suspension. The first Dorman was supplied on 18/8/19 suggesting that earlier cars either did not exist or else were variations on Turners. 14.3hp Tylor engines were offered from mid-1920. The OHV Dorman was an inspired choice, but the adoption of yet another variation of the Rolls-Royce radiator shape was far from original. The firm built its own gearboxes.

VAUXHALL

Luton, Bedfordshire

Named after the area of London where it had first been set up as a marine engineer, Vauxhall had made cars from 1903 and moved to Luton in 1905. In that year Laurence Pomeroy joined the firm and was to become its highly successful chief engineer. He left for America in 1919 (later joining Daimler) and was replaced by Clarence E King, who had worked for Adams and Lorraine-Dietrich. King designed the popular Vauxhall 14/40 and was responsible for the overhead-valve versions of Pomeroy's designs.

In 1920 Vauxhall employed 1400 and made 780 cars. Joint managing director Percy Kidner built up a virtually controlling interest in AC but these

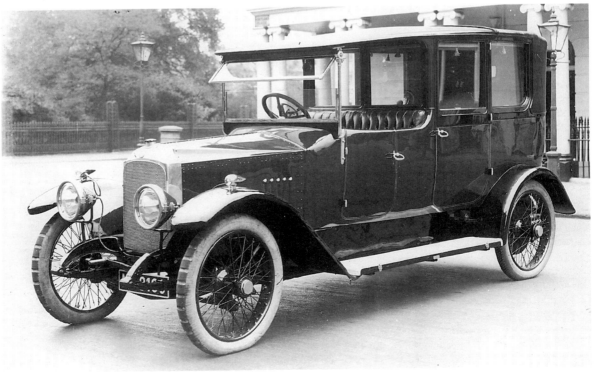

A 25hp D type Vauxhall.

The Vauxhall 30/98 Velox.

80,000 shares were sold to SF Edge in 1925, shortly before General Motors invested £300,000 in Vauxhall.

American influence boosted output to 2587 cars in 1928 (of which 852 were exported) and 8930 cars in 1930, before the arrival of the mass-market Cadet and other cheap models.

D 25. 1913-22 (prod: approx 4500 of which probably 1700 1919-22). Tourer 1921 £1450. S4 SV 3969cc, multi-plate clutch, four speed gearbox with right hand change, bevel axle, semi-elliptic suspension. This was a famous wartime staff car, and 1556 were supplied to the Services 1914-18. Although weighing over 1½ tons it had light controls and was good for 60mph. It was the touring version of the mechanically similar C type Prince Henry, with the same bore and stroke, and was usually seen with heavy and formal coachwork – indeed it was marketed as "the weight carrying chassis".

30/98 E and OE. 1913-22, 1922-28 (prod: 13 pre-war then 270 E followed by 313 OE types. Chassis 1920 £1275, 1925 £950. E S4 SV 4525cc 90bhp, OE S4 OHV 4224cc 112-120bhp, multi-plate clutch, four speed gearbox with right hand change, bevel axle, semi-elliptic suspension.** A development of the famous Prince Henry sporting model, with a fixed cylinder head until the arrival of the OE. The latter car could do 10-82mph in top gear, or up to 100mph with racing bodywork (amongst Vauxhall's own stylish sports tourer bodies was the Velox).

The OE had its most successful year in 1924, when 111 were made. Front wheel brakes came in 1923, and in 1926 hydraulic operation.

Three out of every five 30/98 chassis were sold in Australia. C E King developed the OE in place of a more complex OHC design from Pomeroy.

14, 14/40 (M and LM). 1922-24, 1924-27 (prod: approx 1800, 3500). Chassis 1923 £420, 1927 £395. S4 SV 2297cc, single plate clutch, in-unit three speed (four speed on LM) gearbox with right hand change, spiral bevel axle. Semi-elliptic front, cantilever rear suspension. C E King's new small Vauxhall was unveiled late in 1921. Speed was in the upper 50s (65mph on the LM) and fuel consumption 25-28mpg. As well as four speeds the LM had higher compression pistons and wire wheels instead of discs, gaining four wheel brakes in 1926. Lots were

Vauxhall 14/40 "Princeton" four-seater.

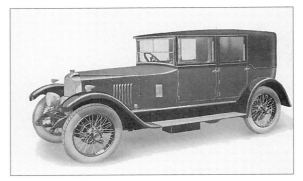

Windover "triple purpose allweather body" on a 25/70hp Vauxhall chassis.

sent in CKD form to Australia, where several survive. An altogether well balanced, well equipped, refined and nicely finished family car. The Princeton tourer shown was a popular style.

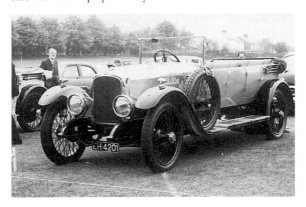

Vauxhall 23/60 OD type "Kington" tourer, 1923.

OD 23/60. 1922-26 (prod: approx 1400). Chassis 1925 £725, various body styles adding up to £575. S4 OHV 3969cc, multi-disc clutch, four speed gearbox with right hand change, spiral bevel axle, semi-elliptic suspension. Vauxhall's first overhead-valve engine was also equipped with a Lanchester harmonic balancer to compete with sixes by then prevalent in the carriage trade. This model was a modernised version of the old 25hp D and had similar non-interconnected four wheel brakes to the OE. For £5 Vauxhall would test the car if it had been bodied by an outside coachbuilder (provided it stayed beneath a 49cwt saloon laden limit).

S 25/70. 1926-28 (prod: approx 50). Chassis 1926 £1050, limo £1675. S6 sleeve-valve 3880cc, multi-disc clutch, four speed gearbox with right hand change, spiral bevel axle, semi-elliptic suspension. This rarity had four wheel hydraulic brakes (non-interconnected) and used the Burt-McCollum licence sleeve-valve system. It was the last new car to be designed by Vauxhall as opposed to General Motors and had a remarkably smooth engine with a ten-bearing, fully balanced crankshaft. 18mpg and

up to 65mph were typical. A distinguishing feature was the transverse Houdaille shock absorbers visible on the front axle.

1929 Vauxhall Velox 20/60hp.

20/60 R and T. 1927-29 and 1930 (prod: 4228 and 1172). Chassis 1928 and 1930 £375. S6 OHV 2762 and 2916cc, single plate clutch, in-unit four speed gearbox with central change, spiral bevel axle, semi-elliptic suspension. Lots of American influences were evident, like coil ignition and central change. Prices and weight were lower and sales higher. The cars were popular in export markets, one such car having stormed up and down a 1 in 2½ hill and then been deliberately somersaulted into a 70-foot pit to show its strength! Many of the old body names were retained (the 1929 Velox shown no doubt upset the traditionalists) and "the Six Super-excellent" was good for 65mph, especially with the larger engine that came in later Rs and the T successor. A Bedford saloon cost only £495, reviving a GM name from Bedford-Buick days that was soon to grace trucks.

VICTOR

Mount Pleasant Road, Ealing, London W15

This 10hp Precision engined cyclecar, which grew from the earlier Dewcar, was available in 1914. In 1915 a four-cylinder 1100cc version was announced and some sources give the Victor as being revived after the war and lasting to 1921. See also Picknell.

Victor cyclecar.

VULCAN

Crossens, Southport, Lancashire

Founded at the end of the last century by the Hampson family, Vulcan had grown into one of the largest makers of cars and commercials in the north west of England. In 1919 Harper Bean had acquired 60% of the firm in exchange for Vulcan buying £150,000 of its shares. C B Wardman (see Lea Francis) was installed as joint managing director.

Wardman's sales arm failed to shift Vulcan's out-put profitably and the whole enterprise foundered. Vulcan's link with the Chiltern car (and possibly with Eric-Campbell) was no more successful and its involvement with Lea Francis brought only temporary respite. One thousand vehicles were made in eight months of 1923 but commercials predominated. A O Lord (see Loyd-Lord), was brought in to revive the cars but, after an unsuccessful small six, production finally ended in 1928. See also French.

Commercials carried on into the mid-1950s despite bankruptcy in 1931 and amalgamations with Tilling-Stevens and the Rootes Group. The factory was later used to make Corgi motor scooters and BMB tractors and still stands, part of it in use with the Phillips electrical group and part with the Dorman traffic cone firm.

16. 1919-23 (prod: approx 1650 incl. Dorman powered 12hp). Chassis 1919 £600, 1923 £420. S4 SV 2610cc Dorman, cone clutch, four speed gearbox with right hand change, worm axle, semi-elliptic suspension. Solid and stolid. Vulcan's blacksmith and anvil mascot was just about the only distinguishing feature. A pity the V8 of 1919 and two- and four-cylinder sleeve-valve models in 1922 were not marketed.

One of the Vulcan 10hp twin prototypes on the 1922 Scottish Trial.

The 16hp Vulcan.

1925 Vulcan 20hp.

Vulcan 12hp saloon.

12. 1920-27 (prod: see below). S4 OHV 1.8/1.5 litre Dorman and Meadows, cone clutch, four speed gearbox latterly in-unit with engine, torque tube, overhead worm axle, semi-elliptic suspension. Vulcan's staple model started with OHV Dorman KNO engines (see 16 entry for combined purchases of Dormans) and later had various engine choices, including, allegedly, Vulcan's own sidevalve 1500 in 1925 – on test one of these gave 34mpg and a top speed of 52mph. A bigger Colonial 14hp in 1925-27 had Meadows 2120cc engines (of which, with some 1795cc units, 77 were bought). A 15.9hp from Hick Hargreaves of Bolton was also tried. The Lea Francis Kirkstone was effectively a Vulcan 12, and 71 were built at Crossens. Engines were Meadows 4ED (twelve used) or British Anzani.

Vulcan's output for Lea Francis was at least 300 cars and in return the Coventry factory made gearboxes and steering columns for Crossens.

20. 1920-22, 1923-25 (prod: n/a). Chassis 1920 £675, 1925 £415. S4 SV 3307cc, 3686cc, cone clutch, four speed gearbox with right hand change, overhead worm axle, semi-elliptic suspension. These models had the same engines and other items as Vulcan 1½ and 2 ton commercial vehicles, initially with fixed cylinder heads. A stylish saloon was available in 1921 for an exhorbitant £1125. Shown is one of the last tourers of 1925, fitted with the luxury of balloon tyres. 1925 marked a profit of £19,000 for Vulcan, which in 1931 was bankrupt to the tune of £926,200.

The larger engined 1923-25 version was sometimes called a 25 but more often "Twenty".

The 1927 Vulcan 14/40 standard saloon.

14/40, 16/60. 1927-28, 1928-29 (prod: n/a). 14/40 chassis £325-400, 16/60 £475. S6 DOHC 1.7 litres, 2 litres, plate clutch, in-unit four speed gearbox (own on VS, Meadows on MVS), spiral bevel axle (VS) or worm (MVS), semi-elliptic suspension (quarter-elliptic rear on MVS). Available as VS "Long Six" and MVS "Short Six", these cars incorporated the unsuccessful "hemi head" twin cam AO Lord six-cylinder engine also utilised by Lea Francis in its 14/40 LFS until the Ace of Spades was ready. The engine suffered from lubrication and rigidity problems and was unnecessarily complex for its modest 45bhp output. It featured magneto ignition and thermo-syphon cooling and the chassis had four wheel servo brakes. Vulcan is also supposed to have tried Calcott and Calthorpe sixes.

A free-wheel and the Humphrey-Sandberg preselective gearbox were optional on cars from late 1926 and 1927 respectively, and saloons with wide bodywork instead of external running boards were an unusual feature from the same era. As Vulcan bought several medium sixes from Meadows for its light coaches and Lea Francis knew the benefits of these, one wonders why Crossens bothered with its own engines in these cars.

WARREN LAMBERT

Petersham Road, Richmond, Surrey

Mr A Warren Lambert was a Morgan agent in Putney who also raced Morgans. In 1912, with help from his father and brother, he offered a rival with four wheels. Built initially at Uxbridge Road, Shepherds Bush, it gained a good reputation in hillclimbs and up to 25 a week were built. Warren Lambert, a Major after war service, resumed production at Richmond in 1920, but as larger rivals got into their stride the supply of bought-in parts such as gears from Moss and gearbox casings from a firm in Bristol became erratic and costly.

The fact that the cars were only available as two-seaters, with primitive features like metal-to-metal brakes and no differential, must have made them unattractive when compared with the cheaper Austin Seven.

The firm had its capital increased to £10,000 in 1920, and when wound up in February 1922 there was a surplus balance of £400.

The Warren-Lambert light car.

10, 11. 1920-22, 1920-21 (prod: 95 in 1920, less afterwards). Complete 1921 £400. S4 SV 1330cc Alpha or 1498cc Coventry Simplex, cone clutch, three or four speed gearbox with quadrant change, torque tube, bevel axle. Semi-elliptic front, quarter-elliptic rear suspension (quarter-elliptic all round on Sports model). Slightly more sporting than many of its rivals, particularly the 65mph Simplex engined Sports with large exposed copper exhaust and four speed gearbox at £575 complete. The Sports retained the flat radiator of earlier types, whereas others received a bullnose shape for 1921.

Two cars were built in 1921 with 1496cc MV engines by Dorman, the make that had been favoured for four-cylinder models in 1914. To help live up to their slogan "The Mountain Climber" many cars had no differentials.

WAVERLEY

Trenmar Gardens, Harrow Road, and Waldo Road, Scrubbs Lane, both Willesden, London NW10

Waverley cars were made from 1910 using French components. British components were mostly specified after the war, and in the later 1920s the "All British Six" with saloon coachwork (often with fabric covering) became a speciality. Most bodies were by E B Hall & Co., which became the Carlton Carriage Co.

The prototype 7hp flat twin Waverley.

The agency for Senechal cars from France had been added, and Waverley luggage trailers were another useful sideline. A few Coventry Victor 7hp powered cyclecars were offered in 1926 but it seems likely that these were some sort of joint enterprise with GWK and nothing came of them. The firm continued in business as general engineers long after the Second World War. Car production probably lasted little beyond the time of the Wall Street Crash, though cars appeared in buyer's guides until 1935.

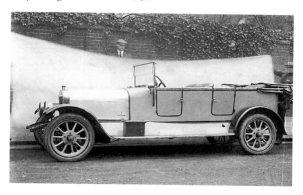

1919 Waverley 15hp tourer.

FIFTEEN. 1919-24 (prod: possibly 350). Chassis 1920 £525, 1924 £400. S4 SV 2304cc (initially 2121cc), cone clutch, four speed (initially three speed) gearbox with right hand change, spiral

bevel axle. Semi-elliptic front and two sets of quarter-elliptic springs at rear. The smaller engine was probably by Chapuis Dornier though Aster was mentioned. The larger was by Tylor and similar to that used by Angus-Sanderson. Smith electric self-starting was present on the Tylor types and both hand and foot brakes were in the rear drums with no transmission brake. The radiator (1919 example shown) with its badge incorporating W in a circle was much as had been used before the war, but gained a slightly more curvaceous top. The double rear spring arrangement was also seen on some Jewels and Citroëns. Though 100 gearboxes were ordered from Meadows in July 1923 only seven seem to have been delivered, suggesting that all was not well at Waverley.

1924 Waverley 12hp negotiating a water-splash.

10/15, 11, 12. 1922-27 (prod: possibly 250). Chassis £340 1922, £195 1927. Various S4 (see below), three then four speed gearbox with cone then single dry plate clutch, Timken spiral bevel axle, semi-elliptic suspension. These models commenced with 1498cc Coventry-Simplex engines, but were enlarged from a bore of 66 to 69mm for the 12. In 1924 there was also a sleeve-valve 1496cc Twelve with Burt-McCollum designed Greenwood and Batley engines as used by Argyll. Perrot front wheel brakes were added for 1924. A sleeve-valve car weighing 22cwt was tested and found to be "turbine quiet" and smooth, with great flexibility and a top speed of 50mph.

A Dorman MVB powered 12 was offered in 1924-25 but only four engines seem to have been supplied.

16/50. 1925-30 (prod: n/a). Chassis 1925 £425, 1929 £400. S6 OHV 1990cc Coventry Climax, cone clutch, in-unit four speed gearbox with right hand change, spiral bevel axle, semi-elliptic front, two

1927 Waverley 16/50 fabric saloon.

sets of quarter elliptic rear springs. The six-cylinder 16/50 was the only Waverley available after 1927 and testers praised its light controls, 55-60mph and 23-28mpg. Weymann type saloons with rather Fiat-like radiators had particularly comfortable seats, with a reclining mechanism for the driver. The engine was especially smooth thanks to a Lanchester vibration damper but, despite fulsome praise from the motoring press and a 70mph Sports version, the 16/50 was up against lots of better-known rivals and ended by being built only to special order.

WEBB

The Tannery, Stourport on Severn, Worcestershire

V P Webb was a member of the Webb seeds family whose thoughts first turned to motor cycles but who settled for assembled light cars in 1922. They stood little chance against the Austin Seven built nearby, and the firm ended its days making bodywork (for Calthorpe amongst others) and milk churns. Victor Webb then moved to Australia.

1922 Webb Super-Nine.

SUPER-NINE. 1922-23 (prod: about 95). Four-seater £220, all-weather £240. S4 SV 1088cc Alpha, cone clutch, three speed Moss gearbox with central change, Moss spiral bevel axle, quarter-elliptic suspension. "Fast but built to Last" was the slogan of the Webb with its royal blue bodywork (built at the Tannery) with maroon wheels and upholstery. Up to 50mph and 45mpg were claimed and sole concessionarire was Autocars Ltd off Bond Street, London, though when sales were disappointing other firms attempted to market the car.

No self-starter was fitted and the 6-volt lighting was by Miller, with a BTH magneto for ignition.

WESTALL

London SW1

An 865cc 7hp single-cylinder cyclecar. Sidney C Westall planned to sell the two-seater for £130 in 1922 but nothing more was heard of the venture.

WESTCAR

Strode Park, Herne, Kent

Major Charles Henry Beeston Prescott-Westcar was a landowner who turned his estate workshops to good use in 1922, having already introduced electricity to Herne from his own Crossley-powered generators. His Westcars had body framing made from ash grown on the estate, brackets from the blacksmith, and electroplating and case hardening from the Major's own facilities. They were otherwise largely "assembled" jobs.

In 1924 one of the cars covered 10,000 miles under RAC supervision in 34 days at 37.19mpg, but neither this nor its handbuilt quality could disguise the fact that it was too expensive and insular to compete.

The Heron (which see), being unconventional, was even less successful. One of the works' last projects in 1925 was a motor tram used on Herne Bay Pier for the next 20 years.

12hp Westcar coupé, 1922.

10/14, 12. 1922-25 (prod: under 100). Chassis 1923 £352, tourer £419. S4 SV 1497cc Dorman, single plate clutch, initially three speed then Meadows four speed gearbox with central change, Moss spiral bevel axle, semi-elliptic suspension. A mixture

of bought-in parts like Alford and Alder front axle, Marles steering, Serck radiator (initially angular then curvaceous) and the Meadows, Moss and Dorman items mentioned above, allied with hand craftsmanship and assembly, spelled good quality but high prices. Regional makes on this small scale rarely survived for long. A 1922 example is shown and one survivor is known to exist, a 1925 Twelve.

WESTWOOD

Lower Ince, Wigan, Lancashire

Made in the Britannia Works, near the home of Pagefield lorries, the Westwood started as a high grade OHV car. It was sold in the south by The London and Parisian Motor Co. of Davies Street W1. The Westwood Motor Co., formed in January 1920 but buying engines in 1919, changed its name to Westwood-Ince in 1924, suggesting some form of financial reconstruction, but to no avail as it disappeared in 1926.

The Dorman engines were supplied by Timberlakes, who were also agents for Little Greg cars and supplied Dorman engines to Pagefield.

The Westwood 14hp all-weather four-seater.

11.9, 14. 1920-23, 1923-26 (prod: 57, 36). Chassis 1922 £575, three quarter coupé (shown) 1925 £495. S4 OHV 1795cc Dorman, 2121cc Meadows, cone clutch, four speed gearbox, spiral bevel axle (latterly by Timken), semi-elliptic suspension. One of the select few with OHV at such an early date, but with little else to make it stand out. Some of the last 14 chassis had pointed-tail sports bodies but, in general, appearance was stodgy and respectable. The 1.8 model ran to chassis A141 and the 2.1 from M4200 to M4233.

WHERWELL

Wherwell, Hampshire

In this tiny village between Andover and Winchester Thompson and Son produced a cyclecar in 1920-21.

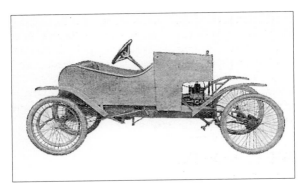

Wherwell cyclecar.

It had friction transmission with chain drive and 7hp Coventry Victor flat-twin engine. Only three are believed to have been built.

WHIPPET

See Willys-Overland and Bleriot

WHITEHEAD

Clayton Lane, Bradford, Yorkshire

Whitehead Light Cars existed in 1920-21 and is believed to have made about sixteen cars. A 1498cc Coventry-Simplex engine with Moss three speed gearbox was used. More unusual features included transverse front suspension and a wooden chassis. A surviving catalogue from Universal Motor Industries, Premier House, Southampton Row, London WC, describes another type of Whitehead, which could conceivably be what became the Whitehead-Thanet. It discloses a 20hp engine with the same bore and stroke of the Ford T and with T-like transverse suspension and epicyclic transmission. It had a distinctive bullnose radiator and cost £230 as a chassis and £275 as a tourer.

The Whitehead of 1920-21.

WHITEHEAD-THANET

Richmond and Ashtead, Surrey

A grandiose plan was hatched by aircraft maker A J Whitehead to sell 100,000 cars per year in 1921. Components were to come from America as well as from an unspecified British engine factory. Other parts were to be from the Whitehead Components factory at Richmond, with final assembly at Ashstead. Output was due to start in 1920 but few, if any, were built. Coachwork was to have been by F J Wraight in London, whose Thanet car may well have been the abortive Whitehead-Thanet, or which may also have been still-born. See Whitehead for a car with distinct American leanings that may have been the first Whitehead-Thanet. A J Whitehead's only specified American component was a chassis from Gray Andrews Corp., possibly something to do with the Gray car, itself a Model T rival.

WHITLOCK

Slade Works, Cricklewood Broadway, London NW2

Whitlock had been a coachbuilder since 1778 and in 1903-06 offered complete cars incorporating its name. The Liverpool-based Lawton-Goodman coachbuilding firm had existed since 1870 and a member of its founding family acquired Whitlock shortly before the 1914-18 War, when 12/16 and 20/30 cars were listed. After production of ambulances and De Havilland aircraft fuselages, complete cars were added in 1922 using a factory close to Bentley's premises.

Output was small, handbuilt and, like Waverley, lasted into the 1930s with a six-cylinder model. Lawton-Goodman's showrooms were in Brook Street W1 with the telegraphic address Metrospeed, whilst that of the factory was, quaintly, Carmenador, Crickle!

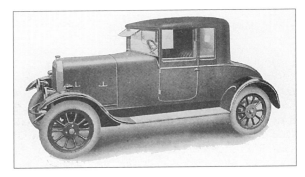

12hp Whitlock coupé de luxe.

11, 12, 12/35. 1922-25, 1923-26 (prod: n/a). Chassis 1923 from £315. S4 SV 1368cc, 1496cc, cone clutch, **three speed gearbox with right hand change, spiral bevel axle. Semi-elliptic front, ¾-elliptic rear suspension.** The smaller engine is believed to have been the work of Coventry Climax whilst the larger was by British Anzani. These were typical assembled chassis, graced with above average in-house coachwork in the standard colours of grey, blue and light blue. The 12 could be had with front wheel brakes from 1924 for an additional £20.

Whitlock 14hp tourer.

14, 16/50. 1924, 1925-26 (prod: few). Complete from £475, £595. S6 OHV 1755cc, 1991cc Coventry Climax, in-unit three then four speed gearbox with right hand change, spiral bevel axle, semi-elliptic suspension. Whitlock's answer to the half-hearted demand for small sixes and a direct competitor to Waverley. Four wheel brakes were fitted, as was safety glass on saloons. There were twin Zenith carbs on the 16/50 and a Lanchester vibration damper.

The 20/70hp Whitlock tourer.

20/70. 1926-30 (prod: 8 see below). Chassis 1927 £600, 1930 £650. S6 OHV 2973cc Meadows (3.3 litres from late 1927), single plate clutch, in-unit four speed Meadows gearbox with right hand change, spiral bevel axle, semi-elliptic suspension. The same engine was used by Bean, Invicta, Chambers, and others including commercial vehicles. Only eight engines for Whitlock can be found in Meadows records, all delivered in 1926-27, and the same sequence through to 1930 has been studied without finding more.

A 5-65mph top gear and a Bentley style radiator seem to have persuaded few players in the Star, Sunbeam, Crossley league to choose a Whitlock. In 1929 or 1930 a flatter radiator with winged badge and large cut-out W (actually two overlapping, one of which faced downwards) on a dividing bar was substituted. One such car exists as the only known surviving Whitlock.

WHITWORTH
See Hammond

WIGAN-BARLOW

Lowther Street and David Road, Coventry, Warwickshire

Capt. Barlow is linked with firms after the Great War called Kolchester Manufacturing Co. and Coventry Motor Co., which may have been forerunners of Wigan-Barlow Motors Ltd. This had a brief existence in 1922-23 and was a typical assembler of the period. Eight cars are known to have had 1496cc Meadows engines, and one or more had 1368cc Coventry Simplex units. Wrigley rear axles and other proprietary parts were used. A 1922 11/40 at £450 is shown.

1922 11/40hp Wigan-Barlow, costing £450.

WILLYS-KNIGHT

Heaton Chapel, Stockport, Lancashire

Another one of the Willys-Overland-Crossley marques, Willys-Knight arrived in Britain a little later than Overland because of licensing agreements – Daimler having previously had exclusive rights to British use of the Knight engine.

The marque was launched here in October 1921 and sold well through the decade, a poppet-valve Whippet being added in 1930. Willys-Overland-Crossley collapsed in 1933 and R H Collier in Birmingham acquired the spares (as he had done for so many victims of the Depression).

There was much confusing badge-engineering

in the latter stages of the company. For example, the Willys Light Six was a version of the (Overland) Whippet Six (for which Willys-Overland-Crossley bought 2000 smaller Lycoming engines), the Crusader was a variation of the model 56 for 1929, and the Palatine of late 1930 was named after a Manchester suburb. Another Willys brand, the Falcon Knight, accounted for an assembly batch of about 40 cars at Heaton Chapel.

Willys-Knight Six saloon, 1927.

SIX. 1926-30 (prod: n/a). Complete 1927 £375-£850. S6 sleeve-valve 3874cc 25/60hp (3881cc 27/65 from 1929), dry plate clutch, in-unit three speed gearbox, spiral bevel axle, semi-elliptic suspension. This was typical of the various Knight engined Willys models offered after the "fours" ended in 1925. There were also smaller 21hp sixes and even some poppet-valve derivates of the Whippet. In November 1925, by which time 180,000 Willys-Knight engines had been built in total, Willys-Overland-Crossley announced a successful top gear trip from Land's End to John O'Groats. This Knight was far cheaper than the equivalent Daimler and equally prone to exhaust smoke when worn.

WILSON

Leicester Road, Loughborough, Leicestershire

W Wilson had designed cars for Coltman of Loughborough before the war but it is unlikely that any of his 11.9 Wilsons of 1922-23 were sold. They were listed as two- or four-seaters at £325 and £450, with a British Transmission Co. three speed gearbox and spiral bevel axle. The engine was supposedly the Dorman MV but very few were bought.

In 1925 Wilson Brothers of Aldermanbury, London EC2, were intending to make an 8hp cyclecar and approached John Dorman of the Meadows engine firm for gearboxes. One much altered version survives, but whether more were built, or whether there was any connection with W Wilson, is unknown.

WILTON

High Street, Tooting, London SW

C F Halsall is said to have built a three wheeler in 1901, followed in 1912 by four wheelers which were made for a couple of years with what was claimed to be Wilton's own four-cylinder 9hp engine but was probably a Chapuis-Dornier in a Malicet et Blin frame.

Postwar offerings from Wilton Cars Ltd were larger and fairly ordinary, with proprietary engines, though the use of worm driven axles was more unusual. The bicycle business from which Wilton grew later sold radios, etc., and still survives. The Halsall family also ran a garage in Hanworth from 1916 to 1946.

The 11.9hp Wilton.

11.9. 1919-24 (prod: about 100, see below). Chassis 1920 £425, 1924 £325. S4 SV 1490cc 24bhp Dorman, plate clutch, three speed Moss gearbox with right hand change, worm axle. Semi-elliptic front, cantilever rear suspension. Early cars had 1496cc Meadows units, after which 1800cc Peters engines were used until the Dormans of 1922 onwards. Only 21 Dorman MV engines have been traced, but 103 chassis numbers were listed from 1922 to 1923. The High Street, Tooting address of 120-124 was a cramped former stables, confirming a limited output. A radiator of rather Palladium-like shape was adopted for the Dorman engined cars.

WINCHESTER
See Storey and Varley-Woods

WINCO
See Stringer

WINDSOR

Lancaster Road, Notting Hill, London W11

James Bartle and Co., founded in 1854, made coachwork and iron castings (its manhole covers are still a familiar sight). C S Windsor took control in 1910 and by 1916 had an 1870cc prototype car running. The Windsor car, designed by E Farebrother, was launched at the 1923 London Motor Show. It was unusual in being built almost entirely from the firm's own components, and in having four wheel brakes and pushrod OHV. Sales were organised by F W Berwick, often utilising his Sizaire-Berwick dealers. C S Windsor died in December 1925 and Bartle went out of business in 1927, when machine tool suppliers Alfred Herbert Ltd forced liquidation. Dealers Watkins and Doncaster of Stamford Hill N15 bought the jigs, tools, spares and drawings, and continued to offer cars into the 1930s. Designer Farebrother went to Cluley in 1927 to design its 14.

1924 Windsor 10/15.

10-15. 1923-29 (prod: about 300). Chassis 1924 £295, 1927 £240. S4 OHV 1354cc, dry plate clutch, in-unit four speed gearbox, spiral bevel axle, semi-elliptic suspension. Early types had splash oiling and suffered big end problems, all solved by full pressure lubrication on the S-4 series. The gear gate was "back to front" and testers complained of inadequate four wheel brake compensation. Curiously, Windsor started with coil ignition and then went over to magneto in a complete reversal of the usual trend. Otherwise this was a far better small car than most.

Fuel consumption of 33-38mpg was typical, and a top speed of almost 70mph could be achieved by the 1926 sports model, which had Rudge-Whitworth wire wheels as standard (the normal car did 55-60mph). Polished walnut abounded and the car looked like a miniature Sizaire-Berwick (or Rolls-Royce), with a particularly neat and tidy engine.

WINGFIELD

Norbury Avenue, Norbury, London SE

Though introduced in 1909, the Wingfield was probably not produced until Cars and Motor Sundries Ltd took control in 1912. Thereafter an extensive range was offered and an output of 250 per year was planned. How many were sold is unclear, but one model was revived after the war.

The 23.8 Wingfield chassis.

23.8. 1914-20 (prod: n/a). S6 SV 3920cc, four speed gearbox, bevel axle. Semi-elliptic front, cantilever rear suspension. The pre-war version seems to have had a tri-bloc engine and the postwar a bi-bloc. This was an ambitious size and type of car to launch in postwar conditions, and like British Ensign, Leyland, Sizaire-Berwick and even Napier it was doomed.

WINSON

Rochdale, Lancashire

J Winn and, one can perhaps speculate, his son made this cyclecar in 1920. It could have 8hp Precision or Blackburne engines with friction transmission and chain final drive. Unusually, a form of differential was incorporated.

WOLSELEY

Adderley Park and Ward End, Birmingham

Wolseley had made cars since 1896, originally under the management of Herbert Austin. It was acquired by Vickers, who from 1905 to 1909 employed John D Siddeley as manager. Both Austin and Siddeley of course went on to create their own successful motor firms.

After massive wartime expansion Wolseley had a capacity of 20,000 vehicles per year but almost certainly never exceeded the 12,000 made in 1921

(its chassis numbering from the earliest days reached 92,000 in 1927).

The company was in dire financial straits until it was rescued by William Morris early in 1927. Wolseley was a keen advocate of overhead camshaft engines (based loosely on its wartime Hispano-Suiza V8 aero engine experience), and this feature continued under the new management.

From the late 1920s Adderley Park gradually became the home of Morris-Commercial and Wolseley retrenched into the Ward End factory that had belonged to another Vickers subsidiary which in pre-Great War days had built the Stellite car (Vickers Crayford may also have built some – see Fiat).

STELLITE, 10, 7, 11/22. 1919, 1920-24, 1922-23, 1925-28 (prod: n/a). Complete 10 1920 £545, 7 1922 £255, complete 1927 from £215. All S4 OHC except HO2 SV 984cc 7, others 1100cc and 1267cc, multi-disc clutch in oil (cone on 7), three speed gearbox in-unit with worm axle (spiral bevel on 7), quarter-elliptic suspension. The Stellite was a revival from before the war, the name re-appearing on the Wolseley-Stellite in 1921-22 as a cheaper version of the 10 without electrics.

The 7 was a refined, water-cooled light car similar to models from Rover, Ariel, BSA, etc., and was soon killed off by the four-cylinder Austin and Morris. It could cruise at 25mph and return 45mpg. The coil ignition 10, "the small car of quality", and its successor the 11/22 (with magneto ignition) were

Wolseley 10hp.

refined and relatively expensive. On test in 1924 45mph, 33mpg, light steering, quietness and quality of finish were referred to, and in 1926 50mph and 35mpg were possible with the four wheel braked 11/22. In 1921 one with streamlined bodywork averaged 78.67mph over 250 miles and in 1922 843 miles were covered in 12 hours at Brooklands.

1920 Wolseley 15 touring car.

1925 Wolseley 16/35hp four-door "light saloon".

15, 14, 14/40, 16/35. 1920-27 (prod: n/a). Chassis 1921 £650, 1927 £350. S4 SV and OHC (15) 2.5 litres, multi-disc clutch, three or four speed gearbox with right hand change, worm axle, quarter-elliptic suspension. This family of models shared similar engine dimensions with the 20-24hp sixes. Describing the 15 the *Daily Despatch* called it "what this class of vehicle should be like". Four wheel brakes arrived in 1924, when the brake horsepower was added to the model's appellation, and four speed gearboxes were substituted.

Vickers' metallurgical skills were much in evidence including Vickers-Timken roller wheel bearings. The OHC fours (the 16 and 14 were SV versions) gained much from Wolseley's aero engine experience. The 14 entered production in September 1922 and was guaranteed to do 45mph (against its OHC sister's 55). It averaged 24mpg and was said to be more flexible than the 15.

24/30hp Wolseley with Cole coupé cabriolet bodywork finished in grey with mauve leather interior.

20, 24/30, 24/55. 1920-24, 1923-24, 1925-27 (prod: n/a). Chassis 1921 £1050, 1927 £750. S6 SV 3.9 litres (5.4 litres 24/30), multi-disc clutch, four speed gearbox with right hand change, worm axle (spiral bevel 24/55). Semi-elliptic front, cantilever rear suspension. The 24/30 was a revival of a pre-war type and the others were six-cylinder versions of the 15 family. The 24/55 had four wheel brakes and all cars contained Vickers best steel and other components. Sales were small and dwindled drastically in the last year of Vickers ownership.

The Wolseley 16/45, 1927.

16-45, Viper. 1927-32 (prod: 9958). Fabric saloon 1928 £550, Weymann coupé 1929 £399. S6 OHC 2075cc, single plate clutch, four speed gearbox with central change, spiral bevel axle, semi-elliptic suspension. Launched in September 1926, this was the first sign of the new Morris broom sweeping through Adderley Park. Some stylish designs were offered as well as the six-light steel saloon of 1927 shown. In the final two years, from mid-1930, the model was known as the Viper and had hydraulic brakes, a three speed gearbox and coil ignition in place of the 16-45's mechanical brakes, four speeds and magneto.

The 12-32hp Wolseley de luxe four-door saloon.

12-32HP. 1927-30 (prod: n/a). Chassis 1928 £220, steel saloon £315. S4 OHC 1542cc, single plate clutch, in-unit four speed gearbox, spiral bevel axle, semi-elliptic suspension. A 1½-litre replacement for the old 11/22, with Morris Cowley engine dimensions (but valves overhead) and all steel bodywork, built in what became known as the Pressed Steel Factory at Cowley.

There were three standard colours and a spacious, leather upholstered interior.

21/60, 32/80, 21/60 SIX. 1927-31, 1928-29, 1929-35 (prod: approx 3800). Chassis 21/60 six 1929 £325, 21/60 eight £435, 32/80 £1075. S8 OHC 2.7 litres (21/60) and 4 litres (32/80), S6 OHC 2677cc (21/60 six), single plate clutch, in-unit four speed gearbox with central change, spiral bevel axle, semi-elliptic suspension. The straight eights had teething problems, though the Morris-owned Leon Bollée factory tried to sort the smaller one out in 3-litre form. The absurdly expensive 32/80 got little further

than the prototype stage, and probably less than 600 of these straight eights were built, at any rate in Britain. They had the unusual feature of a vertical shaft between the two cylinder blocks to drive the camshaft. The six with seven-bearing crankshaft was a much better bet, and in 1929 came with all-steel bodywork, Lockheed hydraulic brakes, Triplex glass, chrome plating and, of course, an overhead camshaft. These and smaller models came in standard or deluxe "County" form.

On test in 1928 a 21/60 eight recorded 60mph, 10-50mph acceleration in 33 seconds, 0-60mph in 60 seconds and a 49mph maximum in third gear, but a discreet veil was drawn over fuel consumption (a 1930 test showed 16.8mpg when driven hard).

1930 Wolseley Hornet with Abbey body.

HORNET. 1930-36 (prod: 2500 in 1930). Complete £175-185. S6 OHC 1271cc, single plate clutch, in-unit three speed gearbox, spiral bevel axle, semi-elliptic suspension. A lightweight – some would say whippy – chassis with a trend-setting miniature six-cylinder engine gave 60mph allied to rather suspect roadholding. Initially Morris Minor type bodies were

A straight-eight Wolseley coupé.

worn, but the Hornet soon became the darling of the coachbuilding trade, which was seeing its traditional market decimated by the Depression.

By 1931 over 20 custom body styles were available. The first series of Hornets lasted to 1932, latterly with four speeds, and in all about 40,000 were sold.

WOOLER

Alperton, Middlesex

John Wooler made motor cycles from 1911 to 1955. They were technically advanced, which in some ways was true also of the Wooler Mule of 1920-21. This had independent front suspension and a rotary-valve horizontally-opposed 8/10hp twin-cylinder engine. Primitive features included a hand-wheel gearchange and a surface carburettor. The rear wheels were set very close together and had belt drive.

The 1922 *Motor Car Index* dismisses the contraption with the assertion that it was "not proceeded with, only one or two experimental models being produced". Incidentally this source quotes the engine as being a 1020cc vee-twin.

The Wooler Mule of 1920.

XTRA

London Street, Chertsey, Surrey

This little curiosity existed briefly and was little more than a sidecar mounted on a three wheeled frame with its single rear wheel driven by friction. Chassis numbers commenced at 100 and, one imagines, progressed little further. One completed an arduous continental tour without difficulty.

XTRA. 1922-23 (prod: few). Complete 95 guineas. Single-cylinder SV 270cc air-cooled Villiers, chain drive to friction rollers on Avon rear tyre. Transverse leaf front, coil spring rear suspension. For

The Xtra looked more like a sidecar than a motor car.

Xtra read less, though perhaps this single-seater was intended as Britain's first second car! It was 8ft 10in long and 4ft 6in wide and weighed 3cwt. Equipment included acetylene lighting, and road tax cost £4.

ZEPHYR

Freemantle Road, Lowestoft, Suffolk

E Talbot had worked with Davidson and James at the Adams car firm in Bedford until its demise in 1914. The three then formed their own partnership in the unlikely location of an East Anglian fishing port (where admittedly the veteran Brooke car had been built by a marine engine firm). Whilst at Adams, chief draughtsman Talbot developed his aluminium and steel Zephyr high performance piston, and this became a regular production at Lowestoft for Aston-Martin and others, as well as being fitted to the firm's shortlived car. James, Talbot and Davidson Ltd later made fishing floats.

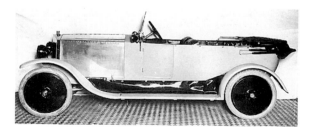

The Zephyr 11.9hp.

11.9. 1919-21 (prod: handful). Chassis 1920 £350, 1921 £500. S4 OHV 1945cc, in-unit four speed gearbox with central change, worm axle. Cantilever rear, semi-elliptic front suspension. In 1914 Zephyr had intended to produce a 9hp car but the postwar offering was far more interesting, with the modern features of Zephyr's own pushrod OHV 2-litre engine and four speed centre change box. Supply difficulties were given as the cause of failure, but the high price must have deterred customers.

Foreign makers
who sold cars in Britain

UNITED STATES

By making popular cars at a realistic price American makers had persuaded one in nine of the adult population of the USA to own a car by the end of 1923. In Britain the figure was one in a hundred, so not surprisingly the US became by far the most important foreign producer of cars for the British market. Its sales to Britain in the period 1922 to 1930 inclusive were 81,348 (of which a few thousand were re-exported). As the US industry was also backing most of Canada's exports, and of course made Ford, General Motors and Chrysler cars in Britain, its influence cannot be underestimated. Ford arrived here even before the vintage decade, during which GMC had its own UK assembly operations and also acquired Vauxhall.

The watershed year of 1925 (McKenna duties were re-imposed that July) saw the peak of the US invasion of Britain, with 18,534 cars sold here, a figure that had fallen back to 6941 in 1930 in the face of protectionism and the after-effects of the Wall Street Crash.

The activities of the major players are covered in the A-Z section, to which should be added the firms that either didn't establish assembly operations or else did not get very far with them, like Maxwell, which became Chrysler and died soon afterwards – though

its natural successor with four-cylinder cheap cars was the new Plymouth brand of 1928. Walter Chrysler bought Dodge in 1928, the year in which the companion De Soto brand was launched. Chrysler in 1924 became one of the first with hydraulic four wheel brakes, admittedly of the contracting variety.

As with the Chrysler empire, it is difficult to establish which of the General Motors makes were produced, or at any rate partially assembled, in Britain. Suffice to say that the principal brands involved were Chevrolet, Cadillac, Buick (some Canadian built models being called Buick Dominion), La Salle, Marquette, Oldsmobile, and Oakland from which grew Pontiac in 1926. Finally there was Scripps-Booth, which under GM control from mid-1918 used Chevrolet and Oakland parts.

Ford tended to plough a more lonely furrow but had a luxury arm in the shape of Lincoln to rival Cadillac and Chrysler's Imperial.

W C Durant, who had built up GMC, and Chevrolet when it was independent, started his own Durant brand in 1921 and added many other names including Eagle, Flint, Princeton and Star (known as Rugby in Britain and the Empire to avoid confusion with the Wolverhampton variety). Most of these were in the lower price range, and there was a Durant-owned British HQ at Slough and then in London NW8. To

1921 Alsace 20hp "interior drive saloon".

1920 Anderson 6: body was made from firm's own trees.

1919-20 Apperson 5.4-litre V8 tourer.

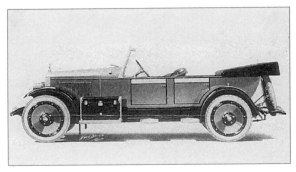

1922 Auburn Beauty Six sport model.

1930 Buick Master Series 60.

1928 Auburn 6-66 sedan.

1924 Buick Master Six.

1927 Cadillac V8 with Brunn coupé coachwork.

1929 La Salle V8 convertible coupe.

1926 Chrysler Six 23-75hp two-seater.

1923-24 Case 55hp six-cylinder.

gain a more luxurious and hopefully profitable line, in 1922 he acquired Locomobile from a group that included Mercer (one of the few well-known makers not represented in Britain). Unfortunately Locomobile was killed by the Wall Street Crash and Durant itself went out of business in the early 1930s after some quite substantial British sales.

Another of the big names to enjoy success in Britain was the old wagon builder Studebaker, which also had a large Canadian factory. President Albert R Erskine launched the 2.3-litre sidevalve six Erskine in Europe as a companion brand in 1926 and this enjoyed modest success until being axed in 1930. From late in 1924 Studebaker helped Chrysler, Horstman and Triumph to pioneer hydraulic four wheel brakes in Britain and by the late 1920s called itself the largest builder of straight eights in the world.

Of similar intention to the Erskine but a little earlier was the Essex, a cheap four-cylinder rival to the Model T launched here in 1919 by Hudson. As noted in the A-Z, Hudson had some assembly facilities in Britain and was a pioneer of enclosed "coach" saloons at a lower price than tourers – an Essex Coach was only £295 in 1924. Hudson Essex sales were handled initially by the well-known London motor dealers Shaw & Kilburn.

Another well-known name in Britain was that of J N Willys, some of whose cars were made here in collaboration with Crossley. Overland became the best-known brand here (one model even having Morris running gear), but there were several Knight sleeve-valve types including Willys-Knight, Stearns-Knight (some with straight eights) and Falcon-Knight.

Even the "small" American makes turned out to be a lot bigger than some British front-runners. For example the Allen, sold here briefly, was said to have found 20,000 customers in its homeland between 1914 and its demise in 1922. Continuing alphabetically we come to Alsace, a small right hand drive car made by Piedmont for the Automotive Products Co. of New York in 1920-21 and intended specifically for export. The 22.5hp AMCO of 1919-20

could have right or left hand drive and was advertised by American Motors Ltd of Holborn as mainly British (though local content was actually wheels and bodies!). The Anderson was unusual in coming not from the industrial north but from Carolina. A 25hp model was listed here in 1920 and though total output was nearly 2000 in 1923 no further attempts were made to interest the British market, where it had been handled by HC Motors of Great Portland Street, London. The Apperson listed here in 1919-22 was unusual in being a V8 – the unit was made by Apperson in Kokomo, Indiana, and had a displacement of 5.4 litres.

Auburn is thought of as being a stylish constituent of the Cord empire in the 1930s, but it was in fact acquired by E L Cord as early as 1924 and was available here for some five years before that. In the Cord era it was handled in London by speed ace Malcolm Campbell, who also looked after Duesenberg's sales.

The Briscoe, sold here in 1919-22 and named after a former head of Maxwell, was designed in France and should thus have been particularly suitable for European conditions with its 2.5-litre engine. Sales however were disappointing, and it had even less impact in Britain in 1923 under the name Earl.

Case is a well-known name in farm machinery circles, but its Continental engined cars offered here in 1923-24 were seldom seen and even in their homeland they were dead by 1927.

A high grade car from Cleveland, Ohio, was the Chandler, notable from 1924 for its constant mesh "easy change" gearbox. It was sold here initially by H G Burford (ex-Mercedes, Humber, New Orleans, etc.) and then by the ill-fated BMTC (see Bean, Lea Francis, etc.) It had a cheaper sideline in the shape of the six-cylinder Cleveland, offered here in 1919-26 but actually defunct in America a year earlier. Chandler itself vanished into Hupmobile in 1929, a make that enjoyed some limited success in the UK and had its peak US production year of almost 66,000 cars in 1928. The well-known motor agents Normands

1928-29 Chandler 8 sedan.

c1920 Chalmers 20hp six-cylinder tourer.

1930 Chrysler 77 4.4 litre.

1923 Columbia Six 25hp tourer.

1921 Comet Six tourer.

handled Hupmobile sales here, in London. Cleveland was represented in London by Salmons, the coachbuilders (see NP), who also looked after King.

The Cole, from a former carriage builder in Indianapolis, was sold here up to 1924 by an apparently unconnected Cole & Sons of Hammersmith Road, London. With a 39hp V8, the Cole Aero Eight cost £1375, falling to £950, and latterly had Westinghouse air assistance to the suspension.

The 25hp Continental engined Columbia was available here 1921-22 and hailed from a firm in Detroit that expired in 1924, a year after acquiring the Liberty, itself a make briefly offered here.

The Commonwealth was a 15/20hp car sold here in 1921 with the unhelpful RAC hp rating of 19.6. Its makers achieved more lasting fame for Checker taxicabs.

In a curious case of coals to Newcastle, Bramco of Coventry was the importer of the Cotay in 1920-21 – a rare example of an American cyclecar, and one that was doomed to failure at any price (and particularly at £425-£485!).

Another light car was the 1920-21 Moller, made on European lines with 1.5-litre engine and right hand drive. Better known was the Saxon with 1.4-litre engine sold by L C Rawlence at £110 in 1914 but £495 in 1919 and £550 in 1922, after which Saxon disappeared in its homeland.

The Crown Magnetic employed Entz electrical transmission and reached these shores via the Owen Magnetic Motor Car Corp, Wilkes-Barre, Pa, in 1919-22 (see also British Ensign). On the subject of the British variety of Owen, it has been alleged that the American Kenworthy might have done duty as one of its models. The Davis, available in Britain 1920-25, was from a former wagon firm and included the colourfully named Man o'War Tourer.

The Diana was an offshoot of Moon, made 1925-28, and like the Moon had a radiator shape almost identical to Minerva. A 29hp model was offered in Britain in 1926 and, like so many products of the lesser known American makers, it sold in dime numbers. Moon cars were available from North Western Motors of Liverpool throughout the decade (a 20hp·chassis cost £325 in 1925-26) and in 1927 were said to have British lamps, tyres and coachwork and to be assembled here. Moon's eight-cylinder Prince of Windsor model in 1929 fell foul of Buckingham Palace because of its unauthorised use of the Royal Coat of Arms. Early cars were interesting in being made specifically for export with Falls engines whereas their American sisters relied on Continental power.

The Dixie Flyer was an assembled car which expired in America in 1923 and was available in Britain in the early 1920s. It was in the same group as the National, also briefly available. The Dort was offered 1919-24 in 19.6hp or 23.4hp forms – Joshua

1921 Cole Aero-Eight Sport Coupe.

1920 Cotay 11hp four-cylinder air-cooled.

1924 Dodge Brothers 24-35hp saloon (£435 complete).

1927 Dodge Senior six-cylinder 3.7 litre.

1929 Dodge 8 sedan.

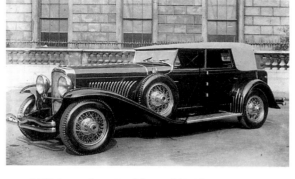

1929 Duesenberg Model J 265bhp (chassis £2300).

c1923 Durant 15.6hp four-cylinder tourer.

1926-27 Elcar 34hp "In Line 8".

1928 Erskine Six by Studebaker (16/40hp).

1927 Essex 17.3hp Six.

1929 Franklin Air Cooled Six.

1929 Graham-Paige Model 615.

Dort being another wagon builder who switched to cars as late as 1915 and went out of business in 1924, bringing down the Canadian Gray-Dort based on the American car soon afterwards.

America's most powerful car, the Duesenberg, arrived on these shores in 1929. It was known here as the 45/265, and a chassis could be bought for £2380 from Malcolm Campbell's London showrooms which, as noted earlier, also handled Auburn.

DuPont was another exclusive brand, lasting from 1921 to 1932 in its homeland but only making 537 vehicles. It was available here 1928-30 with chassis prices up to £875. Elcar's peak was 4000 cars in 1919 though very few were exported, even if sixes and eights were listed here 1926-28. The Fergus is covered under OD in the A-Z section, whilst the Franklin was a valiant attempt to market a high quality air-cooled car, enjoying some success here thanks to L C Rawlence & Co. of Albemarle Street, W1 (also involved with the Saxon). The Gardner from St Louis derived from another wagon business and was a luxury car with a Lycoming engine.

The Glover was an English design marketed from Leeds but made from parts manufactured in America, like several rivals in the A-Z such as Perfex, Vandy, Morriss-London, Thor and London Pullman.

Graham became better known here with the Lammas-Graham of later in the next decade, but Paige cars had been sold here before the Graham brothers (whose Graham Brothers trucks were part of the Dodge empire) took over Paige to create Graham Paige in 1927 (handled in London by Wolseley and Lorraine "Silken Six" distributors Eustace Watkins, who made a big feature of its twin top gears). Like the Gardner, the Graham Paige was an unusually early American car to have internal expanding brakes. Grant lasted only from 1913 to 1922, but initially attracted the Whiting's London department store to sell them as Whiting-Grant before T B André became distributors (see Marlborough).

The Gray of 1922-26 was an attempt by ex-Ford men to make a rival to the Model T. S Crabtree Ltd of Todmorden sold examples here for £260 complete. Six-cylinder Haynes cars were available 1920-22 with 29.5hp engines and a chassis price of £1100. The Huffman, from Elkhart, Indiana, was little known in America where only about 3000 were made, but a hopeful garage man in England acquired the distribution rights before the firm folded in 1925.

The Jordan was available here throughout the decade (Stiles Ltd of Baker Street W1 describing themselves as sole concessionaires in the late 1920s). Edward S Jordan was a marketing man whose lyrical advertising of the freedom that came with the automobile is remembered in the famous slogan "somewhere west of Laramie". The advertising here was more prosaic and the £500-£700 cars lasted little beyond the Wall Street Crash.

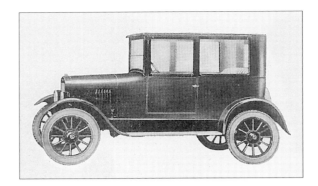

1924 Gray 20/25 four-cylinder sedan.

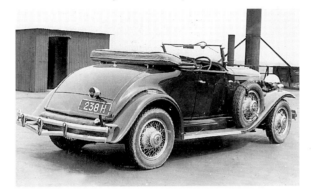

1930 Hudson Super Eight two-seater.

Jordan Great Line Eight Victoria coupe.

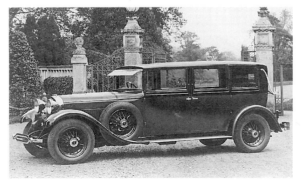

1930 Lincoln with Maythorn coachwork.

1923 Essex 18.2hp Coach.

1925 Locobobile Junior Eight (by then Durant controlled) 25hp eight-cylinder belonging to golfer Walter Hagen.

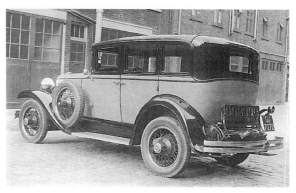

1929 Marmon Roosevelt.

1919-20 Maxwell cabriolet.

1924 Maxwell Club Saloon.

The King's reign in Buffalo ended in 1924 but the marque was notable for being handled here, like the Cleveland, by Salmons (see NP in the A-Z). The Kissel came to an end in 1931 and is remembered for its Gold Bug sports car. Its UK spares ended up with Jordan's at Wm Clarke (SP) Ltd, Marshalsea Road SE1, who also handled spares for the eight-cylinder Elcar.

Maibohm, an assembled car from Sandusky, Ohio, was yet another to be listed but as it changed its name to Courier in 1922 (not apparently available here) very few cars can have been sold. Another fleeting visitor was the Lyons of 1920, with Rolls-Royce shaped radiator and Midland Motors as distributors. Historians are not sure which factory built it.

Far better known here was the Marmon, whose UK spares ended up with those of Jordan and Kissel, but whose Bentley-rivalling cars were sold through the decade by Pass & Joyce Ltd, Euston Road NW1. A cheaper sister brand called the Roosevelt existed briefly at the close of the decade.

Mitchell was another carriage maker that had turned to cars. It bowed out in 1923, when Nash acquired its factory. Nash cars themselves were sold here from 1920 by Charles Jarrott and Letts, with six-cylinder chassis prices starting at £1000 and falling to £290. Their founder in 1917 was Charles W Nash who, like W C Durant, had been a key figure in GMC.

Leonard Williams & Co. Ltd, of Great West Road, Brentford, sold the six- and eight-cylinder Packards from 1926, starting at £650 for a chassis. The other great American "P" cars were also available here: Peerless between 1920 and 1929 at prices from £1110 for a complete car, and Pierce-Arrow throughout the decade, latterly from Henlys. Its cheapest 39.2hp model cost £1095 in 1930.

Pilot of Richmond, Indiana, sold a few smallish cars here before it collapsed in 1924, whilst continuing down the alphabet Reo, like Peerless, was best known in Britain for its commercial vehicles. These and Reo's cars were offered by Harris & Hasell Ltd of Bristol from 1925. After car production ended in 1936 our old friend William Clarke added the spares to his other American orphans.

The ReVere luxury car was made 1917-26 but only figured here briefly, in 1921, at a prohibitive £1800 complete. The Regal was known as the RMC here and was sold until 1920 by Seabrook (see A-Z). The Rickenbacker from US racing driver and air ace Capt. Eddie Rickenbacker was announced here in 1926 but had no time to become established before the American factory closed in 1927 after building 34,500 cars. The Roamer had a radiator like a Rolls-Royce but was an assembled car which plainly proved difficult to sell, its price falling from £1350 in 1919 to £695 in 1922, its last year in Britain.

The Eastern Export Co. Ltd of London EC3 handled the short-lived Rollin. In 1925-26 it cost £320-£360 and was built for European tastes in the Cletrac tractor

1925 Nash 25hp six-cylinder two door sedan.

1921 National 30hp six-cylinder bodied in Los Angeles.

1926 Oldsmobile six-cylinder 18.1hp Coach (£280 complete).

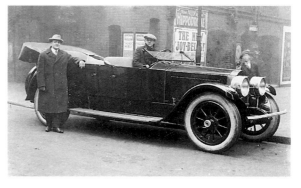

1920 Packard Twin-Six tourer.

1921-22 Oakland 20hp six-cylinder tourer.

1929 Packard Eight limousine.

1929 Peerless Custom Eight seven-seater sedan.

1927 Pierce-Arrow Series 80 limousine with division.

c1920 Pilot 75 six-cylinder tourer.

factory to the design of Rollin White, formerly of the White vehicle business (which curiously was little known here). Rolls-Royce was, of course, built in America, but not exported here at the time, though many have arrived subsequently.

The Scripps-Booth four-, six-, and eight-cylinder range was offered briefly by Whitings after General Motors acquired the factory in 1918. The Seneca from Fostoria, Illinois, was an assembled car made at the rate of a few hundred per year from 1917 to 1924. At £425-£595 quite a few were sold here – indeed half of Seneca's production was allegedly exported.

The Stanley steam car was available here to 1926 (and in the US for another year) from the grandly named Steam Car Corporation of Great Britain, not based in the West End but at Radford Fields in the hostile export territory of Coventry.

Former racing driver Warwick Wright, later associated with Rootes products, was the agent from 1927 for the Stutz, often endorsed in advertising by his friend Henry Segrave. Examples ran at Le Mans, where one finished second in 1928. Prices started at £995, or £735 for the Black Hawk of 1930.

The high quality Templar from Cleveland died in 1924 but was briefly offered in Britain, where it was hoped its overhead-valve engine might appeal.

The Velie was made to 1928 but was scarcely known here, despite American backing from the John Deere Plow Co. and British sales in the unlikely hands of Delaunay Belleville Motors Ltd of Maida Vale. The Westcott was a high grade assembled car which cut little ice in Britain and, as we considered Willys at the start of this section, it marks the end of the enormous choice of American automobiles. In a way it was just the tip of the iceberg, as there were dozens of other transatlantic car makers looking for European sales – no doubt a few of which appointed garages with insufficient resources to benefit anyone.

CANADA

Second only to the United States in its car sales to Britain came Canada. In the period 1922-30 inclusive, 50,964 cars (less a few for re-export) arrived from Canada, the peak year being 1923 with 10,177. Sales had dwindled to 1641 in 1930, when all the big players had their own British operations.

Under USA we noted that General Motors, Chrysler, Dort (Gray-Dort), Studebaker and Durant all had Canadian factories which served Britain and could provide parts for local assembly. The fact that Canada was a Dominion linked by the Crown to Britain gave these manufacturers a considerable tax advantage over their American counterparts.

Just about the only significant indigenous car was the 1923-26 Brooks, from Brooks Steam Motors Ltd of Stratford, Ontario. Only about 300 were built. At £936 complete from D McCormack with an office in Piccadilly, sales must have been minimal.

1929 Reo Series 15 (Continental engine) tourer.

1926 Rickenbacker eight-cylinder 100bhp Super Sports saloon.

1919 Roamer 24/30 tourer.

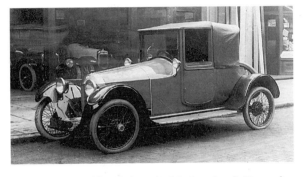

1919 (or possibly a little earlier) Scripps-Booth (General Motors) 2.9-litre six-cylinder OHV.

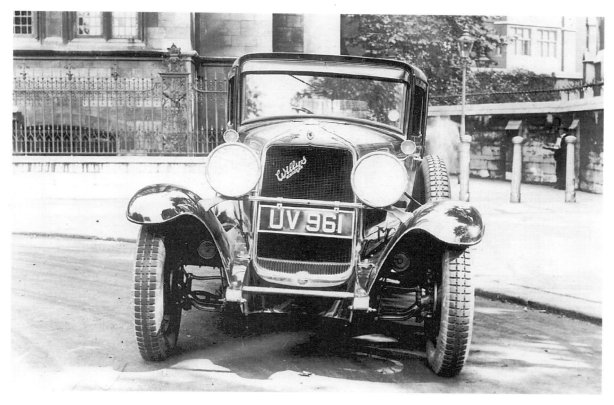

1929 Willys Great Six with Knight sleeve valves.

1929 Studebaker Commander Eight.

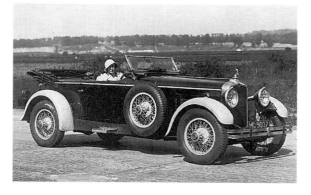

1928 Stutz Black Hawk Six sports.

1919-20 Templar OHV four-cylinder tourer (included Kodak camera and compass as standard).

1929 Viking (Oldsmobile brand) V8 36hp.

FRANCE

Since the earliest days of motoring France had been one of Britain's principal suppliers. Firms like Renault, Peugeot, Panhard-Levassor and de Dion Bouton helped to pave the way for long term success. With 47,744 cars sold 1922-30 inclusive – the best year being 1925 with 13,028 and the worst 1930 with 1255 – France was by far the largest European supplier to Britain. In the 1920s both Citroën and Renault established assembly operations here and de Dion Bouton had a British company at Great Marlborough Street W1 looking after its sales. Servicing and the fitment of British accessories and bodywork were undertaken at de Dion's Woodside Works in North Finchley, London. De Dion started the decade with everything from a 12hp at £895 to a 25hp V8 at £1810 and expired in 1931, when its cars cost as little as £395. Spares were acquired by W T Botten & Co. in Finchley. Though there was a French Aster company making engines it was only in the earliest days that it had any direct connections with the London firm of Aster that made cars in the 1920s. Likewise the Anglo-French Sizaire-Berwick is covered in the A-Z, it being an example of one of the numerous French firms which had British financial involvements.

In fact the Charron car from France was also sold here to 1929 (despite the unconnected Charron-Laycock) and the Marlborough (see A-Z) started off as a French machine. Another example was Clément-Talbot, or London Talbot, which started with French links and then in 1919 joined Sunbeam and Darracq in STD. French Darracq had a works here making, amongst other things, bodywork for Talbot. Its cars were known as Talbots in France and Talbot Darracqs in England up to 1929, when they became simply Darracqs.

Bugatti offered its highly successful sporting range from Brixton Garage and Crossley built a few examples of one of its models. The Blériot Whippet's only link with France seems to have been the Blériot-type aeroplanes that its backers had formerly built.

Hotchkiss had famous links with Britain, thanks to the armaments factory it established in Coventry in the 1914-18 war. Afterwards this made engines, toyed with a light car and then became the Morris Engines factory. The French original, run up to the 1950s by Englishman Harry Ainsworth, had sales handled by London & Parisian Motor Co. off Oxford Street (who were also agents for Westwood). The Hotchkiss was available here throughout the decade, culminating in the excellent 3-litre six-cylinder AM80 at £600-£650 in 1929-30.

Morris followed Austin's lead into France (Austin made tractors there from 1919) by buying Léon-Bollée in late 1924. Before that Bollée's expensive and old-fashioned cars had appealed to a small British clientèle and afterwards, as thinly disguised Morris cars, they were not seen again here, and expired in France in 1933.

1925 Amilcar CGS sports coupé.

1922 Amilcar in Scottish Light Car Trial.

1919 Berliet VB 3.3-litre SV tourer at Fondation Marius Berliet.

1925 Berliet 10/20 OHV saloon.

1922 Charron 8hp one door saloon.

1928 BNC 527 type with 1100cc engine.

1926 Ballot 2LT sports saloon.

1925 Chenard-Walcker 12/25 sunshine saloon.

1929-30 Cottin-Desgouttes 2.6 (four-cylinder, twelve-valve) with all-round independent suspension. Used in Sahara Rally.

Running briefly through the rest, we start with the 20hp Alda, which was made in the Farman works but expired in 1922. Farman itself was an aircraft firm making very expensive cars in the Hispano-Suiza idiom: its 40hp model was sold here 1920-26 starting with a chassis price of £2350 and ending at £1,450. Farman (England) Ltd must have found its Riley agency more lucrative. Hispano-Suiza itself was a serious threat to Rolls-Royce and Bentley and its chassis cost from £2350 in 1920 to £1650/£1950 at the end of the decade. Its famous servo-assisted four wheel braking system was, of course, adopted by Rolls-Royce.

Bentley owed its origin to the DFP, which the Bentley brothers imported and improved. Not that the trade was all one way, as both Darmont and Sandford made variations on the theme of Morgan, and aero engine firm Salmson of Paris acquired manufacturing rights to the British GN in 1919. Three thousand of the latter were made in two years to compete with the dozens of other French cyclecar makers. Salmson then evolved into a maker of proper little sporting cars. These had a strong following in Britain and were sold by SMS (sole concessionaires for the British Dominions) for as little as £158 in 1926 from premises shared with Gwynne. At the end of the decade the former boss of Sizaire-Berwick helped to establish British Salmson, which made cars at Raynes Park in the mid-1930s.

To return to GN, its London factory was the home of the Grégoire importers, Grégoire 10-15hp types being offered here until 1923. Malcolm Campbell was involved in the British Grégoire sales and racing programme and also sold Italas, Bignans, Bugattis, Auburns and Duesenbergs.

Lots of the aforementioned French cyclecars had an impact here in he early 1920s, and some went on to become proper sports cars like Salmsons. Examples included Antoinette, Amilcar, Automobilette, Bédélia, Benjamin, BNC, Derby (called Vernon-Derby here, as the importer was Vernon Balls), d'Yrsan, EHP (whose importers also handled the more conventional Donnet-Zedel range in 1925-30), Kiddy, La Ponette, MASE, Mauve, Majola, Rally, Sénéchal, Zeiller et Fournier and Sizaire Naudin, which survived the departure of Maurice Sizaire to his Berwick involvements but died in 1921 to the tune of touring cars rather than its earlier single-cylinder roadsters. Amilcar was probably the most successful of them all and early in 1928 Derby man Balls announced that Amilcar (GB) Ltd would in future assemble the cars here. Presumably the slump intervened. The aforementioned Sénéchal was sold here by Waverley (see A-Z).

Lots of the traditional French firms' cars had become overweight, old-fashioned and stodgy by the 1920s and few of them survived much beyond the decade. Ariès 8.9 and 17.9hp machines were available

1923 (Talbot) Darracq 15/40 Special Sports.

1920 De Dion-Bouton model 1-D on Jersey.

1919-20 Delage Type CO 4½-litre six-cylinder sports.

1926 Delage 40/50hp Landaulette.

1927 Delahaye 12CV saloon.

1927 Delaunay Belleville 14/40 "The Car Magnificent".

1925 Donnet-Zedel 13.9hp with bodywork by Gaston Grümmer.

1923 Farman 40hp Grand Sports with "aeroplane cockpit".

Grégoire with sporting motorist and ace salesman Capt. Malcolm Campbell.

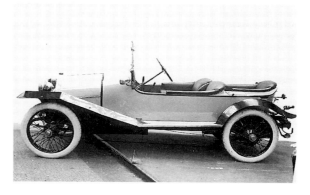

1920 Bugatti Brescia 10/12hp Sports.

1930 Bugatti Type 46 straight-eight 32.5hp Coupé.

1929 Hispano-Suiza H6B six-cylinder 37.2hp with coachwork by Devillars.

in 1925-26 but not the later cars designed by E Petit, ex-Salmson. Bayard cars were seen here in 1920-21 and Bellanger died soon afterwards. Berliet had large premises in a former skating rink in Twickenham and offered everything from 8.9 to 27hp, but one imagines that it was principally commercial vehicles that kept the enterprise afloat here.

Bignan was represented in Britain 1920-25, initially with 17hp cars, then 10hp and latterly with a 2-litre at £565. As noted three paragraphs ago, Malcolm Campbell was involved with Bignan and Grégoire and, confusingly, called the former "Grégoire-Campbells".

The Brasier range of 1919-24 included 12 and 18hp cars sold by Tomlinson of Marylebone. A few Buchets were sold here by a London agent who also handled Automobiles Sigma, and the Italian sounding but French made Butterosi was displayed at Olympia in 1919. Chenard-Walcker fielded a large range via Archie Simons of Great Portland Street W1 (the mecca for car dealers) until 1931. The Cottin-Desgouttes ended its days here in 1929 with all-round independent suspension. From 1923 it had offered overhead valves with three valves per cylinder, which was unusual. The British agent was Peter Crerar in Crieff, which was rather far from London, the traditional market for expensive foreign cars.

Another of the great French names was Lorraine-Dietrich, which despite winning at Le Mans in 1925 and 1926 was forced to abandon car production by 1934. Marius Barbarou designed many of the 1920s cars, having formerly worked for Delaunay Belleville, whose circular radiators had been familiar to British motorists before 1914. Delaunay Belleville suffered a steady decline during the 1920s and was not represented here after 1930, its importer Delaunay Belleville Motors Ltd of Maida Vale having turned to the American Velie in 1927 in an attempt to make ends meet. The Donnet-Zedel was sold here from 1925 in 9.5 and 13.9hp forms by the London sales outlet for French Laffly commercial vehicles.

Gladiator just staggered into our period with 12 and 25hp models at up to £1200. Hollingdrake of Stockport sold the traditional La Buire whilst nearby Timberlakes Garage sold the Hinstin as a Little Greg (it also sold Grégoire – see Westwood and GN in A-Z). Hurtu, which had originally spawned the Belsize, made the sorts of cars that could be bought a lot more cheaply from Citroën, Renault and Peugeot, as well as British makers, before expiring in 1930 (and in 1926 here at the premises of Ardon Engineering of Camberwell). Peugeot itself did well, particularly with its light cars, which cost as little as £140 in the later 1920s.

The Jouffret at £350 was virtually unknown, whilst La Licorne earned a small reputation for its principally light cars in the early 1920s. The Mass was named after its sponsor Masser-Horniman from Weybridge,

1927 Hotchkiss 15.9hp four-cylinder saloon.

c1926 La Licorne (8, 10 and 12hp models were offered from 1922).

1926 Léon Bollée Type M (12/35hp) saloon.

1925 Lorraine 20/60 "Silken Six" (six-cylinder) saloon.

1914/19 Peugeot Bébé 6hp two-seater.

1919 Panhard 12/16 sports torpedo.

1926 Panhard 14/20 two door saloon.

1929 Panhard 20-60hp six-cylinder sleeve-valve coupé.

1928 Peugeot Model 183 12hp saloon.

but existed in France under the name Pierron. It lasted until 1923, or a couple of years less than the English representation of the old established Mors car. The final Mors of 1925 cost a prohibitive £1050 for a stodgy 14/20. Motobloc was sold by London lorry dealer W Rinman and struggled through to a £325 10.4hp model in 1926.

It seems unfair to class the illustrious Panhard-Levassor with all these lost causes, but sadly it was no longer competitive in Britain, despite being represented by W & G du Cros (best known as London taxi operators – mostly Panhards – and makers of W & G commercials, by then in the STD group). Like many American manufacturers, the spares of Panhard ended up with William Clarke in Marshalsea Road SE1. Pilain expired in France in 1920, though old stock was still selling at up to £700 for a 10/30 in 1923. The Pilain factory became home to the SLIM-Pilain with 18/40hp ohc four-cylinder engine and air compressor powering starter, jacks, horn, brakes, etc. – a few were seen here by courtesy of L C Engineering Supplies, Palmer Street SW1, who charged £725 to seekers of novelty. Rolland-Pilain, a firm set up by Francois Pilain and his nephew early in the century, was also available here to 1926 – the final model being a £1400 US Continental engined straight eight.

Better known was the Rochet-Schneider from Donne & Willans (1909) Ltd, Kingsbury works (where the Kingsbury car came from), Hendon. It was a typical high grade car in the 12-30hp bracket and was last offered here in 1931. Unconnected was the Th. Schneider, offering some rather more sporting types than many of its rivals. Its distributors were initially the Welbeck Agency, Wigmore Street W1, but sales must have been sufficient for Th. Schneider Automobiles (England) Ltd to be formed off Upper Baker Street – where a trickle of sales continued to 1938.

The 12hp Suère was available in 1925-26 for a reasonable £275 complete from Theo & Co. Ltd, Liverpool. Theo also handled Mathis and later Unic but was more famous for its Theo multiple pumps, which for the first time allowed several grades and brands of petrol to be sold from the same pump.

A car resembling a miniature Rolls-Royce called the Secqueville-Hoyau 10/12hp cost £550 in 1920. In the early days of motoring these difficult to pronounce names were often changed to that of the importer and one would have thought names like "Suère" (swear) and the painful "Hurtu" would have positively discouraged customers!

The Turcat-Méry cost £665 complete in 1925-26 from Warwickshire Motors, Great Portland Street W1, and the Vermorel was available throughout the decade from W G James Ltd, Osnaburgh Street NW1, who lost the franchise when manufacture ended in Villefranche in 1930.

Vinot was another marque to have been sold here

1926 Peugeot Model 117B 12/20 tourer from 165guineas.

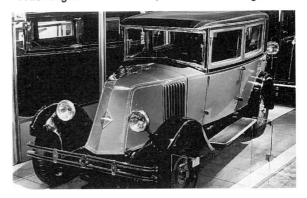

1927 Renault NN1 saloon.

1925 Renault 45hp Phaeton.

1927 Salmson 10/20 fabric saloon.

1928-29 SARA six-cylinder air-cooled 1800cc sports.

1925 Sénéchal 1100cc 8hp sports.

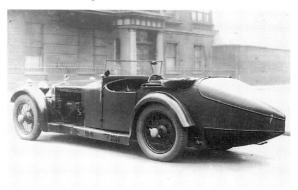

1929 Tracta 80mph sports two-seater with front wheel drive.

1924 Turcat-Méry 16/60, OHV but fixed cylinder head.

1924 Unic 12hp saloon.

since early times. It lasted with Vinot Cars Ltd of Great Portland Street to 1925, the final models being a 12/25 at £465 and a 15/20 at £700.

Maxwell Monson Ltd in Halkin Place SW1, and then Dixons Garage of Putney, dealt with the bizarre Voisins from aircraft maker Gabriel Voisin. In 1919 the chassis price of the 22/30 was £1265, whilst in 1930 the cheapest chassis was the 16/50 at £600 and the most expensive the 32/140 at £1500. At the other end of the scale was the little Le Zèbre at £295 for a complete 10hp model in 1923.

Unic was very well known here for its taxis but its light cars were also available through the decade from Unic Motors Ltd of London and latterly from Theo of Liverpool, the Suère, Mathis and pump firm. Unic and Mathis were direct competitors so the agency for the latter passed later to Gardner Motors of Harlesden NW10.

We will end this long and complex list with three firm British sporting favourites. Ballot's overhead camshaft 2-litre models made a lot of friends, despite an asking price of £1350 for the most highly tuned model in 1925. Ballot also made engines for several other French car firms. Delage and Delahaye were, of course, still independent through our period. The former, like Hotchkiss, was sold by the London & Parisian Motor Co. Its 40/50 six-cylinder chassis cost £1125 in 1926 and some were sold by the Grahame-White organisation. The rival Delahaye 27/50 chassis from the Glasgow & Paris Motor Co., Maryhill, Glasgow, cost a mere £595. Later, Count Heyden took over Delahaye representation in London, whilst the Delage franchise passed to MG distributors University Motors. Plainly there was no shortage of choice, to which should certainly be added the remarkably low-built, front wheel driven Tracta, seen here at the end of the decade by courtesy of Arthur Stuart Auto Services of Vauxhall Bridge Road SW1.

ITALY

With sales of 22,448 cars in the period 1922 to 1930 inclusive, Italy ranked fourth in the import league. As with other countries, its peak year was 1925 (5,007 cars) caused by a last minute attempt to sell cars before the McKenna Duties were re-imposed. The period had started with 2907 cars but this figure dwindled in the difficult years of 1929 and 1930 to 622 and 562 respectively. Plainly Fiat was the major player and, as noted in the A-Z, it employed some limited local assembly.

Another front-runner was Lancia, whose sales were handled by Curtis Automobile Co., Berkeley Street W1, until late in 1928, when Lancia (England) Ltd was formed at Alperton. Its very advanced unitary construction cars had a strong following amongst the motoring press and other cognoscenti. The Lambda cost £725 complete in 1927 whilst in 1929 the Dilambda V8 was priced at £1175.

1923 Vinot 12/25 doctor's coupé "the result of 12 years experience with our famous 70mm bore engine".

1927 Voisin 18hp six-seater with wood and leather saloon body and Voisin's distinctive aluminium bird mascot.

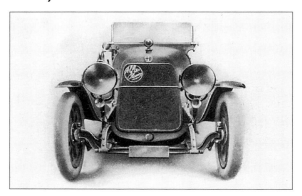

1921 Alfa-Romeo ES 4-cylinder Tipo Sport.

1927 Alfa-Romeo 15/60 6 cylinder 1½ litre Weymann saloon.

c1921 Th. Schneider 16/20 tourer.

1925 Ansaldo Model 4C 12-40hp tourer.

1925 Bianchi 15/50 tourer.

1926 Ceirano 1500cc 150S Tipo Roma sports.

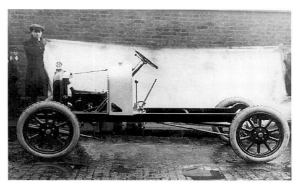

c1921 Chiribiri 12/16hp chassis.

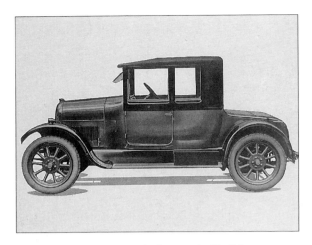

1921 Fiat 501 10/15hp coupé with dickey.

1925-26 Fiat 519 or 510 20/30hp limousine.

Alfa-Romeo British Sales Ltd was based in Baker Street W1, though later, as befitted Alfa Romeo's sporting reputation, the concession was held by Thomson & Taylor at Brooklands racing circuit at Weybridge. Chassis were priced in the upper hundreds and sold in reasonable numbers to discriminating motorists.

Most of the appeal of Italian cars centred on their attractive looks and above average performance. The Ceirano, looking like a miniature Lancia Lambda, was represented by Newton & Bennett (see Newton in A-Z). These agents also handled Nazzarro and SCAT, a factory which was acquired by Ceirano in 1923 to produce the latter cars. A rather similar light sporting car was the 1.5-litre Aurea offered here in 1924-26, whilst even smaller was the two-cylinder Temperino sold in London in 1921-22.

Nazzarro cars made in Turin from 1911 were the product of a former racing driver. A move was made to Florence in 1919, where the cars died in 1923, latterly represented here by the Standard Fruit Preserving Co., whose telegraphic address was CHERIGLACE, LONDON!

CMN lasted in Italy only from 1919 to 1923 and is now remembered for being the company where Enzo Ferrari was test driver before leaving for Alfa Romeo in 1920. The 14hp CMN was available here through F C Cottrell in 1922 at £700 complete.

Ansaldo Motors Ltd of Dover Street W1 represented the products of the massive Ansaldo engineering concern, which had many similarities with Scotland's Beardmore. Ansaldo cars were offered from 1922 well into the 1930s, latterly by L C Rawlence of Albemarle Street W1.

Another significant car available through the decade was the OM, which like so many other Italian firms was soon to be acquired by Fiat. In this context SPA springs to mind. SPA Motors operated in Earls Court Road SW from well before the war to about 1926 and offered a substantial range of 16-30hp types.

Earlier, like the Chiribiri below, it had been handled by Vandervell (see Vandy in A-Z).

Burton Osborne & Taylor Ltd were distributors for Bianchi cars in Belsize Lane NW3, these being competitively priced and mostly in the 10-15hp range. The Soc. Edoardo Bianchi (Engineers) Ltd was also listed in the former Wembley exhibition complex for a time.

Like some Alfa Romeos, Chiribiris had twin overhead camshafts and were of around 1500cc capacity. They were made to 1927 but were seldom seen outside motor shows here and were not offered after 1924. Diatto tried to sell a large 28hp car here in 1919-21 but then concentrated on the Italian speciality of lively light cars before throwing in the towel in 1926.

FAST should have appealed to speed merchants, the letters standing for Fabbrica Automobili Sport, Torino. Its three-litre model was available here through Major Locke, Allsop Street NW1, in 1925-26 at the time of the manufacturer's demise. An ohv FAST engine was tried by Invicta in an early prototype but found to be insufficiently flexible.

The luxury car maker Isotta-Fraschini had a sales agency of the same name in North Audley Street W1 and offered eight-cylinder 6- to 7.4-litre chassis at well over £1000 through the decade. Antonio Lago worked for a time for the London agent and before that had campaigned an Anglo-Italian Restelli (see A-Z). Later he was to buy Darracq from STD when it hit the rocks in the mid-1930s.

Itala's great days had been before the 1914-18 war, but Malcolm Campbell from Sussex Place, South Kensington, did his best to keep the flame alive amongst his French and American offerings with a range of 12 to 26hp cars that ultimately settled on a single 15.7hp six in the later 1920s. Sadly, the market for fast, imported sporting cars slowed to a trickle with the onset of the Great Depression and only the quantity producers survived.

1930 Alfa-Romeo 6C-1750 Gran Sport with Zagato body.

1928 Fiat 503 12hp fabric saloon.

1927 Isotta Fraschini 8A 50/100hp Weymann bodied sports coupé by Touring, Milan.

1927 Lancia Lambda V4 2352cc tourer.

1929 OM 1½-litre sports tourer.

1927 Excelsior 30/100 Albert I six-cylinder d'Ieteren Frères cabriolet de ville.

1926 Imperia driven by company owner Van Roggen in Monte Carlo Rallye from Glasgow.

BELGIUM

Our Belgian neighbours found Britain to be amongst their best customers and sold an impressive 3409 cars here between 1922 and 1930.

In the A-Z the British connection between Imperia and GWK is noted, whilst the Taunton was also to have been an Anglo-Belgian marque.

The engineering group David Brown (famous owners of Aston Martin and Lagonda after the Second World War) were importers of the SAVA from Antwerp but this scarcely survived the Great War and was mopped up by Minerva in 1923 after a period when salvation had not materialised from the ambitious sounding British SAVA Syndicate. Minerva favoured Knight type sleeve-valve engines and offered expensive luxury cars to the potential market for Daimlers and Armstrong-Siddeleys. It typically made 2000 to 3000 cars per year before the Slump, with up to half of them exported. From late 1927 Minerva Motors (England) Ltd was London concessionaire. In the mid-1930s Minerva joined Imperia, which had already acquired Excelsior, Nagant and Métallurgique. All these had been offered in Britain, the Excelsior in particular being a spectacular 30hp machine with a chassis price of £900 to £1300 in the late 1920s. Nagant does not seem to have been revived here after the First World War, though earlier it had enjoyed some popularity as the Nagant-Hobson. Métallurgique had Beauforts Ltd of Lloyds Place, Brompton Road SW3 as its agents until about 1926, and was yet another very high grade car, costing £1225 complete in 1923 for the largest 26hp model and £550 for the smallest 12hp.

H F Pilling of Charing Cross sold the overhead camshaft 12hp Mièsse to 1926, after which its makers concentrated on commercial vehicles.

The ALP light car cut very little ice in Britain, or indeed in Brussels, where it survived only from 1919 to 1921. However, in complete contrast came FN, the important motor cycle, lorry and armaments manufacturer. It made an extensive range of cars in Liège to 1935 but was represented by principally 11hp and 12hp cars to 1930 from FN (England) Ltd of Kimberley Road, Willesden. They were competitively priced at £315 to £440 and usually had British coachwork.

With Belgian car sales in Britain down to only 136 in 1930 the virtual end had been reached. In part this was because the home market was too small to sustain such a large industry when the slump killed exports. The survivors were mostly wiped out because Belgium had become an important assembler of American cars for the Continent, and these proved much cheaper than the country's up-market indigenous marques.

OTHERS

Despite the recent conflict it was our former German enemies who supplied the next largest number of car makes in Britain. However, sales were very limited and amounted to a mere 702 cars between 1922 and 1930.

Adler fielded a large range of 5-24hp cars in 1920 but was forced to withdraw after a couple of years. Benz started quoting British prices in 1922 (£730-£1495 complete). Mercedes offered a diminutive supercharged model from 1921 and printed a catalogue in English to promote it. However it was not until the mid-1920s merger of Benz with Mercedes' parent Daimler that serious inroads could be made by British Mercedes-Benz Ltd of Grosvenor Road SW1. In 1928-29 it offered models with chassis prices of £540 (16/50) to £2000 (36/220) and £2150 for the 38/250 in 1930.

The author can find no evidence that the Ego sportscar, as driven by Rudolf Caracciola and made in Berlin from 1921 to 1926, was marketed here. However he once spotted the remains of one in an Oxfordshire scrapyard so at any rate one must have come here. Another car driven by Caracciola (in 1922) was the Fafnir, offered in Britain up to the Great War and again afterwards from 1919 to 1923.

The Moll light car was made in Chemnitz from 1922 to 1925 and was sold here in 1922-23 by L G

1921 FN 16hp tourer.

1921 Metallurgique 12/14hp.

1929 Minerva 6-litre Speed "Six" drophead coupé with sleeve valves.

1924 Austro-Daimler 26.9 six-cylinder torpedo.

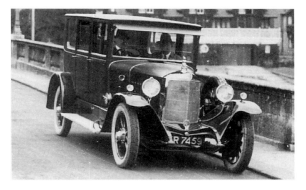

1926 Steyr VII 14/35 saloon.

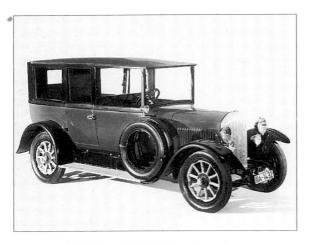

1923 Benz 1030 2.6-litre 30hp saloon.

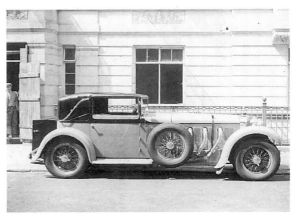

1928 Mercedes-Benz SSK seven-litre sports coupé supercharged to 225bhp.

Hornsted, with its identity hidden by the names of either Hornsted or Summers (see A-Z).

Some sources give Hansa as having an agent in Britain (where it had certainly been sold in 1913-14). NAG cars were listed here in 1922, 1923 and 1926 but without prices in Sterling. They had RAC ratings of 15-17hp.

Stoewer was represented by Caldecote Sons & Co of Birkenhead before and after the war, but later sales must have been sparse as prices were quoted "on application". Many sizes from 8hp to 20hp were mentioned up to 1931, after which spares were held by British Mercedes-Benz Ltd.

Opel had been sold here to 1914 and following the GM takeover was marketed here from 1928. In 1929 its 15/40 cost £310 complete and its 30/60 £435-£510, but despite these low prices the marque then lapsed in Britain until the mid-1930s. Amongst other German makes of car tried here was the luxury Horch, offered in the late 1920s by Johnson Neal, Harrow Road, London W9.

Austria's sales here started promisingly at 192 (six more than Germany) in 1922 but tailed off badly to six in 1930 for an inclusive total of 501. The makes represented were Steyr (called Alpine Steyr here to 1924 by importer Arthur Bray of Davies Street W1). Its 14hp cost £495 complete in 1921 and its 24hp cost £1250. In 1930 an improved range with independent rear suspension cost from as little as £375 for the complete 14hp to £860 for the eight-cylinder 37/100. Latterly distribution was undertaken from Sentinel Steam Waggon's London HQ and then by KMW Ltd (possibly Kennings) of Melbourne, Derbyshire.

Austro-Fiat, under the initials AF, was available from Great Portland Street W1 in 1923-24 at £295 for a 15-9hp chassis.

Austro-Daimler (England) Ltd handled the best known and liked of Austria's exports. Austro-Daimlers were expensive fast cars designed up to 1923 by Ferdinand Porsche and featuring single or

double overhead camshaft engines. Porsche was largely responsible for the ADM model that proved popular in Britain in 100mph sporting guise. Its successor was another to bring independent suspension to these shores in the later 1920s and cost £795-£1250 for the chassis alone.

Next in importance comes Holland, with 117 cars sold in Britain from 1922 to 1930. Double figures were only reached in 1922-26, the latter year being soon after the demise of Spyker, which had sold a 25hp and a 13/30 here in 1919-20 and then embarked on a glorious one model policy that spelled certain death. Its 5.6-litre Maybach engined 30/40 was used by S F Edge to improve his Double Twelve record at Brooklands in 1922. The chassis price was £1,400, which fell to £1100 shortly before the last of 150 examples was built. What the other Dutch cars were is unrecorded though they may have been re-exports from other sources.

Switzerland added 52 to the 1922-30 imports total. Its principal manufacturers were Piccard Pictet, sometimes called Pic-Pic, and Martini. The former was available here to 1922, its 16hp chassis price coming down from £1395 to £900.

Martini had originally been promoted here by Capt. Deasy (whose company became Siddeley-Deasy, a forerunner to Armstrong-Siddeley). In the 1920s Martini was represented by the embryo Rootes Group. Its 20/40 chassis cost £1175 early in this decade.

"Others" account for 842 sales in the period and include 320 from Eire. The rest are not specified, but it is known that three Laurin & Klements from the newly formed Czechoslovakia arrived in 1927 and the first half of 1928, and possibly more before. In the same period one Spanish as opposed to French built Hispano-Suiza was sold here. The rest came from the few other motor producing countries, but not, one can say with quite a degree of certainty, from slumbering Japan.